Arabic Sociolinguistics

Written by four leading experts, this book provides a comprehensive overview of sociolinguistic variation and change in Arabic. It introduces sociolinguistic theory, methods, and data step-by-step, using accessible language and extensive examples throughout. Topics covered include sociolinguistic methodology, social variables, language change, spatial variation, and contact and diffusion. Each topic is explained and illustrated using empirical data drawn from a wide array of Arabic-speaking communities in the Middle East and North Africa, as well as other parts of the world where Arabic is or was spoken, to provide a rich resource of individual dialects, as well as a comparative view of variation in Arabic. Each chapter also contains annotated suggestions for further reading and elaborate exercises. It is an essential resource for students studying Arabic in its social context, as well as anyone wishing to expand their knowledge of variation in Arabic.

ENAM AL-WER is Professor of Linguistics at the University of Essex. A specialist in sociolinguistics, her research focusses on variation and change and dialect contact in Arabic. She is co-author of *A Grammar of Jordanian Arabic* (2022) and co-editor of three books, including *The Routledge Handbook of Arabic Sociolinguistics* (2019).

URI HORESH is a sociolinguist specialising in language variation and change and language contact, especially in Palestine. They formerly held a British Academy Postdoctoral Fellowship at the University of Essex and are co-editor of *The Routledge Handbook of Arabic Sociolinguistics* (2019).

BRUNO HERIN is a lecturer at INALCO (Paris) where he teaches Levantine Arabic and Arabic dialectology. His chief interest is in the description of Arabic vernaculars and minority languages of the Middle East and in linguistic variation. He is co-author of *A Grammar of Jordanian Arabic* (2022).

RUDOLF DE JONG is Director of the Netherlands-Flemish Institute in Cairo. He specialises in Arabic dialectology and has authored several articles and two books on dialects of Bedouin tribes in Sinai (2000 and 2011). He served as General Secretary of the Association Internationale de Dialectologie Arabe (AIDA).

Arabic Sociolinguistics

Enam Al-Wer
University of Essex

Uri Horesh

Bruno Herin
INALCO, Paris

Rudolf de Jong
Netherlands-Flemish Institute in Cairo, Leiden University

CAMBRIDGE
UNIVERSITY PRESS

CAMBRIDGE
UNIVERSITY PRESS

University Printing House, Cambridge CB2 8BS, United Kingdom

One Liberty Plaza, 20th Floor, New York, NY 10006, USA

477 Williamstown Road, Port Melbourne, VIC 3207, Australia

314–321, 3rd Floor, Plot 3, Splendor Forum, Jasola District Centre,
New Delhi – 110025, India

103 Penang Road, #05–06/07, Visioncrest Commercial, Singapore 238467

Cambridge University Press is part of the University of Cambridge.

It furthers the University's mission by disseminating knowledge in the pursuit of
education, learning, and research at the highest international levels of excellence.

www.cambridge.org
Information on this title: www.cambridge.org/9781107182615
DOI: 10.1017/9781316863060

First published 2022

A catalogue record for this publication is available from the British Library.

Library of Congress Cataloging-in-Publication Data
Names: Al-Wer, Enam, author.
Title: Arabic sociolinguistics / Enam Al-Wer, University of Essex [and 3
others].
Description: Cambridge ; New York, NY : Cambridge University Press, 2022. |
Includes bibliographical references and index.
Identifiers: LCCN 2022000817 (print) | LCCN 2022000818 (ebook) | ISBN
9781107182615 (hardback) | ISBN 9781316633731 (paperback) | ISBN
9781316863060 (ebook)
Subjects: LCSH: Sociolinguistics–Arab countries. | Arabic
language–Variation. | Linguistic change–Arab countries. | LCGFT:
Textbooks.
Classification: LCC P40.45.A65 A49 2022 (print) | LCC P40.45.A65 (ebook)
| DDC 306.442/927–dc23/eng/20220228
LC record available at https://lccn.loc.gov/2022000817
LC ebook record available at https://lccn.loc.gov/2022000818

ISBN 978-1-107-18261-5 Hardback
ISBN 978-1-316-63373-1 Paperback

For our teachers and mentors

Peter Trudgill

William Labov

Manfred Woidich

Clive Holes

Jonathan Owens

Gillian Sankoff

Contents

List of Figures   x
List of Maps   xi
List of Tables   xii
Acknowledgements   xiii
Transcription, Symbols, and Abbreviations   xv

1   Introduction   1
    1.1   Arabic Dialectology   1
    1.2   The Variationist Approach to Arabic Sociolinguistics   2
    1.3   Diglossia and Code-Switching   4
    1.4   The Link to Historical Linguistics   5
    1.5   Variation and Change   5
    1.6   Layout of the Book   6
    1.7   Further Reading   7

2   Methodology: Principles and Practice   9
    2.1   Introduction   9
    2.2   Research Design   9
    2.3   The Observer's Paradox   11
    2.4   Interviews, Elicitation, and Other Strategies   16
    2.5   The Ethnographic Approach   19
    2.6   The Subject of Investigation: Linguistic Variables 21
    2.7   Defining a Variable and Range of Variation   24
    2.8   Age   29
    2.9   Analysis   33
    2.10 Ethics   42
    2.11 Further Reading   44
    2.12 Exercises for Chapter 2   45

3   Gender   48
    3.1   Introduction   48
    3.2   General Principles   48

3.3   Gender and the Notion of Standard in Arabic   51
3.4   Local and Supralocal Features   52
3.5   Gender-Differentiated Findings in Arabic Vernaculars   54
3.6   Further Reading   73
3.7   Exercises for Chapter 3   74

4   Education   77
4.1   Introduction   77
4.2   Education as a Proxy Variable   78
4.3   Changes in Educational Opportunities and Experiences   80
4.4   Type of Education: Two Case Studies   85
4.5   Concluding Remarks   88
4.6   Further Reading   88
4.7   Exercises for Chapter 4   89

5   Social Stratification   92
5.1   Introduction   92
5.2   The Classic Social Class Paradigm   94
5.3   Social Network   96
5.4   Regionality   98
5.5   Life-Mode   101
5.6   Community of Practice   102
5.7   Summary   104
5.8   Further Reading   104
5.9   Exercises for Chapter 5   105

6   Religion and Ethnicity   106
6.1   Introduction   106
6.2   Jewish Varieties of Arabic   107
6.3   Druze Varieties in the Levant   109
6.4   Communal Dialects in Baghdad   111
6.5   The ʿArab and Baharna Dialects in Bahrain   113
6.6   Sunna and Shiʾa in Al-Ahsa   117
6.7   Christians and Muslims in Jordan   119
6.8   ʿIzbat Basili, Upper Egypt   122
6.9   Ethnicity, Religion, and Language Shift   122
6.10 Further Reading   129
6.11 Exercises for Chapter 6   129

7   Language Change   131
7.1   Introduction   131
7.2   Historical Linguistics   132

7.3 The Relationship between Variation and Change 135
7.4 Studying Change in Real Time 138
7.5 Studying Change in Apparent Time 141
7.6 Variation without Change 143
7.7 Variation Indicating Change in Progress 144
7.8 Types of Change 146
7.9 Concluding Remarks 150
7.10 Further Reading 151
7.11 Exercises for Chapter 7 152

8 Spatial Variation 156
8.1 Introduction 156
8.2 Language and Geography 156
8.3 Linguistic Atlases: An Overview 159
8.4 Atlases as a Source of Data 161
8.5 Waterways as Carriers of Linguistic Features 175
8.6 Focal and Relic Areas 178
8.7 Arabic-Based Creoles 185
8.8 Further Reading 187
8.9 Exercises for Chapter 8 187

9 Contact and Diffusion 189
9.1 Introduction 189
9.2 Regional Standards 189
9.3 Diffusion across the Language Barrier 191
9.4 Borrowing and Substrate Effects 192
9.5 Areal Groupings 197
9.6 Types and Models of Diffusion 201
9.7 Transitional Zones and Interdialectal Forms 206
9.8 Summary and Concluding Remarks 211
9.9 Further Reading 211
9.10 Exercises for Chapter 9 213

References 214
Subject Index 227
Place Index 234
Name Index 237

Figures

2.1 Sample coding spreadsheet   37
3.1 Percentage use of weak and strong palatalisation in Cairo   56
3.2 Cross-tabulation of (dʒ) by age and gender in Medina   57
3.3 Percentage use of [ɛ:] by age and gender in Mecca   58
3.4 Percentage use of [i] by gender and age in Saḥam   60
3.5 Percentage use of [l] by gender and age in Saḥam   61
3.6 Index scores of speakers for (ɛ:) in Korba by gender   62
3.7 Percentage use of [l], *-ik*, and [k] in Sūf   64
3.8 Percentage use of [a] and [a:t] by gender in Ha'il   66
3.9 Percentage use of [ɹ] in Damascus by age, gender, and
neighbourhood   68
3.10 Percentage use of [dʒ] in Qalʿat Siker by age and gender   70
3.11 Percentage use of [dʒ] in Qalʿat Siker by contact and gender   71
3.12 Percentage use of [dʒ] in Dammam by age and gender   72
4.1 Percentage use of weak and strong palatalisation for women in
four social classes   86
5.1 Social class and style for weak palatalisation among women   95
5.2 Social class and style for strong palatalisation among women   95
5.3 Percentage use of rural variant *-u*   97
5.4 Percentage use of [ɹ] by age and life-mode in Damascus   103
6.1 Eimi language use across age groups   123
6.2 Realisation of (dʒ) as [dʒ] by age for the Ajam community
in Kuwait   125
7.1 Progression of a hypothetical change from Form A to Form B   135
7.2 The S-curve   136
7.3 Percentage use of [ɹ] by age and life-mode in Damascus   145
8.1 Aerial view of the Sinai Peninsula   170
9.1 Transition from [q] to [ʔ] across generations in a Nabulsi family   205

Maps

8.1	Reflexes of /k/	162
8.2	Words for 'money'	164
8.3	Estimated dates of arrival of tribes in Sinai	165
8.4	Tribal migration in Sinai	166
8.5	Mixed forms in Sinai	168
8.6	Dialect groups in Sinai	169
8.7	Clear and dark /l/ in Horan	171
8.8	Reflexes of /ʤ/ in Horan	172
8.9	Reflexes of /k/ in Horan	174
8.10	Distribution of reflexes of /q/ and /ʤ/ in the Nile Delta	177
8.11	The Cairo-Damietta route as a barrier	178
9.1	Areal view of h-deletion in Syria	202
9.2	The Nile Delta as a transitional zone	208
9.3	The diphthongs in the Nile Delta	209

Tables

2.1	Examples of phrases used by youth in Arab cities	30
2.2	Distribution of (q) in Gaza	39
2.3	(q) among Gaza-origin speakers in Gaza	39
2.4	(q) among Jaffa-origin speakers in Gaza	39
2.5	Feminine ending in Al-Ahsa	41
3.1	Distribution of (q) by gender among speakers of Gaza origin	53
3.2	Distribution of (q) by gender among speakers of Jaffa origin	53
3.3	Cross-tabulation of (ʤ) by age and gender in Medina	57
3.4	Usage of [ɑ:] across age, gender, and sect	65
4.1	Percentage use of weak and strong palatalisation in Cairo	85
4.2	Effect of language of education on the lenition of (ʕ)	87
5.1	Regionality Index among the Ghamdi in Mecca	100
5.2	Monophthongisation of (ai) among the Ghamdi in Mecca	100
6.1	Examples of Christian, Jewish, and Muslim Baghdadi Arabic	112
6.2	Examples of ʿArab and Baharna linguistic differences in Bahrain	115
6.3	Percentage use of lowering of the feminine ending in Al-Ahsa by linguistic and social factors	118
7.1	Pronominal suffixes in Amman across generations	143
7.2	Examples of affrication in the stem and the suffix amongst the Najdis in Jeddah	147
8.1	Paradigm of /ra/ 'to see' in Maltese	182
8.2	Paradigm of /qagħad/ 'to stay, endure, fit' in Maltese	183
9.1	Intermediate forms in England	207

Acknowledgements

We have been fortunate to work over the years with a talented group of teachers, colleagues, and students. The preparation of this manuscript benefitted from the generosity and scholarship of a great many people, and we wish to express our gratitude to them publicly. They are

Hassan Abdel-Jawad, Noora Abu Ain, Salah Adam, Sara Al Sheyadi, Deema AlAmmar, Hind Alaodini, Munira Al-Azraqi, Mahmoud Al-Batal, Moayyad Al-Bohnayyah, Aziza Al-Essa, Ahmad Al-Jallad, Areej Al-Hawamdeh, Muna Al-Qouz, Imran Al-Rashdan, Mohammad Al-Rohili, Abdullah Al-Shehri, Alyaa Al-Timimi, Najla Alghamdi, Sahar Aloul, Khairiah Alqahtani, Wisam Alshawi, Doug Arnold, Araali Bagamba, Orit Bashkin, Peter Behnstedt, Adam Benkato, Elabbas Benmamoun, David Britain, Kristen Brustad, Maris Camilleri, Dominique Caubet, Vineeta Chand, Jenny Cheshire, Lina Choueiri, Rebecca Clift, William M. Cotter, Alexandra D'Arcy, Stuart Davis, Penelope Eckert, Shahir El-Hassan, Salifu Faal, Maria Fanis, Karen Froud, Marie-Aimée Germanos, Khaldoun Gharaibeh, George Grigore, Atiqa Hachimi, Chryso Hadjidemetriou, Niloofar Haeri, Batoul Hassan, David Heap, Sam Hellmuth, Reuven Horesh, Abeer Hussain, Bruce Ingham, Hanadi Ismail, Shlomo Izre'el, Wyn Johnson, Michael A. Jones, Petra Jones, Eleftherios Kailoglou, Jonathan R. Kasstan, Paul Kerswill, Reem Khamis, Geoffrey Khan, Ghada Khattab, Maciej Klimiuk, Andromahi Koufogiorgou, Nancy Kula, Moncef Lahlou, M. Lynn Landweer, Mark R. Lauersdorf, Julie Lowry, Christopher Lucas, Stefano Manfredi, Leila Messaoudi, Miriam Meyerhoff, Catherine Miller, Lesley Milroy, Mustafa Mughazy, Naomi Nagy, Hamid Ouali, Peter L. Patrick, Robert Potter, Dennis R. Preston, Stephan Procházka, Andrew Radford, Siham Rouabah, Louisa Sadler, Joseph Salmons, Lotfi Sayahi, Devyani Sharma, Andrew Spencer, Lameen Souag, Sali Tagliamonte, Tariq Tell, Sarah Grey Thomason, Kees Versteegh, Ángeles Vicente, Keith Walters, Janet C. E. Watson, Walt Wolfram, Munther A. Younes, Karima Ziamari.

Of these, we would like to thank a select few who have been particularly generous with their time and expertise in responding to queries and providing material for this book: Deema AlAmmar, Peter Behnstedt, Maris Camilleri, Michael A. Jones, and Moncef Lahlou.

Jonathan Owens, Clive Holes, Lesley Milroy, Peter Trudgill, and David Britain have been extremely influential in reorienting our thinking about many issues presented in the book. In addition to their cumulative scholarly insights, we benefitted from many face-to-face discussions with them in the years leading up to the publication of the book.

Helen Barton and Isabel Collins of Cambridge University Press have been both helpful and extremely patient with us throughout.

Moh'd Bilbeisi has once again generously contributed one of his many magnificent paintings to adorn the cover of this book. We thank him warmly.

Finally, a number of people who have been influential to us professionally and personally are, sadly, no longer with us, and we remember them with fondness: Nahid Hattar, Muhammad Hassan Ibrahim, James Milroy, Ellen F. Prince, and Shlomo Raz.

This project was completed in part during a research leave awarded to Enam Al-Wer funded by the Leverhulme Trust (MRF-2016–075), a British Academy Postdoctoral Fellowship (pf160009) awarded to Uri Horesh and a Leverhulme/ British Academy Small Research Grant (SG160689). We thank these organisations for their support.

As this book was going into print, our friend and colleague Peter Behnstedt, a great fieldworker and linguist, who has been at the forefront of Arabic dialectology for half a century, passed away. His work will continue to stand preeminent, and his collegiality and generosity remembered for many years to come.

Transcription, Symbols, and Abbreviations

Transcription of Arabic examples and sounds, as well as of other languages which do not use the Latin alphabet, is generally presented using the International Phonetic Alphabet (IPA) symbols (www.internationalphoneticassociation.org/sites/default/files/IPA_Kiel_2015.pdf).

Proper nouns, including place names, are spelled in their conventional English spelling if one is commonly used (e.g. Mecca, Fez, Amman). Otherwise, they are written in a broad phonemic alphabet using the conventional symbols listed below:

Symbol	IPA equivalent
ā	aː
ē	eː
ī	iː
ō	oː
ū	uː
ʾ	ʔ
ṯ	θ
j/ǧ	ʤ/ʒ
ž	ʒ
ḥ	ħ
ḫ	x
ḏ	ð
ṛ	rˤ
š	ʃ
ṣ	sˤ
ḍ	dˤ
ṭ	tˤ
ḍ	ðˤ
ʿ	ʕ
ġ	ɣ
č	ʧ
g	g
ḳ	kˤ
y	j

Abbreviations

The following abbreviations are used in the book for grammatical categories. When they appear in the general text, they appear in lowercase letters. When they are included in morpheme-by-morpheme glosses, they appear in SMALL CAPS, as is customary in linguistics, and according to the Leipzig Glossing Rules (www.eva.mpg.de/lingua/resources/glossing-rules.php)

1	first person
2	second person
3	third person
f	feminine
m	masculine
sg	singular
pl	plural
def	definite article
adj	adjective
acc	accusative
dat	dative
ind	indicative
rel	relativiser
pfv	perfective
prep	preposition
prog	progressive
gen	genitive
du	dual

Additional abbreviations used in the book:

N	number of tokens
p	p-value
UC	upper class
UMC	upper middle class
MMC	middle middle class
LMC	lower middle class
RI	regionality index

1 Introduction

This book is intended as a textbook and as a resource for research on variation and change in Arabic. The book was designed with a wide range of readers in mind, including students of Arabic linguistics, scholars in linguistics who may or may not know Arabic, and anyone who wishes to expand their knowledge about sociolinguistic theory and methodology as applied to Arabic data.

In selecting the topics to be covered, we followed two principles: relevance to general sociolinguistic theory and availability of empirical data from Arabic-speaking communities. The material included derives from field research in dialectology and sociolinguistics. These sub-fields of linguistics, as we illustrate throughout the book, are interlinked. They are both grounded in field linguistics and focus on language variation. Dialectology, as the name suggests, is the study of dialects, which began as a formal endeavour in the nineteenth century. Traditional dialectology was concerned with describing dialects and accounting for regional variation across dialects. Works in traditional dialectology were presented in grammars, dictionaries, and linguistic atlases.

1.1 Arabic Dialectology

Around the same time as the first large-scale dialectological projects in Europe were carried out, interest in describing Arabic dialects was on the rise as well, with the first such description (of Egyptian Arabic) appearing in 1880 by Wilhelm Spitta.[1] Subsequently, Gotthelf Bergsträsser (1915) published the first linguistic atlas of Arabic dialects, for Syria and Palestine, followed by Jean Cantineau's (1940) atlas of Horan (see Chapter 8).

Many more descriptions of Arabic dialects followed, as well as (more recently) atlases covering the dialects of certain countries and regions (e.g. Syria, Yemen, Palestine, Morocco) and a four-volume lexical atlas of the whole Arab world (by Behnstedt and Woidich 2010–2021).

---

[1] A detailed history of Arabic dialectology is available in Behnstedt and Woidich (2013).

Traditional dialectology provides the fundamental linguistic background necessary for embarking on sociolinguistic research, while sociolinguistics goes beyond description to refine our understanding of dialectological data, highlighting connections to a general theory of language. Since the earliest days of sociolinguistics, research in the field has relied rather heavily on dialectology, with the link between the two fields gradually increasing over the years. The earliest sociolinguistic studies of English varieties in the United States (Labov 1963) and in the United Kingdom (Trudgill 1974) were anchored in dialectological descriptions and in a sense were conceived of as a natural progression from the traditional studies in dialectology.

1.2   The Variationist Approach to Arabic Sociolinguistics

In research on Arabic, the first sociolinguistic study was Clive Holes's investigation of Bahrain (published in 1987). This study embraces two crucial principles. Firstly, its treatment of variation proceeded on the basis of thorough knowledge and detailed dialectological description of the varieties analysed. Secondly, it approached variation and change in the vernacular as a case of interaction between locally based native varieties. Holes separated the macro-level aspect of variation in Arabic, namely standard versus vernacular, from the domain of variation as it is observed within the vernacular.

These are the principles of sociolinguistic analysis of Arabic that we adopt and advocate because they are in keeping with the foundations of sociolinguistic analysis of *any* natural language, Arabic included. This, unfortunately, is not how Arabic data are always approached. We still find analyses of variation in Arabic based on a preoccupation with diglossia, which assume a priori that change in a given Arabic dialect must be either towards Standard Arabic (in Arabic: *al-fuṣḥā*) features or away from them. Thus, we read about seemingly contradictory patterns within the same dialect, whereby one feature changes from a localised variant to one which is identical to a Standard variant (e.g. [ʧ] > [k]) and another from a localised feature that the dialect shares with the Standard towards a non-Standard variant (e.g. [θ] > [t]). The former is often referred to as 'standardisation' and interpreted as being motivated by the prestige of Standard Arabic. The latter is then referred to as 'colloquialisation' and said to be motivated by the prestigious dialectal norm. What such analyses fail to capture is that changes of the type [ʧ] > [k] and those of the type [θ] > [t] follow a single trajectory, which may be characterised as LOCAL-ISED > SUPRALOCAL. In the example cited above, both target variants, [k] and [t], are the realisations of these two phonemes in the supralocal prestigious dialects of the Levant (e.g. Damascus, Beirut, Jerusalem, Amman). These supralocal dialects happen to share many of their features with the Standard (e.g. [k] for /k/), while other features diverge from it (e.g. [t] for /θ/). The fact that one of them, [k], also exists in Standard Arabic, is merely a coincidence. It is thus clear that the trajectory of change in localised dialects, such as the rural dialects of Palestine, is straightforwardly towards these supralocal urban variants.

Another misleading outcome of a 'standardisation' approach (i.e. the assumption that variation revolves around approximating to features present in Standard Arabic) is that it distracts from the sociolinguistically relevant points. For example, staying with Palestinian Arabic, the variable (q) has no fewer than four different variants: [ʔ], [k], [kˤ] and [g]. Research shows that the trajectory of change is systematically towards [ʔ], which is characteristic of the socially dominant city dialects. Speakers of Palestinian Arabic (as is the case in many other speech communities) generally use Standard [q] in a closed set of lexical items, which are understood to be borrowings from Standard Arabic (e.g. /taqriːr/ 'report'). Analysing variation in this case in terms of standardisation would only account for cases where the speakers vary between [q], on the one hand, and any of the other variants, on the other. Not only is this a false interpretation of the use of this variable, but crucially it distracts from the sociolinguistically relevant variation. What is relevant and socially meaningful in this community is the alternation between the vernacular variants [ʔ], [k], [kˤ], [g].

Additionally, there is a small number of speakers who belong to a well-defined social group (the Druze), for whom [q] is the vernacular variant of /q/. The Druze, too, in interdialectal contexts, tend to shift away from their traditional realisation, even though it is identical to that of Standard Arabic. And when they do, the target variant is, once again, [ʔ]. Another example of [q] being part of a traditional Palestinian dialect comes from a study by El Salman (2003) among speakers of Palestinian descent from the village of Tirat Haifa currently resident in Jordan. Here, too, the results show that younger speakers diverge from the traditional [q] variant to the variants used in Jordan, namely [g] and [ʔ].

This is not at all to say that Standard Arabic is irrelevant to Arabic-speaking communities in countries where it is the official language. Native speakers of Arabic of all backgrounds and creeds revere the Standard variety in various ways. It represents a pan-Arab norm, although its utility as a lingua franca between speakers of different dialects is often exaggerated in the literature and in popular perception.[2] It undoubtedly functions as a stylistic device and is the norm used in formal written and spoken domains. The use of Standard Arabic in these domains is worthy of investigation in its own right, and such research has its own decades-long tradition (e.g. the foundational works of Badawi 1985; Mitchell 1978; El-Hassan 1977). However, as a non-native variety,

---

[2] On this point see Holes (2004: 5).

Standard Arabic does not play a role, nor does it have a normative effect on the structure of variation in the core areas of the grammar of the vernacular (phonology, morphology, and syntax).

Understanding the structure of variation and trajectory of change in Arabic begins with the micro-attributes of the local dialect and the community in which this dialect is spoken, i.e. it begins with the specific and gradually expands to more generalisable trends. Basic to this bottom-up approach is the assumption that generalisations, if there are any, can best be identified through an aggregate of locally based studies in a given region. Importantly, this approach is driven by empirical data.

1.3   Diglossia and Code-Switching

An important, novel contribution to the incorporation of diglossia into the discourse about language variation and change in Arabic is Lotfi Sayahi's 2014 book, *Diglossia and Language Contact*: *Language Variation and Change in North Africa*. In this book, Sayahi makes two important contributions. Firstly, he takes a fresh look at the classic definitions of diglossia, starting with Karl Krumbacher (1902), through to Jean Psichari (1928), William Marçais (1930), Ferguson (1959), and finally, Penelope Eckert, who in a 1980 article analysed diglossia, based on data from Gascon,[3] but with broad applications for general sociolinguistics. Secondly, he couches his analysis of diglossia in the speech communities of the Maghreb within contemporary sociolinguistic theory. He does so through illustrating how diglossia interplays with other phenomena such as code-switching, borrowing (lexical and structural), bilingualism, and language variation.

Sayahi distinguishes between diglossia and bilingualism in the context of the Maghreb. This distinction is based on a widely accepted premise: diglossia is within Arabic varieties, whereas bilingualism involves Arabic and some other language. This distinction lends itself to insights on code-switching as well.

Stemming from this distinction is Sayahi's (2014) reference to 'diglossic code-switching' and 'bilingual code-switching', both of which can be oral or written. Other scholars, e.g. Lahlou (1991), only consider the latter, i.e. the discursive alternation between Arabic and another language, as code-switching. This follows the classic definition of the code-switcher as being a bilingual. According to this definition, monolinguals, such as speakers of Arabic whose everyday speech may include elements of their vernacular in combination with elements from Standard Arabic (but with no interference of a foreign language) *cannot* be code-switchers (see Lahlou 1991).

---

[3] Gascon is a Romance language spoken in south-west France.

Code-switching in Arabic has been studied in detail particularly in the North African context. Studies such as Bentahila and Davies (from 1983 onwards), Lahlou (1991), and Ziamari (2003, 2007) in Morocco and Sayahi (2011) in Tunisia explore the post-colonial effects of French as a component in everyday speech, alongside Arabic. Another type of code-switching is between Arabic and European languages, e.g. Dutch, in Europe itself, among Arabic-speaking immigrants (e.g. Boumans 1998, Boumans and Caubet 2000).

Bentahila et al. (2013: 327) summarise the work in this field as follows:

[W]e can draw a distinction between two general approaches to codeswitching. On one hand, we have the strictly formalistic models, focusing largely on structure, formulating absolute generalizations, and claiming to identify universal principles; on the other, there are more holistic, interdisciplinary approaches that take a wider view, acknowledging the relevance of many other variables and drawing on insights from fields such as sociolinguistics, psycholinguistics, pragmatics, discourse, and conversation analysis.

We refer the reader to Sayahi's (2014) book for full coverage of the relationship between code-switching and language variation and change.

1.4 The Link to Historical Linguistics

Another important sub-discipline to which sociolinguistics is connected is historical linguistics, as both are concerned with the study and understanding of language change. Historical linguistics has traditionally analysed language change retrospectively, i.e. after the change had been completed, while sociolinguistics has devised methods to document and explain language change as it progresses. It was William Labov who in the 1960s pioneered the study of language change in this manner. In addition to allowing for the analysis of change in progress, through such means as the apparent time construct, Labov incorporated the social context of language use in the community as an essential component of linguistic theory (see Chapters 2, 7).

1.5 Variation and Change

Language variation and language change are inextricably linked, in the sense that a change from form A to form B implies a stage in which both A and B coexisted, i.e. a stage of variation. From this perspective, what we think of as 'historical change', e.g. the transition from Middle English to Modern English, is the cumulative effect of incremental stages of language variation. An important goal of sociolinguistics is to explain the mechanisms and the social forces that propel these changes, alongside purely linguistic factors. In practice, sociolinguists are primarily concerned with changes which are ongoing. It is thus necessary to provide thorough explanations of social variation in order to understand change. Over the decades, scholars such as Penelope Eckert have further refined the theory to include the analysis of *social meaning*. While this theoretical innovation has continued to focus on language as the main object of study, it added an additional dimension to the interpretation of linguistic variation, arguing that the usage of different linguistic variants mirrors speakers' social positioning, in much the same way as do other performative behaviours, such as clothing and make-up.

Sociolinguistic research is an empirically based scientific discipline, in the sense that it extrapolates generalisations from attested facts. In order to do this, it is necessary to measure patterns of variation according to objective criteria, such as quantitative analysis of the frequency of forms within and across different social groups. It is important to emphasise that this is a means to an end, not an end in itself. The end, in this case, is to identify the sociolinguistic factors that underpin language variation in a community.

1.6   Layout of the Book

The book begins with a chapter on methodology, which provides a concise introduction to the principles and concepts involved in the design and execution of sociolinguistic research on Arabic. In this chapter we also introduce social variation by discussing age, one of the fundamental speaker variables that sociolinguists include in sampling and analysing variation and change.

Chapter 3 is dedicated to gender, another central speaker variable. Research in Arabic sociolinguistics has only recently begun to incorporate an interdisciplinary approach to analysing gender as a social category in a manner comparable to research on other languages. In this chapter we dispel some myths about Arabic and caution against relying on stereotypes and unwarranted generalisations. We advocate an approach to analysing gender in Arabic-speaking communities that considers it a non-discrete social category, whose social meaning is locally constructed.

Chapters 4 and 5 deal with different ways to stratify speech communities, addressing methodological as well as analytical issues. We begin with a discussion of education, a category that has been used widely in the analysis of Arabic data but whose exact relevance to variation and change in Arabic has been poorly understood. We follow with various measures of social stratification and discuss large-scale categorisations such as socio-economic class, as well as smaller-scale groupings such as social networks.

We have dedicated a separate chapter to religion and ethnicity as social variables because we believe they may play a more significant role than previously recognised, especially in an ever-changing political climate. Chapter 6 presents a fresh approach to these two social factors, reviewing classic and more recent studies in Arabic sociolinguistics where one or both of these factors were found to play a role in structuring variation. We connect findings from micro- and macro-level studies, e.g. phonological change coupled with language shift. We present analyses and re-analyses of Arabic data that go beyond the linguistic differences themselves and focus on the underlying causes and factors that foster sociolinguistic variation along religious and/or ethnic lines.

Chapter 7 deals with language change. It lays the theoretical ground for the study of this process, which is central to sociolinguistics. These theoretical aspects are illustrated with an array of empirically tested investigations of several Arabic-speaking communities. We emphasise and elaborate on the connections between historical linguistics and sociolinguistic approaches to the study of language change.

Chapters 8 and 9 cover topics in variation and diffusion of linguistic features across space. We provide extensive examples of traditional dialect geography by reviewing the seminal works of the early Arabic dialectologists. We proceed by introducing recent studies, highlighting the continuity and innovations in the description and cartographic representation of regional variation and the theoretical insights that emanate from them. In Chapter 9 we focus specifically on language contact (and dialect contact) as a necessary precursor to diffusion across space.

We have made every effort to render this book accessible to a wide readership while maintaining a high standard of academic rigour, factual accuracy, and sound intellectual reasoning.

1.7 Further Reading

The following list of recommended reading includes articles and chapters that introduce Arabic sociolinguistics and critically survey research in the field. These resources approach the subject matter from a perspective similar to the approach adopted in this book. We list them here in chronological order to reflect the evolution of the field.

> Holes (1995) – A discussion of koineisation in the dialects of three Arab cities.
>
> Haeri (2000) – On the nexus between Arabic sociolinguistics and linguistic anthropology.
>
> Owens (2001) – A critical review of research in Arabic sociolinguistics to date.
>
> Miller (2007) – An overview of linguistic developments in different types of urban centres.
>
> Owens (2011) – An introduction of Arabic sociolinguistics for scholars in Semitic linguistics.
>
> Owens (2013) – A historico-philosophical perspective on Arabic.

Al-Wer (2013) – A critical review of research in Arabic variationist sociolinguistics focussing on methods and analytical frameworks.

Horesh and Cotter (2015) – A survey of works to date focussing on the sociolinguistics of Palestinian Arabic.

Horesh and Cotter (2016) – A critical survey of variationist research in Arabic, intended for a broad audience of linguists.

Al-Wer and De Jong (2018) – A concise introduction to macro-sociolinguistic aspects of Arabic and the geographical classification of its varieties.

Holes (2018) – An extensive, summative account of historical Arabic dialectology.

Al-Essa (2019) – A critical synthesis of works on phonological and morphological variation in Arabic dialects.

Al-Wer and Horesh (2019) – An epistemology of Arabic sociolinguistics.

Haeri and Cotter (2019) – An update and addendum to Haeri (2000).

Herin (2019) – A coherent illustration of the concept of traditional dialects as applied to Arabic.

Horesh (2021) – An up-to-date evaluation of variationist sociolinguistics contextualised within Arabic linguistics more broadly.

Al-Wer et al. (2022) – A synthesis of recent findings from several Arabic vernaculars and their implications for a general theory of language change.

2 Methodology
Principles and Practice

2.1 Introduction

This chapter provides an introductory coverage of the major issues involved in designing and executing sociolinguistic research with a focus on Arabic – in particular, research that aims to investigate variation and change in spoken Arabic in natural settings. For this type of research, what is required are samples of the *vernacular*. The vernacular corresponds to everyday spontaneous speech as opposed to written language or prepared speech, which is influenced by notions of 'correctness' (see Section 2.3).

Students of Arabic sociolinguistics will find this chapter helpful in designing and executing research projects. It discusses and explains the fundamental principles that have guided research since sociolinguistics emerged as a sub-discipline of linguistics in the 1960s. Further resources that explain specific issues are provided in the Further Reading section at the end of this chapter. These include general principles and methods in sociolinguistics, guidelines for learning and developing skills in statistical modelling and using computational tools, and technical guidance for recording and archiving data.

2.2 Research Design

The first step in embarking on sociolinguistic research is to decide on the investigation topic (i.e. a range of linguistic phenomena) and the community in which to investigate it. The topic of research and the choice of the community are interdependent in that the topic of investigation has to be one which is salient in the speech of that community. For instance, in one of the earliest variationist research projects, Labov (1966) investigated the presence or absence of the sound /r/ in expressions like 'fourth floor' in New York City. While this feature was suitable for research in a community such as New York, where there was significant variation, it would be pointless to do such a study in London, where /r/ is systematically absent, or in California where it is always pronounced. Similarly, it would be futile to investigate variation in an Arabic vernacular that categorically has [g] for /q/ in everyday speech (e.g. Riyadh) or

[ʔ] for /q/ (e.g. Beirut). However, in communities where more than one variant of /q/ is used in casual speech (e.g. Amman, where both [g] and [ʔ] are used), it is viable as a topic of investigation.

Sometimes for personal or practical reasons you might wish to work on your own community. There may be advantages in doing this (see Section 2.3.1), but in this case you need to identify linguistic features which are relevant to that community. On the other hand, you might wish to investigate a particular linguistic phenomenon, e.g. the presence or absence of interdentals, in which case you must choose a community which exhibits variation with respect to that phenomenon. Researchers decide on the linguistic features or phenomena they want to study on the basis of observation or simply on the basis of their intuition. However, the research project must provide concrete evidence to support or refute your initial observations. In making these decisions, reading previous studies can be very useful. Such studies may help you identify topics worthy of further investigation in a community of your choice.

The success of research depends on careful design of the methods of data collection. The task of designing research from scratch may at first appear to be daunting and time-consuming, but it is without a doubt a most exciting, productive, and rewarding experience. You end up with a precious reward, data that you can call your own, which you will be able to draw upon for future research endeavours as well. Because sociolinguistic research often involves relatively lengthy stays and frequent interaction with members of the local community, you also end up forming a special bond with the place and its people.

When deciding on which method of data collection to follow, the rule of thumb is that the *methods should be dictated by the objectives of the research.* The methods may involve only minimal intervention by the fieldworker, as in the methods that involve observation of interactions in which the fieldworker does not participate, or maximal involvement as in the case of conducting face-to-face interviews with the participants in the research. But while there is wide variation in the methods of data collection, all types of sociolinguistic research embrace the following fundamental principles.

The most important of these principles is that analysis of language should be *descriptive* rather than *prescriptive.* In other words, the analysis should be based on the way language is actually used rather than the way (someone thinks) it should be or can be used. To achieve this objective, analysing a language requires *empirical data* and these data must be collected *in the field.* The field of research is not a laboratory or an office but a community of people who live in a certain locality. The locality itself can be a neighbourhood or any such sub-area within a town, village, or a large city. Therefore, all types of sociolinguistic research require the fieldworker to enter a community, select speakers from that community, and collect samples of their speech. Relying on the researcher's intuition or the intuitions of native speakers (as opposed to their actual usage) as the primary source of data is unacceptable.

Secondly, while researchers may formulate hypotheses or assumptions about what some of the results might turn out to be prior to collecting and analysing the data, their aim of conducting the research is never to *confirm* these hypotheses but to *explore* them (and maybe uncover new ones). In other words, the aim of research should always be *exploratory* rather than *confirmatory*. After the data have been collected and analysed, the researchers can then check their hypotheses against the actual results.

In the next section of this chapter, we address the 'observer's paradox', a central problem in sociolinguistic research, in particular the type of research that aims to investigate linguistic variation and change.

2.3 The Observer's Paradox

In research aimed at investigating linguistic variation and change, it is necessary for the pool of data to contain samples of *vernacular* speech. Labov defines the vernacular as 'the form of language first acquired, perfectly learned, and used only among speakers of the same variety' (Labov 1984: 29). Speakers normally use the vernacular when they are least conscious of their speech and thus monitor it least closely. Studies of variation and change are interested in obtaining samples of vernacular speech because it is thought to be the maximally *regular* form of speech and therefore the source of systematic linguistic change.

This form of natural, unmonitored speech that is free of conscious interference from other forms of language normally only emerges when the context of speech is informal and in interactions among close associates, such as family members and close friends. The conundrum is that collecting data involves the presence of a researcher and recording equipment, which automatically increases the formality of speech. Therefore, the paradox with which the researcher (the observer) is faced is this: *to observe the way speakers talk when they are not being observed.*

To what extent the observer's paradox influences the quality of the data collected will depend on a number of factors. Firstly, it depends on the relationship between the researcher and the community. Some researchers investigate their own communities and their own dialects and are thus seen as 'insiders'. Being an insider, an immediate member of the community under investigation, has the benefit of reducing the formality of the data collection event in several ways. For instance, the speakers are more likely to trust the researcher and to be more relaxed in their presence. The researcher is also likely to be a native speaker of the same dialect as the speakers, which may encourage the speakers to maintain their normal linguistic behaviour. The social distance between the researcher and the speakers is also likely to be reduced in these circumstances. Most often researchers are associated with institutions of higher education, and their educational achievement can be intimidating for some speakers. In cases where the researcher is an insider to the community, this intimidation is likely to be reduced (but not necessarily so). Overall, researchers who investigate their own communities have a more straightforward task in finding speakers, getting them to agree to take part in the research, and generally in maintaining informality. At the same time, however, being an insider carries with it some obligations, which can, depending on the community in question, interfere with the pace of the research. For instance, one of the authors, Enam Al-Wer, reports that while conducting research in various localities in Jordan, she found that it was much easier to stick to the fieldwork schedule in the towns where she was a 'stranger' than in localities where she had considerable familial or friendship connections because in the latter cases she was expected to socialise with the community, not just conduct research and leave. The sociolinguistic literature contains a wide range of similar fieldwork anecdotes.

The advantages of being an insider are considerable, but this neither means that insiders necessarily make better researchers nor that it is necessary to be an insider to the community to conduct research in that community. In actual fact, there are very many studies in sociolinguistics that were carried out by outsiders rather than by insiders. In Arabic dialectology, the seminal works were carried out by researchers who were not just outsiders to the specific communities they studied but also non-native speakers of Arabic. Regardless of the researcher's relationship to the community they are interested in, and whether or not they are native speakers of the language they investigate, the skills required are the same. A researcher must learn and fully familiarise themselves with the language, as well as with the structure of the community and its social values. In order to acquire a thorough knowledge of the community, extensive preparatory work is necessary prior to collecting linguistic data. Once in the field, such knowledge can be augmented through ethnography (see Section 2.5).

There are important skills that a researcher needs to have regardless of their personal relationship with the community of their investigation. The fieldworkers' research skills, in particular their ability to build a good rapport with the speakers, helps reduce the formality of the context and hence reduce the effects of the observer's paradox. The setting or the venue where the data collection takes place is another factor that can affect the quality of the data. Researchers often prefer a home setting, rather than a public place, to conduct their interviews. Normally the data collection event takes place in the speakers' own homes where they are likely to feel more relaxed and less formal. Finally, the topic of discussion can have a significant influence on the extent to which the data obtained are a close representation of the vernacular, as explained below.

2.3.1   Reducing the Effect of the Observer's Paradox

It may appear that the best way to eliminate the effect of the observer's paradox is to record the speakers without their knowledge. Surreptitious recording of speakers as a solution to the observer's paradox is not an option in academic research. Such a practice is considered unethical and, in many countries, illegal. It is incumbent upon researchers to find solutions to research problems that are not only practical but also adhere to research ethics (see Section 2.10).

Eliminating the effect of the observer's paradox completely may be untenable. The various strategies and refinements to existing methods, such as the ones explained in this section, focus on ways to *reduce* those effects. We will first cite techniques suggested by some of the founders of sociolinguistics, who have gathered data in English-speaking countries. We later turn to techniques based on our own and colleagues' experiences, spanning years of fieldwork in Arabic-speaking communities.

Labov has suggested a number of ways in which the sociolinguistic interview itself can be controlled to divert the attention of the speakers from the fact that they are being interviewed and that their speech is being recorded. One such method was specifically designed to engage the speakers in narratives (storytelling) of personal experiences. The idea is that when speakers are involved emotionally, they pay less attention to their speech and consequently lapse into casual speech. This strategy is popularly known as the 'Danger of Death' question, named after the actual question that Labov put to the speakers in his New York study. The original exact wording of this question was as follows: 'Have you ever been in a situation where you thought you were in serious danger of being killed – where you thought to yourself *This is it*?' (Labov 1972: 113).

If the answer to the question was affirmative, Labov prompted them to recount the story by asking them 'what happened?' This method proved to be successful in eliciting what was considered by Labov as 'casual' speech in his research. In recounting life-threatening experiences in these interviews, the speakers showed signs of tension, which was taken to signify their emotional involvement.

While the method of posing provocative questions in order to obtain spontaneous speech has been widely used in sociolinguistic research, the content of the question has been modified to suit different communities in different research. For instance, in Peter Trudgill's study in Norwich, the parallel question was the following: 'Have you ever been in a situation, recently or some time ago, where you had a good laugh, or something funny and humorous happened to you, or you saw it happen to someone else?' (Trudgill 1974: 51). Trudgill reported that his informants found this question natural and acceptable, especially since he posed it at the end of a series of questions about

Norwich and whether it was possible to have a good time in the city. In this study, too, the method proved to be successful. Getting the speakers to tell a story, here involving a comical incident, produced a casual type of speech.

The 'Danger of Death' question in the form used by Labov is nowadays considered inappropriate. For many people, being asked to recount incidents where their lives were endangered can cause considerable distress. Students of sociolinguistics are strongly advised to avoid raising topics that may in any way cause harm, emotional distress, or embarrassment to their informants. In the Belfast research, which was conducted by Lesley Milroy at a time when violence was commonplace in the city, she did not find the question helpful in eliciting casual speech, but she also recounts an incident from her fieldwork to highlight the inappropriateness of the question in Belfast at the time:

During a conversation with a working-class family about the general hardships of life, it emerged that one nineteen-year-old man had already had a number of narrow escapes from death. First, as a merchant seaman he had almost drowned in the Baltic ... then he had been held up by gunmen in a Belfast alley-way; arrested and beaten up by troops ... and two months before the period of the research he had been shot in the legs.

(L. Milroy 1987: 40)

Other ways of controlling the interview that have been tried and proven successful in diverting attention and producing casual speech include the following. The researcher can allow the recorder to run outside the context of the formal interview, e.g. before the interview starts, after it has finished, and during break times (while the formal interview is suspended). Sociolinguists argue that there is no deception involved by following this method since the speakers are aware that they are being recorded and the recording equipment is visible to them. If it turns out that the excerpts recorded outside the interview contained information that the speakers did not wish to include as part of the material they agreed to supply, the researcher is under obligation to erase these parts immediately.

As mentioned above, sociolinguistic interviews normally take place in the informants' homes. Sometimes a third person enters the room wanting a quick word with the participant or the participant answers the phone. Researchers report that such interruptions, where the participant addresses a third person (who is normally a member of their family) encourage the production of vernacular speech. This part of the interview is usually included as part of the data collected from the participant.

Finally, it sometimes happens that speakers digress from the topic of discussion. Researchers encourage such digressions, which often involve the speakers choosing to tell long stories about their favourite topics. In Trudgill's research in Norwich for instance, he reported that the older speakers in particular digressed considerably from the subjects of discussion and he encouraged them to 'continue with their reminiscences, stories and favourite topics' (1974: 51). Digressions of this sort can provide data similar to those obtained through the 'Danger of Death' question since more often than not speakers in such circumstances tell emotive stories that involve their personal lives. An elderly woman in one of our studies spent two hours telling stories about her family, which provided a rich sample of spontaneous speech. Clearly, these methods cannot be planned ahead of the interview since it is not possible to predict developments of this sort. A skilled fieldworker knows how to make use of opportunities when they arise in the course of the interview.

A partial solution to the observer's paradox is to ask the speakers to record themselves without the presence of the fieldworker. This method was used in a number of studies. For instance, in a study in Glasgow, Scotland, Jane Stuart-Smith (1999) asked her speakers to record themselves in pairs without her presence. This method eliminates the effect of the presence of the researcher, but it does not eliminate the effect of the presence of the recorder. Also, because the researcher has no control over the interview, the method has limitations. For instance, it is impractical for studies that require elicitation of different styles of speech through deliberate manipulation of topics of discussion, manipulation of task (reading versus speaking), elicitation of certain structures or forms through using pictures, etc.

There are considerable advantages to be gained from interviewing speakers in groups (with the researcher present). The presence of other members of one's friendship group tends to reduce the formality of the event and may put the speakers at ease. In such interviews, attention is often diverted away from the fieldworker, who may assume the role of a participant or simply a keen listener, while the group members interact with each other. The study by Labov and his associates in the New York City neighbourhood of Harlem and the research by Walt Wolfram and his team in North Carolina used group interviews. Group interviews are very rewarding as far as the quality of the data is concerned, and they certainly help reduce the effect of the observer's paradox. They are, however, considerably more difficult to analyse. For instance, it is sometimes difficult to keep track of who said what in the interview, though in recent years high-quality, affordable video equipment has become readily available, which can help alleviate this obstacle. Also, some participants may dominate the conversation and thus cause the database to become imbalanced in terms of amount of data per speaker. Even if the researcher predicts this imbalance while the recording is taking place, e.g. by noticing that one or two speakers dominate the discussion, it is still difficult to rectify the situation without attracting the attention of the participants, which in turn can counteract the purpose of interviewing the speakers in groups in the first place.

One of the significant refinements to sociolinguistic methodology is the *ethnographic approach*, which involves gaining a thorough knowledge of the local culture, structure of the community, and its dynamics, as well as establishing contacts and becoming closely acquainted with members of the community under investigation. Therefore, the fieldworker normally invests a considerable amount of time living in the locality under investigation and interacting with its members before making the recordings. Having established local contacts, the fieldworker is introduced to potential speakers through the local contacts as a 'friend' or as a 'friend of a friend', rather than as a researcher. This method of introduction proved to be very successful in Milroy's study in Belfast. Being introduced to the community as a friend of their friend gained her trust among the participants and subsequently their permission to run her tape recorder in their homes while they were going about doing what they normally do. In this part of the research in Belfast, the data were not collected through face-to-face interviews but through recording ordinary daily interactions in the homes of the participants during which the fieldworker, Lesley Milroy herself, was present and in which she participated. In this approach, the 'observer' becomes also a 'participant', which is why the method is commonly known as 'participant observation'. Notice that in this approach to data collection the two aspects of the data collection event that give rise to the observer's paradox are addressed through (i) positioning the fieldworker as an insider through careful preparation prior to data collection and (ii) replacing the face-to-face interview with recordings of ordinary day-to-day interactions.

The benefits of the ethnographic approach in sociolinguistic research are far-reaching and significant not only at the level of improving the quality of the data obtained but also at the levels of analysis and interpretation of data. The knowledge gained through doing ethnography in the community is often the key to interpreting the results. We further elaborate on the ethnographic approach in Section 2.5.

2.4   Interviews, Elicitation, and Other Strategies

Although many researchers follow alternative methods, some of which have been mentioned above (e.g. participant observation), the face-to-face recorded interview has remained the standard method of data collection in sociolinguistics. The interview method has been refined over the years to improve the quality of data and, as we have seen, the design of the interview contains various strategies to reduce the effect of the observer's paradox. The standard interview format normally includes different sections depending on the nature of the linguistic variables under investigation and the range of speech styles the investigator wants to elicit. The various strategies explained in Section 2.3.1 are geared towards reducing the formality of the interview situation in order to obtain samples of speech that resemble the vernacular as closely as possible. This style of speech is considered 'casual'. In many studies, 'style' is considered a variable, and therefore the researcher needs to obtain a range of styles in order to investigate the effect of change in style on variation. In the earlier landmark studies by Labov in New York and Trudgill in Norwich, different styles were elicited through changing the task, from speaking to reading. The reading task itself was further manipulated to include different types of material (e.g. reading passage, minimal pairs). We must remember, however, that for Arabic, reading styles are not on the same continuum as speaking styles, and therefore reading tasks as a way to elicit different styles in the vernacular should be carefully thought out ahead of time. For instance, asking the speakers to read a text written in the Standard variety is likely to render normativised standard pronunciations. Such data cannot be compared to spontaneous speech uttered in the vernacular itself. One way around this can be to design reading tasks that are based on texts originally written in the vernacular, such as text messages and social media posts.

We now turn our attention to problems that are not so much associated with the *formality* of the interview situation but with eliciting data that contain specific types of variables. Normally, a long enough interview (1–2 hours) provides a sufficient number of tokens, or instances, of pronunciation features. However, for variables at other grammatical levels, during a free interview, where the speakers are mainly responding to questions put to them by the interviewer, only a few tokens of the required variables may occur. This is especially true of syntactic variables in general, simply because they do not occur frequently enough in spontaneous speech. For instance, Cheshire (2005) reports that in 32 interviews only 144 instances of 'multiple negation' (*I don't want nothing*) were obtained, an average of 4.5 tokens per speaker. Compare this to a study of the STRUT-FOOT distinction in Manchester English by Turton and Baranowski (2020), where the number of tokens obtained for this phonological variable averaged 62 per speaker.

There are more specific syntactic features that may not occur at all in an interview situation. Rickford and Wasow (1995) suggest two solutions to this problem. One solution is to observe and record data from the speech community over an extended period of time. The other solution is to use corpora of spoken data where available. Corpora (plural of *corpus*) are collections of attested utterances, which nowadays can be accessed electronically to search for particular features. There are several online corpora that include transcribed speech in Arabic dialects.

Sociolinguistic research on languages such as Arabic faces additional complications of a different nature in data collection. For instance, in some Arabic dialects, there are certain syntactic, morphological, and morphophonemic features that inflect for gender and number. In order to elicit such features in natural speech, interactions have to include a group of female and male speakers. Therefore, a one-to-one interview conducted by either a male or a female researcher will not elicit the range of data required.

A stereotype often propagated about 'Arab societies' concerns restrictions on the interaction between women and men outside the family circle. This is sometimes used as an over-generalisation that ignores the wide variability that exists in Arabic-speaking communities. Some Arab societies are indeed strict, to the point of prohibiting such interactions, while in others it is not an issue at all. In the context of conducting research on Arabic, conventions based on stereotypes often discourage researchers – especially young researchers – from exploring the actual norms of the specific community they intend to study and adjusting their methods accordingly. In many cases, the researcher will find that the restrictions they had presupposed are either non-existent or not as rigid as originally thought. Even when such restrictions do exist in a given community, the researcher should try to explore alternative methods to ensure sufficient representation of all social categories in their locality of interest.

In Aziza Al-Essa's research (2008) in Jeddah, Saudi Arabia, she was faced with both types of complications, namely the need to alternate the interview setting according to the grammatical data required and social restrictions that prevented her from conducting the interviews with male speakers outside her family circle. She dealt with the problem of interviewing male speakers by recruiting interviewers from both gender groups. To obtain data for the plural verbal endings *-ūn* (m) and *-in* (f), which required plural addressees, she conducted group interviews (2–3 people) and used picture elicitation. The speakers were asked to describe what they saw in pictures which were designed specifically to elicit the variables under investigation. To obtain data for the 2nd person singular feminine ending variable (*-ik*), she used two strategies. First, in order to maximise the number of tokens elicited from men, she trained two women to interview male members of their own family.

Commenting on obtaining data in his own research in Bahrain, where he faced obstacles both as a man and as a foreigner, Professor Clive Holes offers the following advice:[1]

It can be a big problem accessing data from females, particularly elderly ones in conservative communities, if you are male. I found that a very effective way round this was to train proxies. I trained male relatives of elderly females (their mothers, aunts, grandmothers) in communities I could never otherwise have had access to, or younger educated female relatives (university students, teachers). I was interested in obtaining recordings of relaxed conversation. The proxies told their relatives that they wanted to record them on behalf of a foreigner interested in the culture they had known in their youth, without mentioning any linguistic motivation. I would say that about 60% of the proxies proved adept at getting their interviewees to relax, and had the skill to draw

---

[1] We are grateful to Clive Holes for offering us these insights via email in 2020 and consenting to their inclusion in this book.

them out. Others were either not very skilled, or chose uncommunicative informants or couldn't operate the recording equipment effectively or several of these shortcomings. But I got some fantastic and very natural data this way.

2.5   The Ethnographic Approach

Research begins by selecting a locality and community. As mentioned at the beginning of this chapter, the size of the locality can range from a large city with a very large population to a small village with a few hundred inhabitants. Researchers may target a specific community in that locality, such as a certain neighbourhood within a city that is previously known to be inhabited by a group of people who share certain characteristics, such as a group of migrants from a specific background or a specific ethnic or religious group.

Once the locality and the community have been identified, researchers begin a process of data collection, which we shall call *ethnography*. It begins by gathering as much background information as possible about the place and the people. This will include historical information and historical events that may have affected the place and the demography (wars, migration, etc.); the local economy (growth, industry, employment); the physical environment (layout of buildings, layout of residential quarters); anthropological information (descriptions of people, their social structure and social dynamics, their cultures, customs and habits); who lives where; what languages/dialects they speak; and so on. Additionally, previous records of the dialect under investigation or of related dialects need to be consulted. These records may be previous linguistic studies, dialectological descriptions, and linguistic atlases (see Chapter 8). The extent to which the records are relevant to the research being planned will depend on the peculiarities of each case and on the available resources.

Naturally, the amount of background information available for different communities varies quite widely, and localities for which there is little or no documentation pose a challenge for the researcher. In such cases, relevant information may be gleaned from talking to the local residents, especially the older generation. In many societies around the world, oral tradition, rather than written documents, is the normal channel through which information is passed down the generations. Even in places that have efficient state institutions that gather population and historical data, some of the data are inaccessible for political reasons. Cases in point are Levantine countries which have directly experienced the turmoil of the Palestinian forced migration and, more recently, the rise of religious fundamentalism. In Jordan, for instance, it is not possible to find statistics based on census data regarding ethnicity and religion. In Palestine itself, much of the historical and archival material is controlled by the Israeli occupying authorities, who have banned access to most records related to the *Nakba* and the displacement of Palestinians. In order to overcome these restrictions, researchers in the region have relied on personal experiences, living memories, stories passed down, informal oral histories, and the like. Some of these personal recounts are available in print or online, but in many cases the researcher needs to find ways of obtaining and verifying such information during their fieldwork.

Ethnography is not an add-on to the gathering of linguistic data but serves as a broad methodological framework. It entails the researcher immersing themselves in the community in order to gain well-rounded knowledge of that community, including its history, local dynamics, practices, and values, and to incorporate this information into the analysis of sociolinguistic variation.

Language variation is most often socially meaningful. Whether intentionally or not, speakers make use of variation in language to position themselves within their community. Discovering this social meaning is a fundamental task for the researcher. This can be demonstrated through Leila Messaoudi's analysis of variation and change in Rabat, the capital of Morocco, where she traced contact and koineisation between speakers of the old urban dialect of Rabat and the rural dialect of Zaer (on the outskirts of Rabat), resulting in the formation of the new dialect of Rabat (Messaoudi 2019). This new dialect has features from the old dialect as well as features from the neighbouring rural dialect, which are used variably. One of the interesting variables is (q). The old dialect has [qʰ], the rural dialect has [g], while the new dialect has [q] and [g] variably, depending on context. The alternation between [q] and [g] is so full of social meaning that the use of one variant or the other implies a bundle of characteristics, including labels used pejoratively to target certain groups. The neutral term for a native of Rabat is *rbaṭi* (associated with [qʰ]), but speakers of the new dialect (who alternate between [q] and [g]), coined the term *rbiṭi* – literally 'little Rabati' – to mock the group who speak the old dialect, which contains [qʰ]. Those who consider themselves the original community of Rabat, speakers of the old urban dialect, call the newcomers *mrabbeṭ*, which connotes 'fake Rabati; Rabati wannabe'.

This example demonstrates how social meanings emerge and how they relate directly to linguistic usage. The ethnographic approach to researching a speech community enables us to discern social meaning, as it involves paying attention to fine details, both of linguistic practice and of the social evaluation it receives within the community. Penelope Eckert, whose work among teenagers in suburban Detroit epitomises the ethnographic approach to sociolinguistic research, summarises this succinctly:

The sociolinguistic enterprise involves, importantly, the investigation of the local deployment of linguistic resources as they are imbued with social meaning [...] Because meaning is made in day-to-day practice, much of it tacitly, the study of social meaning requires access to this practice.

(Eckert 1997b: 54)[2]

---

[2] The full text can be found at web.stanford.edu/~eckert/PDF/whyethnography.pdf (accessed 2 February 2022).

2.6 The Subject of Investigation: Linguistic Variables

For the subject of their investigation, researchers choose linguistic features that have more than one way of being realised by native speakers. Such features are called 'linguistic variables'. The different forms or different realisations of a linguistic variable must have the same *referential* meaning. For instance, in Jordanian varieties of Arabic, the pronunciations [ɡɑmɪħ] and [ɡɑmʊħ] both refer to 'wheat', i.e. they have the same referential meaning. However, this alternation only occurs in northern Jordanian dialects, while elsewhere in the country only [ɡɑmɪħ] is used. Therefore, it is a *variable* in the north, which we may signify as (u). Note that we use parentheses to denote linguistic variables, and the symbol used between the parentheses usually represents the broad quality of the variable but need not be phonetically precise. This variable has two *variants*: [ɪ] and [ʊ]. We use IPA symbols between square brackets to denote variants. This information is usually conveyed in the following manner:

(u): [ɪ], [ʊ]

The example above concerns a *phonological variable*, which simply means that the variation is one of pronunciation. Linguistic variables can be found at every level of grammar. Below are some examples of morphophonemic, morphological, and syntactic variables from varieties of Arabic.

2.6.1 *Morphophonemics*

In the dialect of the Šammar tribe in Ha'il, Saudi Arabia, studied by Deema AlAmmar (2017), the plural feminine ending -*āt* can be realised in three different ways: [aːt], [aːh] and [aːj]. Note that the pronunciation of /t/ as [h] or [j] only occurs in this morpheme; other occurrences of the phoneme /t/ are not affected, such that /t/ in /ktaːb/ 'book', for instance, is not variable. For this reason, we refer to this variable as a *morphophonemic* variable.

2.6.2 *Morphology*

In some Arabic dialects, the paradigm of verbs includes separate forms for feminine and masculine plural, while others use one form only to refer to both genders. For example, in the verb *rāḥ* 'to go', some dialects use a form such as *rāḥu* 'they went' for agents of both genders, as follows:

(1)   li-wlād rāḥu 'the boys went'

(2)   l-banāt rāḥu 'the girls went'

Other dialects have a separate form for the feminine plural, as in the following example:

(3)   li-wlād rāḥu 'the boys went'

(4)   l-banāt rāḥin 'the girls went'

Many Arabic dialects show variation, and some are in the process of change, whereby the feminine plural form is being gradually eliminated from the paradigm. For instance, consider the following examples from a Bedouin dialect of Fazzān, in southwestern Libya (D'Anna 2017: 106), which demonstrates this variation.

(5)   **žan**   n-neswān   fi   ḥōš   el-maṛa
        came.3.F.PL   DEF-woman.PL   in   house   DEF-woman
        idīru   l-ʕers   yōm-ēn
        3.make.M.PL   DEF-wedding   day-DU
        'The women came to the bride's house to celebrate the wedding for two days.'

(6)   **ižu**   n-nesāwīn   iwāṭō   l-hen   l-bēt;
        3.come.M.PL   DEF-woman.PL   3.unload.M.PL   for-them.F   DEF-tent
        yugoʕden   **yəbnen**   f   əl-bēt ...
        3.stay.F.PL   3.build.F.PL   PREP   DEF-tent
        'The women arrive and (the men) unload for them the tent. They (the women) set up the tent.'

   The verbs in bold in examples (5) and (6) all refer to women. Note that while the verbs *žan*, *yugoʕden*, and *yəbnen* have the feminine ending *-n*, showing agreement with the feminine subject, the verbs *idīru* and *ižu* do not overtly indicate feminine gender and are identical to the masculine plural forms.
   Numerous Arabic dialects, including in Libya itself, have in fact lost gender distinction in the 2nd and 3rd plural paradigms, including verbal suffixes, pronominal suffixes, and independent pronouns. Variation as in examples (5) and (6) can be taken as indication of change in progress and thus worthy of sociolinguistic investigation (see Chapter 7).

2.6.3   Syntax

In Palestinian dialects of Arabic, the relativiser *illi*, which is used in an invariant form (i.e. it does not inflect for gender or number), traditionally only occurs following definite nouns, while relative clauses following indefinite nouns prohibit the occurrence of a relativiser. Consider the following two examples.

(7)   l-walad illi sākin žambna 'the boy who lives next to us'

(8)   šift walad 'īdo maksūra 'I saw a boy whose arm was broken'

But the following example is ungrammatical:

(9)   *šift walad illi ʾīdo maksūra 'I saw a boy whose arm was broken'

On the other hand, Palestinian Arabic–Hebrew bilingual speakers produce sentences where *illi* is used with indefinite nouns, as in (11). Consider the following examples from the central Palestinian dialect of Taybeh.

(10)   b-iħtaːʒ-u   la-mustaʃaːr   mihni   Ø ʕand-o   maʕrife
        IND-need-3PL   DAT-advisor   professional   Ø PREP-3M.SG.GEN   knowledge
        'They need a professional counsellor who has knowledge.'

(11)   ʔana   ʔinsaːn-e   illi   ħasˤal-et   ʕala   laqab   θaːliθ
        I   human-F   REL   obtain.PFV-1SG   PREP   degree   third
        'I am a person who has obtained a doctorate.'

Examples (10) and (11) show that following indefinite nouns, speakers either use an overt relativiser or not, i.e. it is neither prohibited, as in the traditional dialects, nor required. It is likely that this expansion in the use of the relativiser to contexts of indefinite nouns is a result of contact with Modern Hebrew, which obligatorily uses the relativiser *še-* with all nouns, regardless of definiteness.

In a recent study of the dialect of the *Yāl Saʿad* tribe in Oman, Sara Al Sheyadi (2022) examined variation and change in an intriguing syntactic feature, the marking of definiteness with or without an overt article. A somewhat similar feature is reported for Bahrain and for Central Asian varieties of Arabic.

The variable involves variation between the overt article *l-* generally used to mark definiteness in the dialect and the absence of an overt article in semantically and syntactically definite nouns. Consider the following examples:[3]

(12)   n- rabbī- hin   fi   Ø-bēt.
        1PL-raise- 3PL.F   in   Ø-house
        'We raise them [the cows] in [the] house.'

(13)   mā- ṭlaʿ   mi- l- bēt.
        NEG-1SG.go out   from-DEF-house
        'I don't go out of the house.'

(14)   a- tšōf   ʿa   Ø-bāb.
        1SG-look.PROG   at   Ø-door
        'I was looking at [the] door.'

---

[3] The authors are grateful to Sara Al Sheyadi for providing these examples from the data she has collected.

(15)   mā- fitaḥ-ni   l- bāb,   a- fitḥ- i   l- bāb?
        NEG-open-1PL   DEF-door   1SG-open-3SG.M   DEF-door
        'We haven't opened the door; shall I open the door?'

In all of these examples, the clause-final nouns *bēt* and *bāb* are definite. In examples (13) and (15), the definiteness is marked by the overt article *l-*, whereas in examples (12) and (14), this article is absent. One of the challenges in the analysis of this variable, and syntactic variables in general, is to define the range of variation (see Section 2.7). Specifically, not all nouns lacking an overt article are definite, and not all definite nouns *can* occur with a null article. Al Sheyadi conducted an intricate analysis of all tokens, first in order to determine which of them to include in the quantitative analysis, and then to conduct the analysis and arrive at conclusions (see Al Sheyadi 2022, chapter 7).

2.7   Defining a Variable and Range of Variation

2.7.1   *The Dependent Variable*

When analysing linguistic variation, the first task is to define the linguistic variable and its range of variation. A linguistic variable is a linguistic unit that has more than one way of being realised. For example, in Amman, the phoneme /dʒ/ can be realised as either [dʒ] or [ʒ]. Therefore, we can define (dʒ) as a linguistic variable in the Ammani dialect. On the other hand, there are other dialects where this phoneme is not variable and only has one possible realisation, e.g. Beirut, where it is always realised as [ʒ], and Aleppo, where it is always realised as [dʒ]. Therefore, in the dialects of Beirut and Aleppo, /dʒ/ is *not* a variable.

Once you decide that a certain feature is variable, you move on to identifying the range of variation. What this principally means is to identify the contexts in which the linguistic feature is variable and the contexts in which it is not variable, i.e. where only one of the variants occurs categorically. The contexts in which the feature is variable are what we are interested in exploring. Since in most cases, a subsequent step will involve quantitative analysis, we shall refer to such variables using statistical terminology and call them *dependent variables*.

Defining the linguistic variable and its range of variation requires a close examination of the data to determine where the linguistic feature in question is variable and where it is not. You will come across expressions that contain a certain realisation of the variable, but in these expressions themselves, the feature is not variable. For instance, in Jordan, the phrase /l-marħale θ-θaːnawijje/ 'secondary school' is invariably realised with the sound [θ], even among speakers who do have variation in other words, such as [θaːni] ~ [taːni] 'second'. Several such words and expressions, which are clearly borrowings from Standard Arabic, are used in specific contexts and in discussing certain topics. Occurrences of the invariable items in the data should be *excluded*, as they do not fall within the *range of variation* for this variable.

In more complex cases, defining the variable requires examining the grammar of the dialect more closely. In the dialect of Damascus, the variable (h), which was studied by Hanadi Ismail (2007) concerns the presence or absence of /h/, i.e. (h): [h], Ø. This variation is confined to a particular morpheme and a specific phonological context (therefore we call it a *morphophonemic* feature). Morphologically, the variation between [h] and Ø is only possible when /h/ occurs in the 3rd person suffixes *-ha* and *-hon*, but it does not affect /h/ in the stem of the word. For example: variation can occur in /ʕammha/ ~ /ʕamma/ 'her uncle' where /h/ is part of the suffix; but not in /hoːn/ 'here' where /h/ is part of the stem. Secondly, it is constrained by the preceding vowel; /h/ cannot be dropped after /aː/. For example, variation occurs in /ixtha/ ~ /ixta/ 'her sister', but not in /ramaːha/ 'he threw it (f)', where /h/ comes after /aː/. So, the range of variation of (h) in Damascus contains only the tokens that are *potentially* variable, namely suffix /h/ when it is not preceded by /aː/. All tokens in which no variation is possible are excluded, i.e. in which /h/ occurs categorically (stem /h/, and suffix /h/ after /aː/)

In several eastern Arabic dialects, historical /k/ was affricated, resulting in [ʧ] or [ts]. This affrication, however, affected /k/ when it occurred in the environment of a front vowel [i], [e], [a], or in some dialects a high back vowel [u]. Nowadays, these affricates are undergoing change to the velar stop [k], as in the following examples.

(16)   ʧam > kam 'how many' (Sūf, Jordan)

(17)   ʧeːf > keːf 'how' (Sūf, Jordan)

(18)   tseːf > keːf 'how' (Qasim, Saudi Arabia)

(19)   jabtsi > jabki 'he cries' (Qasim, Saudi Arabia)

Because not all occurrences of historical /k/ became affricates in these dialects, in the reverse process of affricate-to-stop that is in progress currently, not every occurrence of [k] that we find counts as a token of this variable. For example, in Jordanian Arabic, the [k] in the word /kumm/ 'sleeve' was never affricated, and therefore its occurrence in this word is not a result of de-affrication. Similarly, in the Najdi dialect of Qasim, [k] in /djuːk/ 'roosters' was not affricated to [ts] in the first place and thus is not a legitimate token of the variable. Therefore, in designing a study to investigate these features, all the words in which /k/ was not historically affricated have to be excluded, and the range of variation for this variable will include all items that can potentially occur with either variant.

Having defined the linguistic variables and ascertained the range of variation for each of them, we can begin the process of analysis, starting with identifying the *independent variables*. The independent variables are the set of factors that we hypothesise may have an effect on the probabilities of occurrence of the different realisations (variants) of the dependent variables. They consist of two types of factors, or constraints. The first type is called *linguistic constraints* because it concerns factors that are internal to the linguistic system being studied. The second type of factors is *non-linguistic*, external to the linguistic system, and consists of *social* factors, such as age, gender, and socioeconomic class, and *contextual* factors that indicate the *style* of speech. These concepts will be explained in the next sections.

2.7.2   Independent Variables

Variation in language is not random but *structured* by language-internal (linguistic) constraints and language-external constraints (social and stylistic). We begin with the linguistic constraints – what they are and how they function.

2.7.2.1 Linguistic Constraints   Linguistic constraints are internal constraints, i.e. they are dictated by the grammar of the dialect concerned. In variationist sociolinguistics, we often encounter constraints which do not permit a generalisation of certain rules. These constraints result in grammatical rules, which apply variably within the speech community. We refer to these as *variable rules*. A variable rule is not much different from a regular grammatical rule, except that it is not categorical, and a speaker – or an entire speech community – only apply such a rule under certain constraints, some of which are internal to the language itself. Sociolinguists use a variety of methods to determine the applicability of variable rules. Some of these methods are qualitative, but the gold standard for determining the precise salience of internal and external factors governing a variable rule has been, for several decades, the use of multivariate statistical analysis (see Section 2.9).

By way of illustration, the palatalisation of /k/ mentioned earlier is constrained by different rules in different Arabic dialects. In traditional rural central and northern Palestinian dialects, /k/ is realised as [ʧ] categorically. Thus, one finds /kalb/→[ʧalb], 'dog', /diːk/→[diːʧ], 'rooster', /kbiːr/→[ʧbiːr], 'large', and /djuːk/→[djuːʧ], 'roosters'. On the other hand, in many dialects in the Arabian Peninsula, e.g. Najdi, /k/ is palatalised to [ts] in front vowel environments only. For example, in Najdi Arabic: /diːk/→[diːts], 'rooster', but /dju:k/→[dju:k], 'roosters'.[4] In the Horan region of the Levant, which stretches from south of Damascus to the outskirts of Amman, /k/ is palatalised to [ʧ] most often in the environment of front vowels: /kalb/→[ʧalb], 'dog', /ka:n/→[ʧa:n], 'if'. In some cases, it is also palatalised in the environment of high back vowels, as in /dju:k/→[dju:ʧ], but not in /jkūn/→*[jʧu:n], 'he is'. Contrary to the cases of rural Palestinian and Najdi, recent analysis suggests further that in Horani, palatalisation of /k/ is sometimes lexically governed (rather than phonologically productive).[5] For example, in the word /miklabe/ 'dog-like behaviour' (i.e. bad behaviour) /k/ is palatalised to /ʧ/, as would be predicted by the surrounding environment (viz. front vowel); thus in Horani: /miklabe/→[miʧlabe]. Nonetheless, in the word /ke:le/ 'cup', where /k/ also occurs in the environment of front vowels, palatalisation, /ke:le/ →*[ʧe:le], does not occur.

At first glance, it may seem as if the rural Palestinian dialects described above, and the Najdi dialect, would not benefit much from the kind of variationist analysis explained here. The Palestinian dialect simply has a consonantal shift of /k/ to [ʧ].[6] And the Najdi dialect illustrates a rather straightforward phonological rule, whereby velar stops are palatalised in the environment of front vowels.[7] Only the Horani dialect appears to have more complex conditioning rules.

However, this description is highly simplistic, as it ignores the realities of everyday life in the greater speech communities described. For instance, rural Palestinians do not interact solely with other rural Palestinians. Many of their communicative dealings are in fact with urban Palestinians and speakers of other rural dialects that lack palatalisation. Additionally, it has been established that palatalised [ʧ] is a socially stigmatised feature outside of its native dialect area, and therefore it is quite common for Palestinian speakers who palatalise /k/ to de-palatalise this phoneme when speaking to non-palatalising speakers. Similar complications prevail in the case of Najdi dialects. For example, Al-Essa (2009) has found that in dialect contact situations, Najdi speakers residing in Jeddah are motivated to de-palatalise [ts] to [k]. In all of these cases, de-palatalisation can and has been shown to occur in virtually any phonological environment. However, the retention of palatalisation within

---

[4] Najd is the central region of the Arabian Peninsula and is currently part of the Kingdom of Saudi Arabia. Najdi dialects are the subjects of Bruce Ingham's detailed investigation of the dialects of central and north Arabia (Ingham 1994).

[5] See Herin (2010) and Herin and Al-Wer (2013).

[6] This is likely to be so, because rural Palestinian dialects have an additional shift of /q/ to [k], leading to the conclusion that this is a consonantal chain shift.

[7] The other velar stop in Najdi, /g/, is palatalised to [dz] in the same environment, e.g. /gidər/→[dzidər].

each speech community is constrained to those environments in which it was dictated by the original grammatical rules of the respective dialect. Whether the original rule was categorical, as in rural Palestinian Arabic, or conditional, as in Najdi Arabic, its application in the newly formed variable rule is now contingent upon the combination of these internal grammatical factors and the social and stylistic factors, which will be discussed more fully in the next section.

We often encounter linguistic features that exhibit two different kinds of alternation in the speech of native speakers. The first kind is what we called above a *regular* grammatical rule, which is a rule that applies, under certain conditions, across the board. The other kind involves deviations from these regular conditions. These deviations are not categorical, by which we mean that the same speaker may sometimes adhere to the regular rule, and at other times deviate from it. We call this kind of variation *intra-speaker* variation. Similarly, we may find this pattern of variability across speakers within the community, which we refer to as *inter-speaker* variation.

A good illustration of these two types of alternation for a single variable working in tandem across the same community is the case of the feminine ending in central and northern Jordanian dialects. In the traditional dialects, there is a regular phonological rule, according to which the feminine ending in pausal positions is raised from [a] to [ɛ]. Whether or not this vowel is raised is determined by the place of articulation of the preceding consonant, such that the vowel is raised only after coronals or in the presence of an /i/-type vowel in preceding syllables. So, the vowel in a word such as /gahwa/ 'coffee' is not raised, but the vowel in /farʃɛ/ 'mattress' is raised. Up until two generations ago this feature was not variable in Jordanian cities, as all speakers adhered to this phonological rule. Nowadays, the younger generations vary between the traditional pattern as described above and the pan-Levantine pattern found in most city dialects in the neighbouring countries, Syria, Lebanon, and Palestine.[8] In the pan-Levantine norm, the vowel is always raised except after emphatic, emphaticised, and post-velar consonants. Thus, according to this rule, both words cited above are pronounced with a raised vowel: /ʔahwe/, /farʃe/, but a non-raised vowel occurs in a word such as /mni:ħa/ 'good (f)'. Sociolinguistic studies over the past two decades have reported that the younger generations in the city of Salt vary in their realisation of this vowel between the traditional Jordanian pattern and the pan-Levantine pattern. The same speakers were found to use both realisations in words such as [gahwɛ] ~ [gahwa], [ħuku:mɛ] ~ [ħuku:ma] 'government'. If we wish to conduct a variationist study on this feature in this dialect, we will only consider contexts in which the traditional Jordanian and pan-Levantine patterns differ, mainly after labials.

---

[8] The pan-Levantine pattern has also become the norm in the newly formed dialect of Amman.

In both examples above, the linguistic constraints have to do with the effect of the surrounding sounds – also known as the *phonological environment* – on the realisation of the variable in question. Other types of phonological constraints may involve syllable structure, stress, and intonation. Some other linguistic factors are non-phonological, such as part of speech (noun, verb, etc.), morpheme boundaries (stem versus affix), tense–mood–aspect, and definiteness.

2.7.2.2 Extra-linguistic Factors   In addition to linguistic factors, variation is influenced by extra-linguistic factors, which include speaker variables (also known as social factors), such as age, gender, social class, social network, religion, and ethnicity. Another type of extra-linguistic factor is style of speech. In the next section, we elaborate on one of the speaker variables, age, because in addition to being a social factor, it is also a means of simulating time. This is based on the assumption that the speech of different age cohorts represents the state of language at different points in time. Age is also the first criterion that sociolinguists use in their sampling methods. In Chapter 7, where we explain the relation between linguistic variation and linguistic change, we will provide further details about age as a diagnostic of language change.

Other key social factors are explained in detail in Chapters 3, 4, 5, and 6.

2.8 Age

The clearest example of different age groups using different linguistic forms is in the choice of lexical items or expressions. For instance, in every language there will be words and expressions which tend to be used almost exclusively by the younger generation. In some cases, existing words may acquire new meanings. As examples, consider the English adjectives *wicked* and *terrific*. The word 'wicked' comes from the Old English word *wicca* 'sorcerer' or *wicce* 'witch' but is now widely used by the younger generations to mean 'outstanding'. The word 'terrific' comes from Latin *terrificus*, which meant 'very frightening', but its contemporary reference means 'excellent'. A similar transformation in meaning, but definitely unrelated to the English case, occurs in various Levantine Arabic dialects, where the word *rahi:b* 'frightening' is used by the younger generation to mean 'marvellous' or 'excellent'.

Words and expressions which are age-specific may also take the form of creations using existing linguistic material, which come about as a result of shared experience or shared lifestyle among a group of people of similar ages. This is neatly illustrated through contemporary computer and internet terminology, borrowed from English and moulded into Arabic morphology, e.g. *fazbak* 'wrote on Facebook', *farwad*, 'forwarded [an email or a text message]', *biyhannig* 'hung, stalled'.

Additional examples of lexical items used in semantically shifted meanings by the younger generation have been recorded by Hassanein (2009). Table 2.1 summarises several interesting examples reported by Hassanein, including words from the dialects of Kuwait, the United Arab Emirates, and Cairo. We have added to this list expressions from Ammani Arabic.

In sociolinguistic research, age is used to give the investigation a depth in time. The assumption is that the linguistic behaviour of different age groups represents different stages of evolution in the language itself. Therefore, differences in linguistic usages between different age groups are taken as indicators of linguistic change (see Chapter 7). The use of age differences as a substitute for time in studying language change is widely followed in sociolinguistics for practical reasons, since it provides instantaneous results, but is not without problems. This practice is known as the *apparent time* method.

The main problem with the assumption that every linguistic difference between the speech of the young and the old is an instance of language change is due to the phenomenon of *age-grading*. This refers to the possibility that speakers may change their linguistic behaviour as they grow older, and hence the linguistic differences observed between the young and the old at a particular point in time may not be permanent, but temporary alternations that are abandoned later on in life and are not transmitted to the next generation. Age-graded variations tend to recur in successive generations. It is because of age-grading that sociolinguists warn that even though generational linguistic differences are symptoms of change, they are not hard and fast evidence of it. The phenomenon of age-grading and the issue of 'variation without change' are explained in full in Chapter 7.

Table 2.1 *Examples of phrases used by youth in Arab cities*

Word	Literal translation	New meaning	Dialect
dabbuːr	wasp	playboy	Cairo
ʕasˤfuːra	bird	squeeler	Cairo
ʔarnab	rabbit	a million Egyptian. pounds	Cairo
sanfuːr	smurf	freshman	Amman
bass balaːʃ	enough don't	get outta here!, I don't believe you!	Amman
insaːni u-xud ʕinwaːni	forget me and take my address	don't call me again! It's over!	Cairo
ʔaruːh malħ	I'm going like salt	I melt	Kuwait
ʔinta taksi	you're a taxi	you're a playboy	Kuwait
gitˤʕa	piece	a beautiful girl	UAE

2.8.1   Age Divisions

Age is measured in units (years), or it is represented in terms of life stages (childhood, adolescence, adulthood). The divisions between different age groups in units can be arbitrary. The investigator may simply decide that a ten-year gap provides a realistic overview of the progression of a linguistic feature over time.

Life experiences of individuals, as well as expectations of how one should behave, are different at different stages of their lives. At the same time, it should be pointed out that life experiences and society's expectations at different life stages vary across cultures. Therefore, the connotations of the divisions into childhood, adolescence, and adulthood are likely to be culture specific. For instance, in some parts of rural Africa, life stages are not conceptualised in terms of chronological age but are stratified in ways which are culturally meaningful to the local community. An interesting story on this topic is cited in Bagamba (2007: 39). He writes:

> when my American colleague and I were investigating Swahili bilingualism among the Bila of Ituri, some Mbuti pygmies … asked us to look at their beards or count their children as a means of determining their age. When I insisted that a middle-aged man who had three sons give me an estimate of his age, 'I'm ten', he said. And how old is your first son? I asked. 'He is fifteen'.

In this community, the system of conceptualising age in terms of years is meaningless, as shown by the response of the Mbuti informant who was pressured by the researcher to conceptualise age in a way that was strange to him. Similarly, among the Hema of the Democratic Republic of Congo, life stage is largely determined by the social role performed by the individual; here, childhood stretches from birth to marriage, and a single man in his thirties is considered a boy, but one who is fifteen years old and married is a mature man who can take on the social roles ascribed to mature men (Bagamba 2007: 41).

Even in societies where age is commonly conceptualised in terms of childhood, adolescence, and adulthood, with different roles and expectations at each stage, the cutting chronological age between the stages may vary. In Middle Eastern societies in general the divisions of life stages are similar to those found in Western societies but only at the conceptual level. In practice, and generally speaking, youngsters socialise separately from their families and form their own friendship networks at a later age than in Western societies; so, in Jordanian society, for instance, the social life of a twelve-year-old may be similar to the social life of a seven-year-old in Britain. In sociolinguistic research, it is important to incorporate a sophisticated understanding of the social meanings of age divisions and life stages so that it can be shown that the sampling techniques and the analytical tools are motivated in some way, for instance by the community's social practices.

Eckert (1997a) refers to two specific approaches: the *etic* approach, which arbitrarily groups speakers into age cohorts in predetermined equal intervals, as in some of the classic sociolinguistic studies (e.g. Labov 1966 and Trudgill 1974), and the *emic* approach. The latter 'groups speakers according to some shared experience of time. This shared experience can be related to life stage or to history' (Eckert 1997a: 155). The examples Eckert provides for emic approaches include studies of American and Australian English which classified speakers' ages according to life stages such as 'childhood, adolescence and young adulthood', and research on Québécois French that used historical events such as the Great Depression of North America and World War II as defining historical events for the sake of the age grouping of the speakers they had studied (Eckert 1997a: 166).

The emic approach can be demonstrated through a detailed case study among Palestinian communities. Extremely significant historical events have affected the Palestinian community at the following intervals: 1948, the *Nakba*, 'catastrophe', a term referring to the massive relocation of much of Palestine's indigenous population and the establishment of the State of Israel; 1967, the *Naksa* 'setback', i.e. the Israeli occupation of the West Bank and the Gaza Strip, among other regions; 1987, the *Intifada*, the first Palestinian uprising; 2000, the second uprising. It is crucial for sociolinguists to pay close attention to these historical events for the purpose of age divisions, not only because of the social impact these events have had on the speech communities and the population movements that resulted from them, but also because they are far enough apart from one another to coincide, for the most part, with natural generation gaps.

Research on variation in Palestinian Arabic has taken the history of the Palestinian community into consideration, from the early stages of sample design. Cotter (2013, 2016) studied Palestinian speakers in Gaza, some of whom were refugees from Jaffa; Horesh (2014, 2015) examined the Jaffa community itself, which at various stages had been influenced by an influx of Hebrew speakers; and Al-Wer (1991, 2007, 2020) has been working on unearthing the outcomes of the historical events on the Jordanian dialects of Arabic, as millions of Palestinian refugees, mostly in 1948 and 1967, fled to Jordan and assimilated into that country's populace and, crucially, contributed to the emergence of a new dialect, especially in the capital city of Amman.

Within Palestine, different communities have responded differently to the abrupt demographic changes caused by the arrival of displaced Palestinian populations. For example, unlike the pan-Levantine pattern, in the traditional Gaza dialect the feminine morpheme -*a* is always pronounced [a], without vowel raising. A large proportion of the current population of Gaza are refugees from the 1948 war and their descendants. Many of these refugees originate in Jaffa, where the dialect spoken is of the pan-Levantine urban variety mentioned above. In this dialect the vowel in the feminine suffix is raised to [e] after non-back consonants. Cotter (2013) reports that only a minority of older women, most of whom were born in Jaffa itself, maintain this phonologically conditioned raised pronunciation. Most of the rest of the refugee population, comprising offspring of people born in Jaffa, have predominantly acquired the Gaza pattern of non-raising.

With regard to Jaffa, its population nowadays is roughly 60 per cent Hebrew-speaking and 40 per cent Arabic-speaking. The indigenous Palestinian population in the city were compelled to learn Hebrew, leading to widespread Arabic–Hebrew bilingualism, especially in the generations that began school from 1948 onwards.

In a study that has taken all of these factors into account and divided the Jaffa speaker sample according to historical events, Horesh found a clear correlation between age group and the lenition (or weakening) of the voiced pharyngeal fricative sound /ʕ/. This lenition is a direct result of contact with Modern Hebrew, a language which by and large has lost the /ʕ/ sound. Thus, speakers educated predominantly in Arabic prior to the 1948 war were found most likely to retain the pharyngeal pronunciation of /ʕ/. Speakers educated after the 1967 war, on the other hand, were exposed to Hebrew since child-hood, and some of them were also educated in Hebrew; speakers in this age group were found more likely to delete Arabic /ʕ/ or pronounce a weakened variant of it, e.g. a glottal stop [ʔ]. We see, therefore, that from the outset of the research it is essential to incorporate as much background information as pos-sible on the community under investigation. We caution against using ready-made formulae, even if they were found viable for other communities, without ensuring their suitability for the community that is about to be studied.

2.9   Analysis

You will notice in the literature that people often refer to two different types of analysis, one which is called *quantitative* and the other known as *qualita-tive*. Quantitative analysis involves one or more methods of statistical analysis, which in sociolinguistics is used to calculate the probabilities of linguistic forms occurring under each of the circumstances defined by linguistic, social, and stylistic factors. This type of analysis requires a systematic sample of speakers within a speech community and a large enough number of speakers and linguistic tokens to ensure reliable results. In qualitative analysis the size of the sample may be smaller than for a quantitative study, but close attention is paid to the content of the speech act as well as to the linguistic forms reflected in it.

The separation between quantitative and qualitative is often an artificial one in sociolinguistics. While in some cases, quantification of the data is not viable, for example because of small token numbers, the nature of certain linguistic variables, and unbalanced distributions of social groups in the sample, a qualitative analysis of at least part of the data is always warranted. The interrelatedness of the two types of analysis in sociolinguistics can be demonstrated in cases where one or two speakers from within a large sample show atypical linguistic patterns relative to the rest of the members in their cohorts. From a statistical point of view, it may seem that these speakers are merely outliers whose data should be excluded. But in our experience, an in-depth examination of their personal circumstances, as reflected in the content of their narratives, can provide invaluable explanations of their own linguistic behaviour as well as innovative interpretations of the overall results for the speech community.

2.9.1   Why Quantify?

If, in a given speech community, *all speakers* used different variants at the same rate, and if each speaker exhibited the same linguistic behaviour *in all situations*, we would not need quantification to describe the linguistic usage of these alternating variants in this community. The fact is, however, that in sociolinguistic variation, rates of use of variants are rarely uniform across the community or across different contexts within the speech of an individual.

How, then, do we describe the system in cases where members of a given community show one of the following patterns in their usage of the Arabic phonemes /k/ and /q/?

1. All members of the community *sometimes* use [k] for /q/ and at other times use [g] or [ʔ] for /q/; they also sometimes alternate between [k] and [ʧ] for /k/.
2. Some members of the community consistently use [k] for /q/ and [ʧ] for /k/; other members follow the pattern under (1).
3. Some members of the community *sometimes* use [k] for /q/ and at other times use [g] or [ʔ] for /q/; they also vary between [k] and [ʧ] for /k/ in certain situations.
4. Some members of the community use [k] for /q/ consistently but vary between [k] and [ʧ] for /k/ in certain situations.

The list of possible variations is much longer than this. Notice that in the few possibilities described in points 1–4 above, there is interaction both between variants of each phoneme and between the two phonemes described. Furthermore, the combinations of who will use which variants in which contexts is infinite. Indeed, for a dialect to vary according to who is speaking it, to whom, and in which contexts is the normal state of affairs. Quantifying these patterns and calculating the *probabilities* of each combination of factors to occur allows us to accurately describe the system as a whole and to make informed predictions about ongoing and potential changes and their trajectories.

This kind of variation requires us to treat the two phonemes, /q/ and /k/, as linguistic *variables*, using the notation mentioned earlier, namely (q) and (k). In order to fully describe this variable system, we would need first to determine the potential linguistic and extra-linguistic factors (i.e. the independent variables) that are likely to interact with the variable linguistic behaviour (i.e. the dependent variables). For instance, it is necessary to identify what the social make-up of this community is so as to define the social factors. As mentioned earlier, we will probably divide the sample into age groups. Any further groupings (e.g. gender, ethnicity, religion, occupation) will be determined based on the specific characteristics of the community. We will also include linguistic factors that we hypothesise may affect the choice of variants. Since the variables (k) and (q) are phonological variables, the linguistic factors may include preceding and following segments, syllable structure, and morpheme boundaries. The number and nature of linguistic factors depend on the variable and are discerned based on general linguistic principles and knowledge of the structure of the language or dialect under investigation. Once these potential factors are determined, the processes of transcription and coding can begin, as explained in the following section.

2.9.2   *Transcription*

When we transcribe data, we use a standard transcription system accessible to most linguists. The two most commonly used systems for Arabic data are the International Phonetic Alphabet (IPA) and a simplified system often used by scholars of Semitic languages.[9] Transcription is time-consuming. It is therefore a good idea to decide on the level of transcription that you need for your specific project. If you are interested in fine-grained phonetic detail, you will probably opt for a narrow transcription. The IPA will allow you to do this with maximum precision by using the full range of diacritics available in this system. If phonetic detail is not particularly important for your project, but phonemic distinctions are, you may choose to use a broad transcription. For some projects, you may need to delineate morphemes, which in the transcription will be separated by dashes or dots, depending on the types of morpheme boundaries.[10] A further consideration to bear in mind is how much of the collected data you should transcribe. Ideally, you will transcribe

---

[9] For detailed guidelines regarding these two systems and their applicability to Arabic data, see the introduction to *The Encyclopedia of Arabic Language and Linguistics* (Versteegh et al. 2006–2009).

[10] Guidance for this kind of morphophonemic transcription, as well as morpheme-for-morpheme glossing is available at www.eva.mpg.de/lingua/resources/glossing-rules.php [(accessed 2 February 2022).

all of what you have recorded. Realistically, though, every project is confined by time and resources, and a prudent researcher allocates sufficient time to all tasks involved, resulting in the need to be selective regarding the data to be transcribed.

2.9.3   Coding

Prior to analysing the data, it will be necessary to organise them in a manner that will enable us to easily read and retrieve them and allow us to refer back to the recording. Additionally, in preparation for running statistical models on the data, it is crucial that the data be formatted in a way that is compatible with the specific statistical package you intend to use. Usually, you will first organise your data in a spreadsheet, such as the ones used in Microsoft Excel. When dealing with more than one variable, it will usually make sense to devote a separate spreadsheet to each variable. In this spreadsheet, all instances (tokens) of the dependent variable are entered by means of a *code*, or symbol, that indicates which variants the speaker actually used. The spreadsheet also includes coding for all the independent variables and any additional notes you may wish to keep a record of, e.g. the full phrase or sentence in which the variable occurs or a time stamp that will help you locate the token in the recording.

   To illustrate these points, we present a partial snapshot (Figure 2.1) of a token file that was used to analyse the lenition and deletion of the voiced pharyngeal fricative – the variable (ʕ) – in two Palestinian cities: Gaza and Jaffa.[11]

   This simple spreadsheet displays the following information:

A. Pseudonym of the speaker
B. Age group (in this case, by year of birth)
C. Sex
D. Community: Gaza or Jaffa
E. The dependent variable, coded '0' for deletion, '1' for pharyngeal realisation; 'other' for lenited variants
F. Simplified transcription of the token
G. The location of the token in the recording

The details are repeated in the spreadsheet multiple times for each speaker, based on the number of tokens each of them produced for this variable. In this case, the full spreadsheet from which this excerpt is taken has 709 tokens representing the speech of fourteen speakers, seven from each city. This particular token file was formatted to be used with the statistical program Rbrul (Johnson 2009), but the information it includes can be rearranged for any statistical software for multivariate analysis.

---

[11] The results of this study were published in Cotter and Horesh (2015).

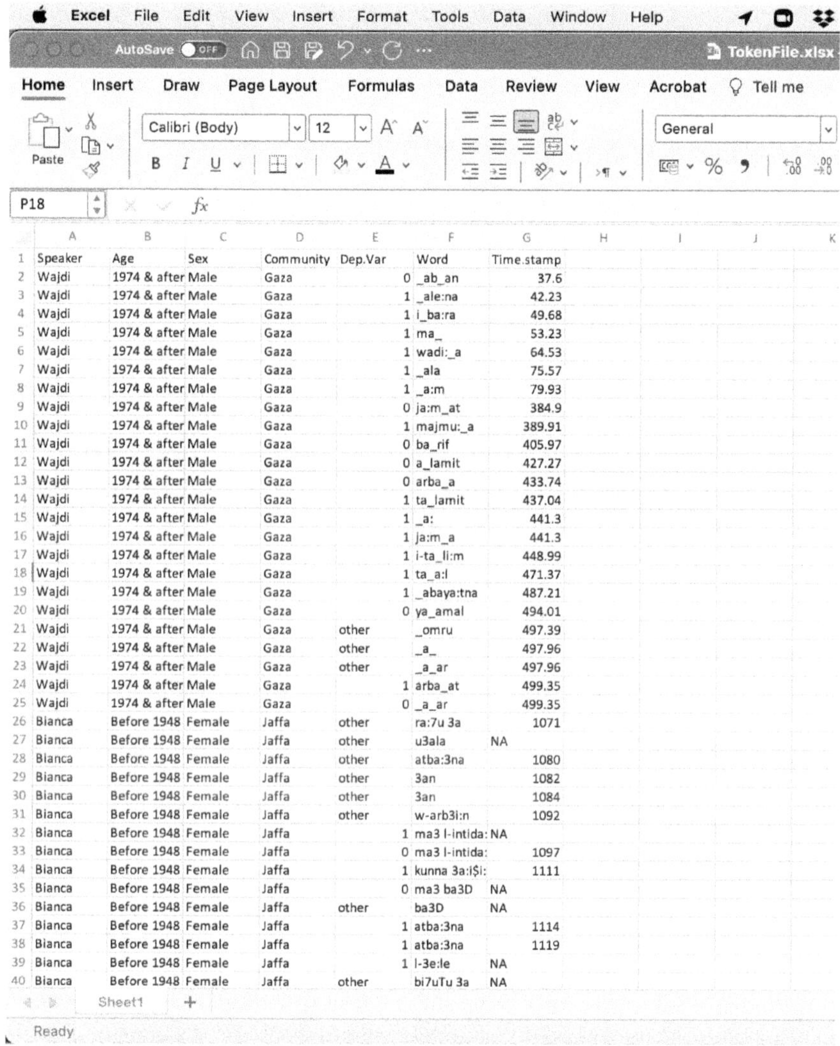

Figure 2.1 Sample coding spreadsheet

2.9.4   Eyeballing the Data

Once the coding process is complete, it may be useful to sift through the token
files. This will help you spot coding errors, which can cause problems at the
statistical modelling stage. Spending some time inspecting your data manually

in this manner can also help you identify patterns that may lead you to formulate additional hypotheses or discard assumptions you may have had at the outset of the research.

2.9.5   *Auditory and Acoustic Analysis*

When dealing with sociophonetic variation, we must listen carefully for the pronunciation of each variant of the variable in each token that we have recorded. In many cases, an auditory (or impressionistic) report of the sounds we hear (e.g. [k], [?], or [g] for the variable (q)) will suffice. In cases where we are unsure of the exact quality of the sound we hear, or if we wish to measure the duration of a sound (e.g. to examine whether some vowels are longer than others and by how much, or what the realisation of geminated consonants is), we may need something other than our ears to help us decide what we have heard.

In this type of analysis, that which pertains to the precise phonetic properties of sounds, we may benefit from instrumental analysis of sound waves, for instance using a spectrogram. For this purpose, it is important to ensure, at the recording stage, that the settings on the recording device are compatible with the software we will be using for the acoustic analysis, and that the quality of the recording is adequate for the level of acoustic accuracy that we wish to document. This can be achieved by reducing background noises (e.g. fans, air conditioners, wind, cars, and crying babies), as well as by saving the sound files in uncompressed formats.

2.9.6   *Modelling*

In order to formulate the grammatical rules that faithfully capture the way language is actually used, i.e. as a vehicle of human communication and as social practice, we need an objective analytical tool. Statistics can provide us with such a tool. The use of statistics is common not only in linguistics, but also in other social sciences. The advantage of using statistical tools, where appropriate, to analyse language variation and predict trajectories of language change lies in the ability of such tools to impartially consider large amounts of data. Since these data are constrained by multiple independent variables, statistical tools are designed to test the effect on linguistic behaviour of the multiplex of independent variables simultaneously. The outputs of such statistical tests are numerical values which represent the probability that each independent variable will affect the occurrence of the dependent variable. These probabilities are then used by the linguist to interpret the linguistic structure as it interacts with elements of social structure. This kind of analysis is referred to as *multivariate analysis*. While the multivariate analysis itself is done by whatever statistical software the analyst uses, the *modelling*, i.e. the set of components fed into the program, is decided upon by the analyst themselves.

Statistical analysis includes two types of treatment of the data. One type, *descriptive statistics*, involves counting occurrences of the dependent variable, calculating overall means (averages) and conducting simple cross-tabulations of two (or sometimes more) independent variables. To illustrate a very basic form of descriptive statistics, consider Table 2.2, based on Cotter (2016), which presents the raw numbers of tokens of each variant for the variable (q) in Gaza, as well as the percentages of occurrence of each variant. Such basic counts provide a quick overall report of the distribution of variants.

A more detailed account of the distribution of these data can be seen in Tables 2.3 and 2.4, where two independent variables are cross-tabulated with

Table 2.2 *Distribution of (q) in Gaza (based on Cotter 2016: 237, Table 3)*

[g]	[ʔ]	Total
412	163	575
71.7%	28.3%	100.0%

Table 2.3 *(q) among Gaza-origin speakers in Gaza (based on Cotter 2016: 239, Table 5)*

	Gaza Speakers			
Age	[ʔ]	[g]	%ʔ	Total
65+	1	64	2%	**65**
40–64	7	154	4%	**161**
17–39	46	105	30%	**151**
				377

Table 2.4 *(q) among Jaffa-origin speakers in Gaza (based on Cotter 2016: 239, Table 6)*

	Jaffa Speakers			
Age	[ʔ]	[g]	%ʔ	Total
65+	47	2	96%	**49**
40–64	25	21	54%	**46**
17–39	37	66	36%	**103**
				198

the dependent variable. These independent variables are heritage dialects (i.e. Gaza and Jaffa) and age group.

Descriptive statistics such as those displayed in Tables 2.3 and 2.4 have limited explanatory power because what they tell us is only the distribution of data in this particular sample. What we ultimately want to know is the probability of these variants being used under similar circumstances among all speakers of the dialect in this community. For this purpose, we need a more powerful tool known as *inferential statistics*. This involves a computational process that yields a response to the following question: is the distribution of the variants for a given variable a matter of chance, or does it reflect a pattern that is predictive of the linguistic behaviour of the community? While there are many ways to calculate this probability – using different statistical software packages that include different computational steps – what they all have in common is that they provide us with an estimate of *statistical significance*. If an independent variable is found to be statistically significant, we may interpret this to mean that the pattern vis-à-vis this variable is *not* due to chance, and thus the probability of this pattern recurring in a comparable study of the community, using different speakers to draw the speech sample, is high.

Statistical significance is usually inferred by a number between 0 and 1, called the *p*-value. It is common to interpret a *p*-value lower than 0.05 as indicating statistical significance. This is not to say that in cases of $p \geq 0.05$ the effect of the variable is negligible. It merely means that the data in this sample do not justify the determination that it is statistically significant.

Table 2.5 presents the results of a multivariate analysis of the realisation of the feminine ending in the dialect of Al-Ahsa in Saudi Arabia (Al-Bohnayyah 2019). Examples of the variation in this dialect are as follows.

1. *kibiːr-e ~ kibiːr-a* 'big (f)'
2. *θigiːl-e ~ θigiːl-a* 'heavy (f)'

This model factored in four independent variables: one linguistic (preceding consonant) and three social (age, religious sect, and gender). The dependent variable is the vowel of the feminine ending, which has two variants: [e] and [a]. Since in this dialect [e] is the traditional variant and [a] is the innovative variant, it makes sense to consider the percentages of the use of [a] – the incoming variant – which is reported in the third column of the table. This particular statistical analysis was done in Rbrul, a program devised specifically for the study of language variation, but other options exist as well.

The first column, entitled Factor, lists the independent variables, along with the values associated with them. For instance, for the variable 'preceding consonant', there are four possible values (or factors): pharyngeal, labial, [j], and coronal. The second column, labelled N, lists the total number of tokens for each factor. In the third column, %[a], we see the percentage of N in which the dependent variable was realised as [a]. Finally, the fourth column, Centred

Table 2.5 *Feminine ending in Al-Ahsa (based on Al-Bohnayyah 2019: 170, Table 5.6)*

Factor	N	%[a]	Centred factor weight (FW)
Preceding consonant	**($p \approx 0.000$)**		
Pharyngeal	181	75%	0.85
Labial	227	37%	0.56
[j]	265	22%	0.33
Coronal	669	16%	0.22
Age	**($p \approx 0.000$)**		
Young	660	38%	0.64
Old	682	19%	0.36
Sect	**($p \approx 0.000$)**		
Shia	680	36%	0.61
Sunni	662	21%	0.40
Gender	**($p < 0.0005$)**		
Female	656	34%	0.57
Male	686	23%	0.43

R^2=0.35; Grand mean=0.29

factor weight (FW), includes for each factor a number between 0 and 1. The way to interpret these numbers is as follows. If the number is greater than 0.5, the factor favours the occurrence of the variant [a]. If it is smaller than 0.5, it disfavours [a]. If it is exactly 0.5, it neither favours nor disfavours this realisation. The actual value of the factor weight is important too. The closer it is to 1, the higher the probability of the dependent variable occurring in the given context, and vice versa.

Additionally, the table includes three further important figures: p-values, which are listed for each independent variable, and R^2 and grand mean, which are listed at the bottom of this table for the entire model. R^2 is indicative of the proportion of the variation that is explainable through this model. While the higher the R^2, the stronger the model, a value such as 0.35 seen above is considered adequate to render the model reliable. If R^2 is less than 0.1, it is advisable to consider alternative models. Grand mean simply refers to the percentage of occurrence of [a] in the entire sample, regardless of independent variable.

Note that in this case the p-values for the first three independent variables are almost equal to zero ($p \approx 0.000$). The actual p-values in this case were minuscule numbers, e.g. for age it was 7.75e−13 (i.e. 0.000000000000775). It is customary to only indicate ranges of statistically significant p-values. Usually three such ranges suffice: $p < 0.05$, $p < 0.01$ and $p < 0.001$. For p-values greater than or equal to 0.05, it is usually sufficient to use the abbreviation 'n.s.' (not significant).

The way the data are presented in Table 2.5 is not the only way to present quantitative results, but it is a concise presentation, which includes all of the main components needed for interpretation. When using statistical software, you will often receive outputs that include a great deal of additional information. Not all of this information is crucial to our understanding of language variation, and it is therefore the researcher's responsibility to decide which components of the output to present in their findings. In some cases, it may also be useful to include other forms of presentation of results, such as a graph.

2.9.7   Interpretation

Whichever way one chooses to present one's quantitative results, it is always equally important to provide commentary that highlights the researcher's own observations. The full interpretation of the sociolinguistic situation should, on the one hand, rely on the results of the quantitative analysis, but it must also synthesise all other components of the research. Statistics alone are not the be-all and end-all of sociolinguistic research. We enter a research project with prior knowledge, both theoretical and factual; we amass a great deal of additional knowledge during our ethnographic fieldwork; we then endeavour to use this cumulative knowledge, along with the results rendered by our statistical modelling, to formulate meaningful interpretations about the case in hand but also to contribute to the furthering of sociolinguistic generalisations. A good research project is one that includes insights applicable to future research, be it in the same community and on the same language or in different speech communities. For instance, a study of consonant chain shifts in a Mesopotamian Arabic dialect can potentially lead to better understanding of consonant shifts in language in general. In order for our research to be used in such a way as to be conducive to the furthering of science, it must be presented in a manner that will be coherent to readers who may not be familiar with the specific language dealt with in a given project. It is important to provide plenty of examples from the empirical research, accessible transcriptions and glosses, and references to established knowledge both specific to Arabic and to language in general.

2.10   Ethics

In many countries there are laws that regulate scientific research, and research in sociolinguistics falls within the jurisdiction of such laws. Compliance with these terms goes a long way towards ensuring good practice. In essence, though, research ethics are not about compliance with official legislation but about adherence to a 'moral code of practice'; otherwise participants in research in those parts of the world where no regulations exist, or exist but only on paper, would be denied basic rights. Research ethics are an integral part of research design, not an adjunct to it, and scientific research must not conspire to increase inequality but, where possible, to reduce it. In this section we shall briefly outline the essential components of ethical research as may be required legally and institutionally. We also encourage researchers to think creatively about additional ways to share their findings with the community to enable them to utilise newly acquired knowledge towards solving practical societal problems.

2.10.1 Formal Requirements

Without going into the details of specific regulations in any particular country, but based on the guidelines followed in most institutions worldwide, the broad terms of research ethics stipulate the following:

- Participation in research should be voluntary. The participants should not be made to participate under duress. No recording of data is allowed without the full knowledge and consent of participants. In many cases, it may be wise to ask participants to sign a document in which they confirm their willingness to participate. Some institutions will *require* such written consent. Others may allow for oral consent, for instance at the beginning of a recorded interview.
- The identity of participants must remain anonymous (pseudonyms are used if needed).
- Consent can be withdrawn by the participant at any point in the course of the research. In some cases, you may encounter situations where participants change their minds midway through the interview or afterwards. In these cases, their participation must be terminated and any records thereof destroyed.
- Data should be treated with utmost confidentiality and stored on personal computers protected by a password or on institutionally approved online platforms.
- Access to the data is confined to the researcher(s) and may be extended, with the consent of the participant, to supervisors, in case of research conducted by students.
- Data must be used for the purpose of the research only.
- A description of the research and the research objectives should be made available to the participants.
- Researchers must ensure that participants suffer no harm or any form of inconvenience as a result of taking part in the research.
- Research that involves contact with children or vulnerable adults may require special clearance from the authorities, based on the jurisdiction where the research is carried out.

2.10.2 Principles of Commitment

Part of a true ethical approach to research should, where possible, include activism towards reducing inequality. This is encompassed in Labov's 'Principles of Commitment' (Labov 1982: 172), which go beyond calling for 'ethical research' to supporting an 'advocacy position' (Milroy and Gordon 2003: 84). As a social science, sociolinguistic research carries with it a certain social responsibility. In our research, we often document and analyse linguistic practices which in many societies would be considered inferior and illegitimate. Our stance as linguists is, of course, that all language varieties are valid and worthy of both research and societal recognition. Importantly, speakers must not be discriminated against simply for speaking their own native variety. This is especially true in cases where speakers of certain varieties come from underprivileged social groups, and their non-standard speech often reinforces the negative stereotypes from which they suffer.

Issues pertaining to linguistic discrimination and its impact on the lives and prospects of the groups that are the targets of this discrimination are rarely discussed for Arabic, especially inasmuch as they touch upon societal attitudes towards stigmatised dialects. We have seen the positive impact of bringing to the forefront the issue of Amazigh in North Africa, culminating in the declaration of Amazigh as a national language in two major North African countries (Algeria and Morocco). The relative success of these campaigns is encouraging, but the issue of linguistic discrimination goes beyond the rights of different language groups in Arabic-speaking countries. There is a strong bias against Arabic vernaculars in general and against specific dialects spoken by underprivileged portions of society. As researchers heavily involved in the lives of the communities that we study and in local issues, part of our responsibility is to find ways to disseminate knowledge we gain from our discipline beyond the community of academics. The hope is that such knowledge can help communities confront social injustices.

2.11   Further Reading

> Chambers and Schilling (2013) – This handbook contains several chapters related directly to sociolinguistic methodology, as well as others that provide an overview of sociolinguistic theory.
>
> Eckert (2000) – A monograph containing the details of Eckert's ethnographic study of youth in Detroit.
>
> Gorman and Johnson (2013) – This handbook chapter provides an overview of the practice of quantitative analysis of language variation.
>
> Johnson (2009) – This paper describes the principles that guide statistical analysis using Rbrul.

Labov (1972) – A collection of William Labov's early research, which establishes the tenets of variationist sociolinguistics.

Labov (1981) – In this paper, Labov details the field methods that he and his associates followed in studies of variation and change in American English.

Mallinson et al. (2018) – A collection of chapters, each dealing with a specific methodological topic in sociolinguistics.

Milroy and Gordon (2003) – This is a concise yet comprehensive guide to sociolinguistic methodology, contextualised within questions of theory.

Schilling (2013) – Comprehensive coverage of key topics in designing and executing sociolinguistic fieldwork.

Tagliamonte (2006, 2012) – These two books provide specialist step-by-step guidance to conducting statistical analysis of language variation.

Corpora – For catalogues of corpora that have been compiled for Arabic, we recommend searching the following web pages:

- The CAMeL Lab at New York University Abu Dhabi: nyuad. nyu.edu/en/research/faculty-labs-and-projects/computational-approaches-to-modeling-language-lab.html (accessed 2 February 2022)
- The Linguistic Data Consortium at the University of Pennsylvania: catalog.ldc.upenn.edu/search (accessed 2 February 2022)

2.12   Exercises for Chapter 2

1. **Identifying a Variable:** Most native speakers of Arabic borrow words or expressions from Standard Arabic, e.g. *qism al-luɣāt al-ḥadīθa* 'Department of Modern Languages'. In such lexical items, /q/ and /θ/ are typically pronounced as in Standard Arabic. But does this mean that /q/ and /θ/ are necessarily sociolinguistic variables in the vernacular? Answer this question by observing the occurrence of these sounds in non-Standard words, e.g. /qahwa/ 'coffee' and /kθiːr/ 'much, many' in a dialect of Arabic familiar to you. Use the following guidelines to answer the question.

   a. Are /q/ and /θ/ always or sometimes pronounced differently from the Standard?

   b. How many variants does each sound have in casual speech? What are they?

   c. What seems to determine which variants are used?

   d. Do particular variants of these sounds occur in specific words or phrases?

2. **Obtaining Samples of Vernacular Speech:** Researchers have tried various methods to divert speakers' attention from the formality of the sociolinguistic interview. Think of a specific community in which you are likely to interview speakers. What topics do you think might be suitable for eliciting casual, vernacular speech? How would you formulate questions based on these topics? Are the topics likely to be more appropriate for discussion with speakers of different ages and backgrounds?

3. **Ethnography in Familiar and Less-Familiar Communities**: Think of two possible communities in which you might find yourself doing sociolinguistic fieldwork. One will be your own community or a community that you know well; the other will be a community you know little or nothing about. What would be your first steps towards getting acquainted with the sociolinguistically relevant aspects of each community? Do you *really* know everything you need to know about your own community, or is there need for extensive preparation there, too? How would the preparation differ between the familiar community and the brand new one?

4. **Pilot Study:** You are embarking on a large-scale sociolinguistic study. Do you think conducting a pilot study – with a smaller sample – ahead of the main investigation would benefit your research? Keep in mind the social variables you assume would be relevant, the linguistic variables you anticipate to be salient, and the overall sociolinguistic profile of the speech community.

5. **Determining the Range of Variation**: The features listed below are variable for many Arabic speakers:
   a. Plain interdentals /θ/, /ð/. These may be realised as [t], [d] and/or [s], [z], respectively.
   b. Voiced emphatic interdental /ðˤ/. May be realised as [dˤ] or [zˤ].
   c. Voiced emphatic stop /dˤ/. May be realised as [ðˤ] or [zˤ].
   d. Voiceless velar /k/. May be realised as [tʃ] or [ts].
   e. /q/, which has a wide range of realisations, including [q], [ʔ], [g], [k], [kˤ], [dʒ], [dz]
   f. /dʒ/, which also has a wide range of realisations, including [dʒ], [ʒ], [g], [j].
   g. The feminine ending. In some dialects, feminine nouns and adjectives, e.g. *dʒaːmʕa* 'university', *ħilwa* 'pretty' are realised with a raised final vowel: /dʒaːmʕe/, /ħilwe/.
   h. Diphthongs: /ai/, /au/, which may be realised as monophthongs [eː] and [oː], respectively.

Choose one or more of these potential variables and formulate a hypothesis as to the range of variation they exhibit in a community of your choice. Then test the hypothesis using a small data set – you may use the media as a resource – and finally, refine your hypothesis based on your findings. You may find, for instance, that the features in question are variable only in specific linguistic, social, or stylistic contexts.

6. **Age Grading in a Community**:
   a. Think back to your schooldays. Are there any words or phrases that you and your peer group used frequently, or even invented? Do you still use these words and phrases? Do young people today use them? Have any of them fallen out of fashion? Are there new words and phrases that you yourself may not use but people younger than you have begun using? Provide examples.
   b. Listen to the speech of older members of your community or to older people speaking in the media. Are there words that you have never heard before and perhaps do not even understand? Are there other words that you have only heard from the elderly and that even though you understand them, you never find yourself using? How do you explain this? Provide examples.

7. **Principles of Commitment**. Imagine a research project you wish to conduct in your own community. How would you
   a. involve members of the community during the period of data collection and make the research process relevant and beneficial to the community?
   b. disseminate the results of your research, once completed, with the community, again, emphasising ways in which the community may benefit from sociolinguistic research?

3   Gender

3.1   Introduction

Numerous sociolinguistic studies, including studies on Arabic, have found systematic linguistic differences between women and men. It has therefore become a norm for investigations of linguistic variation to include gender as a variable, as is the case in all social sciences. Furthermore, the findings over more than half a century of research indicate quite convincingly that there are patterns which can be considered general. An important point to bear in mind about these results is that the differences found between male and female speakers are statistical differences. In most cases, the features that are used by the one group are also used by the other but in different proportions.

Students of sociolinguistics will be aware that the term 'gender' has been more widely used than the term 'sex' in sociolinguistics, especially since the 1980s. The change is not simply terminological but reflects increasing sophistication in methods of analysis and interpretation. Chambers (2003: 117) sums up the distinction between the two terms succinctly as recognising 'biological and sociocultural differences'.

In this chapter we introduce and discuss gender-differentiated language patterns in Arabic, focussing on evidence from research within the variationist paradigm. One of the main advantages of studying the interaction between language and gender quantitatively is that it enables us to compare studies from different communities and different languages and arrive at broad, cross-linguistic generalisations.

3.2   General Principles

William Labov (1994) has formulated two main generalisations regarding gender differentiation. We may paraphrase them as follows:
1. Other things being equal, on average, women tend to use standard and/or prestigious linguistic features more consistently than men.
2. In cases of language change, women tend to be ahead of men in using the incoming forms.

It is important to keep in mind that these generalisations are based on quantitative tendencies and do not imply that men *do not* use standard and prestigious features, or that they *never* lead language change. Equally, they do not mean that women do not use non-standard or stigmatised features. It is also important to base our interpretations of gender-differentiated patterns on independent evidence, rather than on stereotypes. In other words, we must not confuse societal stereotyping with scientifically based conclusions. Speakers' perceptions of and opinions about dialects and linguistic features are not interpretations but rather data, which in combination with other types of data, e.g. quantitative results, require an objective analysis. For instance, when speakers of dialect X say that speakers of dialect Y sound 'effeminate', we must keep in mind that this is a subjective evaluation. We cannot dismiss it, but we should also be cautious about taking it at face value. It is our job as researchers to critically examine the data we collect, synthesise them, and arrive at scientifically valid conclusions.

A related point has to do with the use of superficial attributes as if they have explanatory value in and of themselves. In the sociolinguistic literature about Arabic, we often read about a given form being 'masculine, tough, virile, and therefore chosen by men' or 'feminine and soft and therefore chosen by women and avoided by men'. It may be true that such opinions are expressed within the community being studied, but merely repeating such statements does not constitute analysis. Our role as researchers is to discern how such stereotypes originated and evolved, and how they may have contributed to linguistic processes.

For instance, a common characterisation of two variants of (q) in Jordan is that [g] is 'tough', and therefore used by men, whereas [ʔ] is 'soft', and as such used by women. The fact of the matter is that there is nothing inherently tough or soft, let alone masculine or feminine, about these sounds. In dialects of British English, where [ʔ] is a variant of (t), e.g. the word *water* is often pronounced /wɔːʔə/, this variant is associated with the inner city and working classes, as demonstrated in Macaulay's (1977) study of working-class adolescents in Glasgow and many other subsequent studies. Even in Arabic, the social values associated with [ʔ] vary across communities. In Morocco, for instance, it is a hallmark of the traditional dialect of Fez. It is stigmatised and recessive in many other Moroccan communities, but not owing to its association with gender. Equally, there is no association between 'toughness' and the use of [g] in dialects where this is the only variant of /q/ used in the vernacular, e.g. Baghdad, Jeddah, and Manama.

This must mean that whatever social values these sounds are associated with, they must have emerged and been constructed within the community. Therefore, in order to understand the relevance of this meaning to the structure of variation, we must analyse the events that have led to one gender group predominantly using one variant and the other group using the other. We have evidence to the effect that, in certain communities, independent circumstances have led women and men to use different variants. It was only after a period of time during which a large enough number of speakers from each gender group had adopted a variant that the variant became associated with men (and therefore 'masculinity') or with women (and therefore 'femininity').

The historical circumstances of (q) in Jordan are a good example for explaining how social meanings of linguistic forms emerge. Al-Wer (1991) and Al-Wer and Herin (2011) explain that the association of [g] with men's speech and [ʔ] with women's speech that is prevalent in Jordanian communities was established and consolidated in the 1960s and 1970s. Historically, Jordanian dialects only had [g]. The variant [ʔ] was introduced around the early twentieth century with the influx of immigrants from Syria, Lebanon, and Palestine. In the aftermath of the wars in 1948 and 1967, the presence of [ʔ] in Jordan increased markedly with the arrival of millions of Palestinian refugees. Following the 1970 confrontation between the Jordanian state and the Palestine Liberation Organisation, Jordanians (users of [g]) increasingly occupied high-ranking positions in the state administration and in the armed forces. Because women were excluded from this development and its consequences, [g] became associated with the speech of men and with political power. Women, on the other hand, were influenced by a different set of values. Since Jordan until then was the least urbanised of the Levant countries, Jordanians looked to the major cities in the region, e.g. Damascus, Beirut, Haifa, and Jerusalem, for culture and education. The people from these cities represented refinement and progress. Jordanian women saw these urbanites as role models, and therefore increasingly adopted features of their speech, including [ʔ]. Because of this distribution in the usage of the two variants, there emerged an association between [g] and men's speech and between [ʔ] and women's speech. Subsequently, these associations were translated into the stereotype that [g] is 'tough' and [ʔ] is 'soft', which has also led some men whose heritage dialects have [ʔ] to adopt [g] in certain social contexts.[1]

We thus see that social meaning is neither constant nor abstract. It is constructed locally, per speech community, and shaped by patterns of usage, which are often reactions to historical events or other developments. Later in this chapter, we present a number of additional examples where quantitative analysis is combined with speakers' ideologies and societal norms.

---

[1] A more detailed account of the political events that led to the gender associations outlined here is available in Al-Wer (1991) and Al-Wer and Herin (2011).

3.3   Gender and the Notion of Standard in Arabic

A number of early studies from the 1970s and 1980s presented a problematic interpretation of data from Arabic by assuming that (i) the trajectory of change in Arabic vernaculars is in the direction of Classical Arabic, the formal standard; (ii) Classical Arabic plays the same role in Arab communities as that of modern standard European languages in their respective communities. These presuppositions have led to misconstrued conclusions about gender-differentiated patterns. They claimed that Arabic contravenes the general pattern found in other languages in that it is men who use 'standard prestigious' linguistic forms more often than women. This conclusion is flawed for two reasons. Firstly, it is based on the assumption that Classical Arabic, the formal superposed standard, is involved in processes of social evaluation, variation, and change in the vernacular. All of the data that have been analysed refute this assumption and the conclusion to which it leads. In actual fact, the empirical data show that change in Arabic vernaculars is determined by the local varieties, independently of Classical Arabic. Secondly, this assumption led to the interpretation of the occurrence of vernacular features that *happen* to be identical to parallel features in Classical Arabic as tokens of usage of the Classical features themselves. A case in point is the realisation of the interdental fricatives [θ] and [ð]. While it is true that these sounds exist in Classical Arabic and are absent from *some* vernaculars, the fact that they are used in some other vernaculars is unrelated to their use in Classical Arabic. For example, in Palestine, some (mostly urban) dialects have merged these sounds with their dental plosive counterparts [t] and [d], but others (mostly rural) maintained the phonemic distinctions between the interdentals and stops. The fact that rural Palestinian Arabic shares these sounds with Classical Arabic is a coincidence. Thus when a speaker of one of these dialects pronounces [ð] in a word such as /ðanab/ 'tail', they are simply using their own vernacular. Sociolinguistic investigations of change in Palestinian Arabic and other similar dialects (e.g. Jordanian) reveal that these sounds are changing from the rural interdental variants to the urban stop variants. What the speakers are doing in these cases is not diverging from Classical Arabic, but rather from their local, stigmatised dialect and converging with the prestigious dialects of the region. Classical Arabic has different functions in Arabic-speaking societies and is highly valued as a vehicle for formal written and spoken communication; it serves as an expression of political aspirations and attachment to Arab heritage. However, empirical evidence shows that it does not play a role in the dynamics of variation and change. To be more precise, Classical Arabic does not have a normative effect on the structure of variation in the core domains of phonology, morphology, and syntax.

This misrepresentation of Arabic data was rectified by Muhammad Hassan Ibrahim (1986), who made a distinction between Classical Arabic as a superposed formal standard and naturally-formed regional spoken Arabic standards. In Ibrahim's analysis, there is a distinction between the linguistic and cultural role played by Classical Arabic as a pan-Arab norm and the hierarchy of prestige represented by the natively acquired vernaculars. Within the spoken dialects, several varieties emerged naturally as local de facto standard dialects. The local standard is often the dialect of a large heterogeneous city and is typically a levelled dialect containing supralocal linguistic features (see below). For instance, the dialects of Cairo, Beirut, and Tunis function as local standards in Egypt, Lebanon, and Tunisia, respectively. In some cases there may be more than one local standard; for instance in a large country such as Saudi Arabia, the dialect of the city of Jeddah seems to function as a local standard in the western province, and the dialect of the capital city of Riyadh has more influence in the central and eastern provinces. We can thus say that the status of the local standards in Arabic-speaking countries is comparable to the status of standard British English in Britain and standard American English in the United States.

Niloofar Haeri (1987, 1994) and Enam Al-Wer (1997) have elaborated further, presenting empirical data that strengthens the model advocated by Ibrahim. Further details on Haeri's study of the role of women as innovators are presented in Section 3.5.1. Following Ibrahim and Haeri, many other studies confirmed the validity of this approach to the interpretation of gender-differentiated patterns in Arabic. As a result, data from Arabic are now presented not as anomalies but as comparable to findings from other languages.

3.4   Local and Supralocal Features

The generalisation that female speakers produce linguistic features that are closer to the prestigious norms more often than male speakers (see Section 3.2) is by and large valid, bearing in mind that it is based on statistics arrived at through averaged data. It is a useful generalisation provided it is kept in perspective. An important reformulation of sociolinguistic findings of gender-related variation looks at male and female preferences not in terms of standard versus non-standard but in terms of localised versus supralocal features (J. Milroy et al. 1994). Localised linguistic features are ones that tend to be characteristic of a particular dialect or dialects of a particular region and are generally not found in other dialects. Supralocal features are features that can be found in, or have spread to become characteristic of, a larger geographical area. Thus, supralocal features are not peculiar to a particular dialect or a particular group of dialects. It is easy to perceive standard features as being supralocal features insofar as standard dialects tend to be superimposed upon the community nationwide, normally through educational institutions and the media.

Viewed in terms of localised versus supralocal features, generalisation (1) above extends to include patterns of variation in languages where there is a formal standard and de facto standards, such as in the case of Arabic. For example, in research in three provincial cities in Jordan, Al-Wer (1991) found that only the women, especially the younger women, showed variation in the use of local and non-local features. All of the non-local features they introduced in their speech were characteristic of the dialects spoken in the large cities in the region (Amman, Damascus, Beirut, and Jerusalem) and can thus be called supralocal features. The supralocal features that they used variably with the localised features were [ʔ] for (q), [ʒ] for (ʤ), [t] for (θ), [d] for (ð), and [dˤ] for (ðˤ), which are characteristic of the major city dialects in the Levant. In this research there was no variation at all in the speech of the men; they all used the localised features of these variables consistently in the three cities. In a study of the linguistic adaptation in the speech of a migrant group from the Golan Heights in the city of Damascus, Jassem (1993) found that the female speakers were ahead of the male speakers in this group in the use of eight features which are characteristic of the Damascus dialect, whereas the male speakers used the group's traditional features (all localised) more consistently.

Similarly, Jabeur (1987) investigated a number of phonological and morphosyntactic features in the speech of rural migrants in Rades, Tunisia. He found that younger women were ahead in the use of monophthongal variants, which are typical of the Tunis dialect (the de facto local standard). For instance, the localised diphthongal pronunciations of /aw/ and /aj/ were abandoned in favour of the supralocal monophthongal pronunciations [oː] and [eː].

In a study of (q) in Gaza, Cotter (2016) reports variation among two subcommunities: speakers of Gaza origin, whose localised form is [g], and refugees from Jaffa, whose traditional dialect has the usual Levantine city form [ʔ].

Table 3.1 *Distribution of (q) by gender among speakers of Gaza origin (based on Cotter 2016: 241, Table 8)*

Gender	[ʔ]	[g]	%[ʔ]	Total
Female	44	142	24%	186
Male	10	181	5%	191
				377

Table 3.2 *Distribution of (q) by gender among speakers of Jaffa origin (based on Cotter 2016: 241, Table 9)*

Gender	[ʔ]	[g]	%[ʔ]	Total
Female	79	3	96%	82
Male	30	86	26%	116
				198

As seen in Tables 3.1 and 3.2, in both groups, men use the localised Gaza form at much higher rates than women. Women, on the other hand, use the supralocal form, which happens to coincide with the Jaffa heritage form, significantly more than their male counterparts. Interestingly, the men who originate from Jaffa adopt localised Gaza [g] at a rate of 75%, while Jaffa-origin women remain nearly categorical in their use of [ʔ]. For the Gaza-origin group, women still use localised [g] 76% of the time, but they have gradually adopted the supralocal form at a rate nearly five times higher than Gaza-origin men. Furthermore, in Amman, where a new dialect has recently emerged out of contact between Jordanian and Palestinian dialects, Al-Wer (2007) reports that even from the earliest generation of migrants in the city, Jordanian women diverged from their traditional, localised [g] by increasingly adopting the supralocal [ʔ] variant. At the same time, urban Palestinian men of the same generation diverged from their traditional variant [ʔ] to the localised Jordanian [g]. The data from Gaza and Amman show that even in dialect-contact situations, the distinction between localised and supralocal variants is useful in capturing typical gender-differentiated patterns. Data from Arabic vernaculars have thus often strengthened the generalisations previously formulated for other languages.

In the remainder of this chapter, we will present findings from research on variation and change in Arabic dialects. Through these examples we will show how the interpretation of data can be taken a step further to refine generalisations. We shall see that it is always important to link the linguistic findings to the specific social circumstances of each speech community. Our interpretations of language variation and change in Arabic dialects must be based on the supposition that each Arabic dialect and the community that speaks it are intimately linked to one another. They may have specific connections to other Arabic dialects and their respective speech communities, but this connection must be established empirically rather than assumed a priori.

3.5   Gender-Differentiated Findings in Arabic Vernaculars

As mentioned earlier, cross-linguistically, it seems to be the case that women lead most linguistic changes. In studies of languages other than Arabic, a few reported men to be in the lead of linguistic change. Based on these studies, Labov suggested that changes that are led by men are fewer in number than those led by women, and that they tend to be minor changes, e.g. in the pronunciation of a single sound, rather than changes that affect a broader linguistic system, as in the case of vowel chain shifts.[2] In the case of Arabic,

---

[2] A good example of this is the Northern Cities Shift, which has been progressing in the northern United States (and to a lesser extent in southern Canada), which may have started with one or two vowels becoming higher and fronter. This change caused other internal changes in the vowel space, in a chain-reaction mechanism. See Labov (2001) for the full details.

quantification of data is relatively recent, and although there has been a surge of variationist studies of Arabic vernaculars since the beginning of the twenty-first century, the data are still restricted geographically and in terms of the features explored. It is therefore prudent at this juncture to refrain from over-generalising on the basis of the available data. At the same time, it is helpful to keep in mind the generalisations found elsewhere when reviewing the results obtained thus far from Arabic. In all of the studies presented in this section, gender was found to be a statistically significant social variable and thus a factor in determining the structure of variation and a predictor of the trajectory of language change. In some of these studies, the use of innovative or supralocal linguistic features has been found to be led by a specific gender group, while in others the roles of the gender groups vary across age cohorts. The role of gender can also be modified by other social factors, such as social class and dialect contact, and thus cannot be interpreted independently of them. An interesting observation was made by Munira Al-Azraqi (2007: 240) in a multi-city investigation of de-affrication in Saudi Arabia. In this study, she found that men were ahead of women in using [k] rather than affricate variants. Part of her interpretation of these results focusses on the intersection of style and gender. She attributes the increased use of [k], the non-localised variant, to a more formal style of speech used by men when addressing women outside their family circles. By contrast, the occurrence of the localised, affricated variants of /k/ increased in the speech of men when interacting with women within their families. What will become clear as we review the data in the case studies below is that each speech community has its own history and social dynamics, and the linguistic changes that emanate from each community are intimately connected with its local dynamics.

3.5.1   *Palatalisation in Cairo*

We begin with one of the earliest variationist studies on an Arabic vernacular, conducted by Niloofar Haeri in Cairo. One of the features she studied was that of palatalisation of alveolar stops. She identified two degrees of palatalisation: weak and strong. For example, the word /mamti/ 'my mother' can be pronounced as [mamtʲi] (weak palatalisation) or [mamʧi] (strong palatalisation) (Haeri 1994: 88). Figure 3.1 demonstrates that women lead men in the use of both types of palatalisation.

Haeri also looked at the interaction of gender with age, education, and social class. She reports that strong palatalisation increased in the younger age groups, thus indicating change in progress. Regarding social class, Haeri found that palatalisation was an innovation introduced by women in the higher classes. The data suggest that this is a fairly new feature that did not exist in Cairene Arabic, or indeed in any neighbouring dialect, until two generations prior to these data being collected. In the rest of the examples

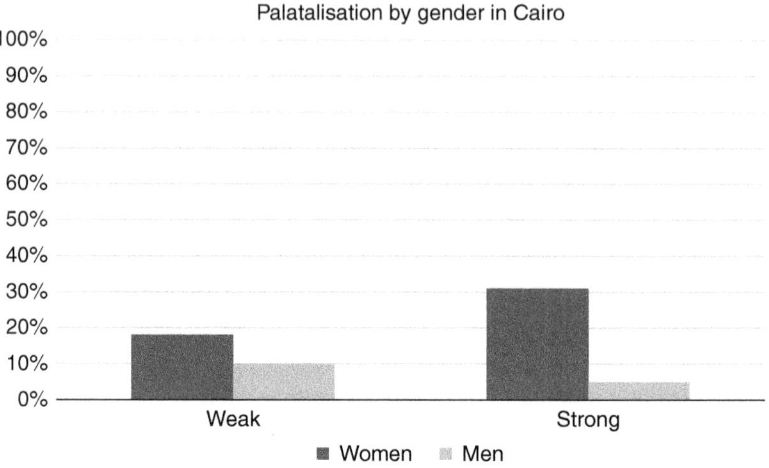

Figure 3.1 Percentage use of weak and strong palatalisation in Cairo (based on Haeri 1994: 97, Table 8)

we discuss, the incoming linguistic features are available to speakers either within their own communities or in communities that have come into contact with them.

3.5.2   Lenition of /dʒ/ in Medina

Our next example is from Abeer Hussain's (2017) study of variation and change among two groups of speakers in Medina: Urban and Bedouin. One of the variables she investigated was (dʒ). This variable has two variants: [dʒ] and [ʒ], as in [nadʒlis] ~ [naʒlis] 'we sit'. The affricate realisation [dʒ] is characteristic of the traditional dialects of both the Urban and Bedouin groups; the fricative [ʒ] is the incoming variant and is characteristic of the dialect of Jeddah, the largest metropolis in the region, and as such enjoys considerable prestige. In studies that explore the diffusion of a feature that originated in another speech community, we typically track the progress of the diffusion by calculating the ratio of occurrence of the incoming variant. In Table 3.3, therefore, we present the percentages for the variant [ʒ].

Looking at the 'Total per gender' row, we see that the rate of use of this variant by women (47%) is greater than that for men (40%); this difference reached a statistical significance rate of $p < 0.01$. Seen as an approximation to the dialect of Jeddah, the behaviour of women in Medina can be described as convergence towards a supralocal, prestigious norm. Once again, we see that women lead men in the use of such features. In order to glean more information about

Table 3.3 *Cross-tabulation of (ʤ) by age and gender in Medina (Hussain 2017: 221, Table 5.9)*

| | % [ʒ] | | | |
Age group	Female	Male	Total per age group	Tokens
Old	8%	15%	12%	515
Middle-aged	38%	42%	40%	519
Adult	56%	47%	51%	575
Young	79%	53%	67%	566
Total per gender	**47%**	**40%**		
Tokens	1102	1023		

Total number of tokens 2175
Grand mean 43%

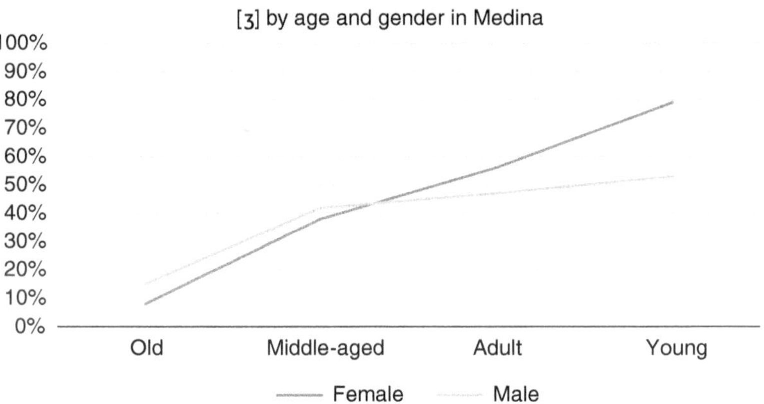

Figure 3.2 Cross-tabulation of (ʤ) by age and gender in Medina (based on Hussain 2017: 221, Table 5.9)

the innovating group and the dynamics of diffusion, it is important to look at the interplay of gender and other social variables. It is useful in cases where linguistic change is in progress to check whether the change is progressing at similar rates across genders; in other words, we can benefit from looking at the interaction between age and gender. In this case, we see that in both gender groups, the younger the speaker, the more they use the innovative variant [ʒ]. However, while in the old and middle-aged groups men use this variant more frequently than women, the gender pattern is reversed in the younger groups (adult and young), where women's rates of use of [ʒ] surpass those of men. We see this crossover quite clearly in Figure 3.2.

3.5.3   Monophthongisation in Mecca

In Mecca, Najla Alghamdi (2014) studied the linguistic developments in the speech of a group of migrants from Al-Baha (of the Ghamdi tribe), whose dialect contains diphthongal realisations [aɪ] and [aʊ] in words such as [baɪt] 'house' and [laʊn] 'colour'. These diphthongs are realised as monophthongs [ɛː] and [ɔː] in the dialect of Mecca, the host community, i.e. [bɛːt] and [lɔːn], respectively. The Ghamdi migrants use three types of variants: their traditional diphthongs, the Meccan monophthongs, and intermediate diphthongal variants. Figure 3.3 shows the use of the monophthong [ɛː] among women and men in four age groups.

The men in the oldest generation in this migrant community initially travelled to Mecca without their families in search of jobs and remained there for up to two years; because of poor transportation options in those days, they only returned home for infrequent visits. They eventually returned to Mecca in old age, after their own children had settled there. We notice that their stay in Mecca while isolated from their families back home resulted in exposure to the Meccan form, which led them to adopt this form variably and at a much higher rate than the women of the same generation.

The second-oldest group (ages 46–61) had a very different experience. Unlike their older counterparts, these migrants relocated to Mecca as families with the intention of staying and becoming residents of the city. They had a positive attitude towards the community, its culture, and the local dialect, and wanted to dissociate themselves from their Hijazi-Ghamdi heritage. They sought permanent employment in Mecca and had no intention of going back

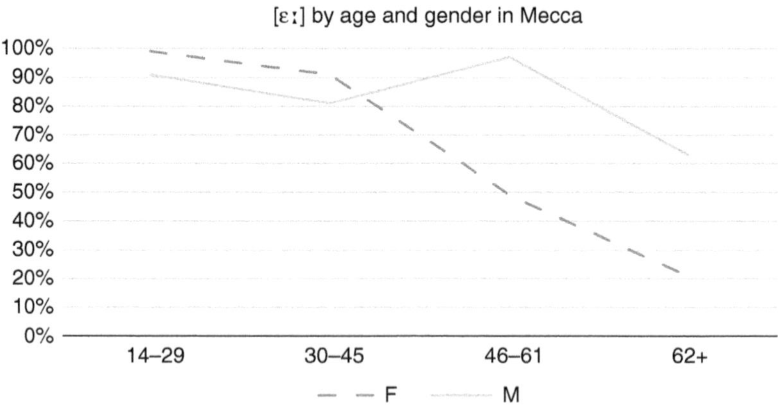

Figure 3.3 Percentage use of [ɛː] by age and gender in Mecca (based on Alghamdi 2014: 77, Figure 4.4)

to Al-Baha. As a result, their friendship networks inevitably included native Meccans. Their positive attitude towards the host community led them to willingly embrace the local Meccan way of life and elements of its dialect. In the case of this particular variable, we see almost categorical usage of the Meccan monophthongal pronunciation in this age group.

The linguistic behaviour of women in this generation moved along the same trajectory as their male counterparts. Their speech, too, was affected by their migration to Mecca, albeit indirectly, mostly through the men in their families. We see a sharp rise in the use of monophthongs compared to women of the previous generation, but unlike the men, this generation of women did not reach the same rate of usage as the men (49% for women; 97% for men). The difference between the men and the women in this generation becomes clear when considering their respective socialisation patterns. While the men extended their immediate social networks to include local Meccans and had frequent face-to-face interactions with them through their jobs, the women mostly tended to their homes and subsequently socialised within the Ghamdi community. In cases where they expanded their social networks, it was with other migrant groups in the city, particularly from Yemen.

The gender pattern in the younger generations (age 45 and under) is reversed, hence the crossover seen in Figure 3.3 for the second-youngest group. While women continue the trend exhibited by the previous generations, namely increasing their ratio of usage of the Meccan form, we see a 17% dip for the men. How can we explain this sudden decline in the rate of use of the monophthongal variant among men of this generation? We find plausible explanations in observations gathered by the researcher during her ethnography.[3] In the younger generations, men, in particular, were aware that the use of their traditional dialectal forms was diminishing. In a conscious effort to assert the distinctiveness of their group and their positive attitude towards their heritage, they revert to traditional linguistic forms, if only variably. In other words, their relative linguistic conservatism compared to the older generation is a symbol of their increased secure position in the host community and, parallel to that, pride in their heritage. We can interpret this as a result of this generation's re-evaluation of negative connotations previously associated with their families' place of origin.

The overall gender pattern in the younger generation, where women lead men in the use of the de facto Meccan standard form [ɛː], is consistent with findings from other Arabic-speaking communities, as well as with well-established tendencies found in other languages. Note that this case is analogous to that of (ʤ) in Medina discussed above. In both Medina and Mecca, not only do we see younger women leading the whole community, but they do so

---

[3] The information on this point was kindly provided to the authors by Najla Alghamdi (p.c.).

following a period during which older women were lagging behind in the use of the incoming feature.[4]

3.5.4   *(u) and (l) in Saḥam, Jordan*

The same pattern of gender differentiation is reported by Noora Abu Ain (2016) in her study of variation and change in the village of Saḥam. This village is home to the northmost community in Jordan, in the heart of Horan. It is only 21 km north of Irbid, a bustling urban centre, which hosts two of Jordan's largest state universities. Abu Ain investigated the use of two salient traditional local features: [u], as in [gamuħ] 'wheat', which alternates with the supralocal variant [i], as in [gamiħ]; and [ɫ], as in [xɑːɫ] 'maternal uncle', which alternates with supralocal [l], as in [xaːl]. Both local variants [u] and [ɫ] are shibboleths of the traditional Horani dialect, whereas these features are often levelled out in the northern city of Irbid (Al-Khatib 1988) and completely levelled out in Amman (see Chapter 6). The cross-tabulation of the use of these features by age and gender is presented in Figures 3.4 and 3.5.

Looking at gender alone (the 'Total' bars), we see that for both variables women are ahead of men (significant at the 0.001 level) in using the supralocal variants [i] and [l]. We also notice that the rate of usage of innovative [l] is much higher than that of innovative [i] (61% versus 24%). It is not unusual in

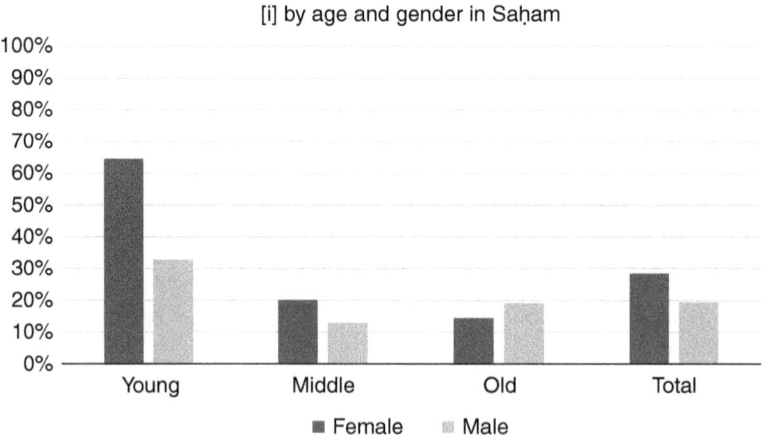

Figure 3.4 Percentage use of [i] by gender and age in Saḥam (based on Abu Ain 2016: 120, Table 4.6)

---

[4] Similar patterns in the western region of Saudi Arabia were found among migrant groups in Jeddah (Al-Shehri 1993; Al-Essa 2009) and in the southwest of the country (Al-Qahtani 2015).

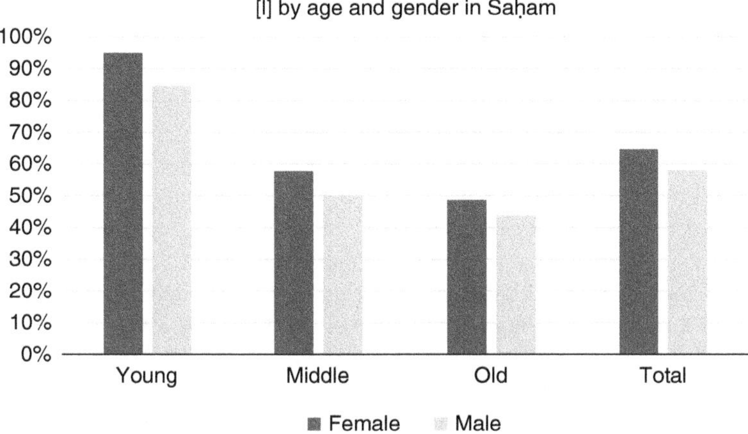

Figure 3.5 Percentage use of [l] by gender and age in Saḥam (based on Abu Ain 2016: 158, Table 5.7)

sociolinguistic research to find that different variables are at different stages of change or even that they pattern differently. This is attributed to social as well as linguistic factors: different variables are evaluated differently in terms of their social meaning and salience, and their grammatical complexity often varies as well. In this particular case, the variant [ɫ] is highly stigmatised as a stereotype outside of the region. This may explain the high rate of abandonment of this variant by the younger generation (90% across both gender groups, with women leading the change at 95%).

This community has undergone radical change in terms of connection to the city; it is now connected to Irbid by a modern road and public transportation. This development has facilitated a transformation of the local economy. Many members of the younger generation commute to the city for work and higher education. Additionally, Abu Ain reports that younger women have expressed discontent with 'traditional rural life' and that their divergence from the traditional dialect can be seen as symbolic of their aspirations for social change.

3.5.5   *(ɛː) in Korba, Tunisia*

Keith Walters (1991) studied a number of phonological variables in the town of Korba, located on Cap Bon, the northeastern peninsula of Tunisia. Among these variables is (ɛː), which concerns the pronunciation of the vowel /ɛː/ in word-final position, as in /mustəwɛː/ 'level'. This variable has three variants in the local dialect:

1. [ɛː], the standard, Tunis-like form
2. [ɪː], a high lax front vowel
3. [ɨː], a lax centralised high vowel with tongue retraction, which is the localised form in Korba

Walters placed these variants on a continuum of 'localness'. Speakers were assigned an index value ranging from 1 to 3, with 1 representing consistent usage of [ɛː] and 3 representing consistent usage of [ɨː]. Only two speakers scored 1, and none of the speakers scored 3. Most speakers thus used more than one variant, and their average scores ranged from 1.07 to 2.52. In addition to gender, the speaker sample represented two age groups, older and younger. Figure 3.6 is a scatterplot of the index scores of each speaker. The X axis indicates speakers' ages; the Y axis, their index scores; light circles represent men, and dark circles represent women. Additionally, the figure includes a trend line for each gender group.

We see that both women and men in the 60–65-year-old age group have, on average, index scores ranging between 2.00 and 2.20, while younger speakers of both genders move in the direction of the Tunis-like standard variant, but the decline in using the localised variants is sharper among men. Note that only men in their twenties scored the lowest, between 1.00 and 1.20. This trend suggests that it is men who are in the lead towards the standard pronunciation. The decreasing use of the localised variant seems to be an outcome of an increase in

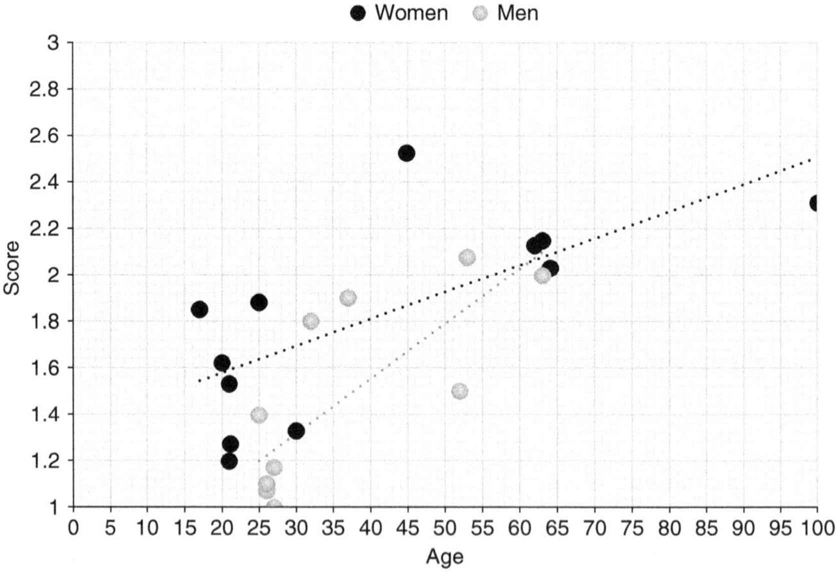

Figure 3.6 Index scores of speakers for (ɛː) in Korba by gender (based on Walters 1991: 211, Table 1)

contact with communities outside Korba, especially in Tunis. This is particularly apparent in cases of contact through higher education, the opportunities
for which have increased over time. Walters also suggests that the raised variants (1 and 2) are associated with a norm that is perceived as 'appropriate' for
women and when addressing women.

There are two outliers in the data. Only one speaker is older than 65. This
100-year-old woman has a score of 2.31. It is difficult to assess whether she
is representative of her generation, as there are no other speakers in this age
range in either gender group. The other outlier is a 45-year-old woman, whose
score is higher than anyone else's in the sample, i.e. she is the most linguistically conservative. Walters provides additional information about this woman,
as well as about her husband, who has the highest score among the men. This
couple lives not in Korba itself but on a farm just outside the town, which may
explain their higher frequency of usage of the localised forms.

3.5.6 *Three Variables in Sūf, Jordan*

Our next example comes from the town of Sūf in northern Jordan. A study
by Areej Al-Hawamdeh (2016) investigated three features in this dialect: the
de-palatalisation of [ʧ] in the feminine suffix -*ik* and in word stems, and the
alternation between [ɫ] and [l] (similar to Abu Ain's study in Saḥam cited
above). She concluded that all three variables were undergoing change from
localised [iʧ] and [ʧ] to supralocal [ik] and [k] respectively, and from localised [ɫ] to supralocal [l]. The results for all three variables are presented in
Figure 3.7

As can be seen, men are in the lead in all three cases. In fact, Al-Hawamdeh
maintains that the women 'speak with a particularly broad local accent' (172),
much more than do their male counterparts. She explains that while the men
of Sūf typically commute for work to one of the two large cities, Irbid and
Amman, most women are employed locally, e.g. as teachers, and at the same
time are expected to transmit and preserve the local culture and traditions.
Maintaining local linguistic features is a symbol of general adherence to such
local norms. In sum, men spend more time outside Sūf, establishing connections with wider and more varied social networks, while the women's activities
and social contacts are much more locally oriented, leading to the linguistic
pattern we see in Figure 3.7.

3.5.7 *Vowel Unrounding in Al-Ahsa, Saudi Arabia*

In many cases, it is important to delve deeper into the statistics by looking at the
behaviour of smaller cohorts of speakers in relation to one another. In the next
dataset, which comes from Moayyad Al-Bohnayyah's (2019) study in Al-Ahsa,
in the eastern province of Saudi Arabia, three social variables were considered

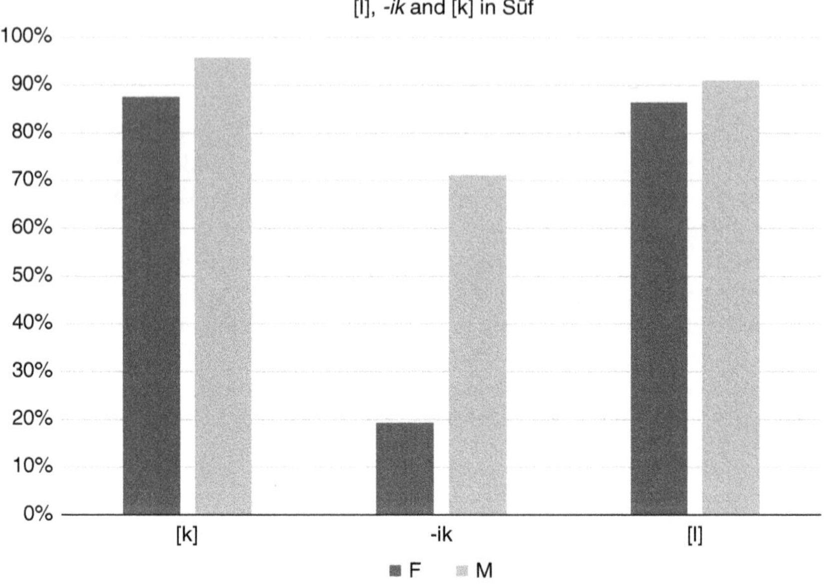

Figure 3.7 Percentage use of [l], -*ik*, and [k] in Sūf (based on Al-Hawamdeh 2016)

in the sociolinguistic correlations. In addition to age and gender, religious sect (Sunni or Shi'a) is also included. All three social variables were found to be statistically significant in this study. For example, one of the features he investigated was the unrounding of the vowel [ɒː], which in most dialects in Saudi Arabia is realised as [ɑː], as in the following examples:

(1)   [didʒɒːdʒ] ~ [didʒɑːdʒ] 'chicken'

(2)   [gɒːl] ~ [gɑːl] 'he said'.

The traditional, rounded variant [ɒː] is a minority variant in Saudi Arabia and a stereotype. It is particularly salient and stigmatised because it is (erroneously) associated by people outside the region with Shi'a speech (see Chapter 6).

The overall statistics regarding gender show men in the lead at 76% (versus women at 57%) in the use of the innovative [ɑː] variant. Let us look at the correlation of all three social variables in relation to the use of the unrounded incoming variant [ɑː]. This is presented in Table 3.4.

Within each sect group, we notice that in the old generation there is a huge gap in the use of the innovative variant between women and men, with men in the lead. When we look at the younger generation, we must treat each sect separately. In the Sunni group, young women have reached categorical use of this variant, while young men are near-categorical. In the Shi'i group, however,

Table 3.4 *Usage of [a:] across age, gender, and sect (based on Al-Bohnayyah 2019: 140, Table 4.7)*

Age	Female	Male	Total	Tokens
Sunni				
Old	26%	72%	47%	534
Young	100%	92%	96%	403
Total	55%	81%	68%	
Tokens	483	454		937
Shi'i				
Old	36%	66%	55%	402
Young	74%	76%	75%	447
Total	59%	70%	65%	
Tokens	403	446		849

neither gender has reached 100% usage, although the gender gap has been reduced considerably. So, by looking at the details concerning the interactions among all three social variables, we see that the conclusion that men are in the lead is a rather superficial one, caused mainly by the older generation, who skew the overall percentage in that direction. We thus see the value of fine-grained examination of the data, through the inclusion of social variables that are relevant to the specific community in which we are interested.

In this community, as in the ones reviewed earlier, socio-economic changes have occurred which resulted in increased contact with a broad cross-section of the population and exposure to supralocal linguistic features. Furthermore, increased face-to-face interactions with a more diverse pool of speakers have raised awareness of the social meanings and stigmas attached to the use of minority and localised linguistic features. While such changes have affected the entire community, women's roles in particular have seen a transformation in the availability of education and employment opportunities. These changes have not only provided access to supralocal features but also increased the pressure upon speakers to abandon their heritage variants. Against this back-drop, it becomes clear why the gap between the older women and the older men is so wide, and why it narrows in parallel to social change. In this way, we can view gender as a sociolinguistic variable that is closely connected with local social dynamics that affect the individual directly.

3.5.8 *Feminine Suffixes in Ha'il, Saudi Arabia*

In the next example, we look at the structure of variation in two variables in the same community. In Ha'il, north-central Saudi Arabia, AlAmmar (2017) examined variation and change in the use of two feminine suffixes among the Šammar tribe. These are the singular feminine ending (ah): [e] ~ [a], as in *milʕage* ~ *milʕaga* 'spoon', and the plural feminine ending (aːt): [aːh], [aːj], [aːt], as in *faːfaːh* ~ *faːfaːj* ~ *faːfaːt* '(television) screens'. The traditional local forms in this dialect are [e] (sg.) and [aːh] ~ [aːj] (pl.). The incoming variants, [a] and [aːt], are characteristic of the pan-Saudi norm, including that of the capital Riyadh, located in the central region.

Figure 3.8 shows the rate of usage of the incoming variants [a] and [aːt] in Ha'il by gender and age. In the case of [a], there has been a sharp increase in the use of this variant by both genders within three generations. The older speakers in the sample barely use it; the middle age group use it just over a third of the time; and the youngest speakers use it over 50% of the time. This generational difference was found to be statistically significant at the $p < 0.001$ level. Speakers of both genders in the middle generation use the incoming variant considerably more than their older counterparts. We see that in this generation men are the ones leading the change, while a generation later, i.e. the young age group, women take the lead. Note that while for women the use of [a] increases steadily across the three generations – we refer to this as a monotonic pattern – men initially spike more sharply in the middle age group and then increase more moderately in the young generation, ending up with lower rates of [a] than the young women. It is important to note as well that overall, regardless of age, women favour the incoming variant with statistical significance at $p < 0.05$.

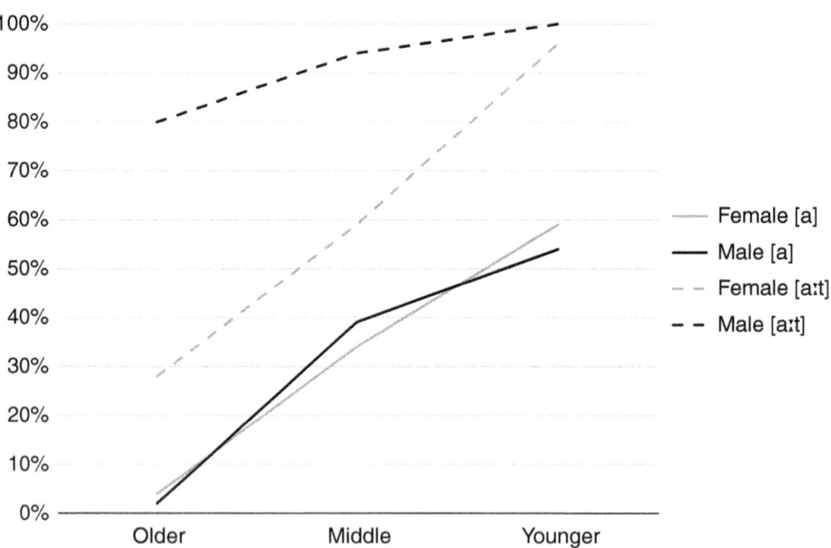

Figure 3.8 Percentage use of [a] and [aːt] by gender in Ha'il (based on AlAmmar 2017)

In the case of the plural variable (aːt), Figure 3.8 also shows that both gender groups increase their use of the incoming variant.[5] The difference between the trends of (ah) and (aːt) is in the rates of change. Note that for (aːt), men in the oldest generation already used the variant [aːt] 80% of the time, rising within two generations to categorical use. AlAmmar attributes this early abandonment of the localised variants [aːh] and [aːj] by men to strong social stereotyping. She maintains that these variants are associated with women's speech and have therefore been mostly avoided by men for quite some time. This is unlike the localised singular suffix variant [e], which does not carry overt negative evaluation for either gender.

Women, on the other hand, started at less than 30% and almost caught up with the men in the youngest generation. The women therefore can be said to have gone through a radical change in a rather short period of time.

The increase from generation to generation reflects the socio-economic change that the community has gone through. In the two older generations, women's access to higher education and subsequently social and economic mobility were extremely restricted. Men used to leave the region to study at universities around the country and eventually work in their acquired professions. Only in the last few decades have opportunities for higher education become available locally. Consequently, for the young women of Ha'il, attaining academic degrees is no longer contingent upon travel outside the region. Women have begun attending the local university (established 2005), alongside a diverse group of students from other regions, which has accelerated the process of levelling out localised features, such as the traditional feminine suffixes discussed above.

3.5.9   Lenition of /r/ in Damascus

In a study of two neighbourhoods in Damascus, Hanadi Ismail (2007) discovered interesting and complex patterns of gender differentiation with regard to the variable (r). In addition to the traditional trill pronunciation [r], she identified a range of lenited variants, the most frequent of which was a palato-alveolar approximant [ɹ]. We shall henceforth focus on the occurrence of this variant. The two neighbourhoods of Damascus surveyed by Ismail are Shaghoor, an inner-city traditional Damascene neighbourhood, and Dummar, a middle-class suburb.

Figure 3.9 shows the percentage usage of the innovative variant [ɹ] by age, gender, and neighbourhood. Let us first look at the inner-city community of Shaghoor, which is one of the oldest quarters of Damascus. We see very clearly

---

[5] The calculations for this variable considered a binary distinction between the innovative variant [aːt] and the local variants, [aːh] and [aːj], combined.

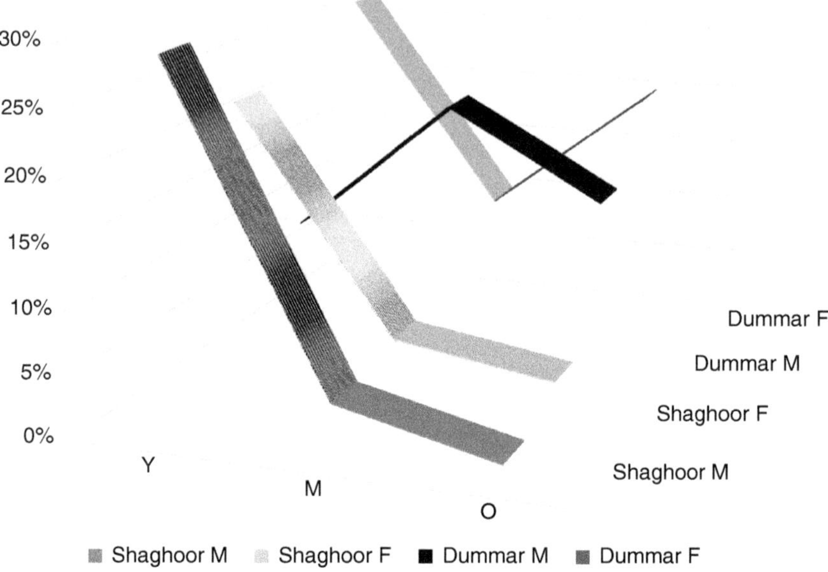

Figure 3.9 Percentage use of [ɹ] in Damascus by age, gender, and neighbourhood (based on Ismail 2007: 206, Figures 9.4–9.6)

that in the old and middle age groups, the use of [ɹ] is extremely low, irrespective of gender. The young age group, however, use it roughly a quarter of the time, with men in the lead at 29%, and women slightly behind at 23%. Ismail describes this pattern as a change in progress that is in its early stages. She explains that the gender pattern in the young generation can be understood by analysing the gender roles in this community, as well as the mode of production. Men in this neighbourhood are almost always the breadwinners, mostly in the traditional family retail businesses. Through this activity, the young men of Shaghoor are exposed to linguistic innovations that may have originated elsewhere in the city. At the time of Ismail's research, only one young woman was employed outside the home. Some women were self-employed locally in traditional occupations such as seamstressing and hairdressing. This difference in the mode of production between the men and women of Shaghoor explains the higher frequency of using the innovative variant among younger men.

The picture is more complex in the suburban community of Dummar. The innovative feature is used more frequently by the old and middle generations in this community than in Shaghoor. This is an indication that this variant has been in use in Dummar for a longer time. When comparing the use of [ɹ] across generations in Dummar, we see that men in the middle age group use it at a much higher frequency (21%) than their older male counterparts (4%). The young generation of men use it slightly less frequently (19%) than the middle age group. The women, however, start relatively high, at 20%. Women in the middle age group only use it 10% of the time, and the youngest women 27%, thus leading the entire Dummar community. This pattern of a dip and following surge in the use of the innovative variant is atypical of changes in progress and requires a closer examination of the data obtained through the ethnographic fieldwork (see Chapter 2).

Ismail explains that the women in the old age category in her sample were 'wives of "important" men' (209) and 'home-refiners' (rather than 'house-wives') (208). In other words, these women work on the image that goes with the family status, which is determined by what their husbands do and who they are. This leads to the hypothesis that these women of Dummar attach a posi-tive social meaning to this variant and may be consciously adopting 'trendy' features used by younger people.

Figure 3.9 shows an additional group whose adoption of [ɹ] appears to be exaggerated, namely the men of the middle age group in Dummar. Their use of this variant (21%) is higher than both the younger men (19%) and the women in their own age group (10%). The behaviour of this group of speakers also suggests that /r/ weakening is a trendy feature. Ismail describes them as single, educated men in their thirties, mobile, and financially independent. In terms of social behaviour and ideologies, they are 'progressivists'.

While the use of the innovative feature in the inner-city neighbourhood of Shaghoor was confined to the young generation (of both women and men), in Dummar the older and middle generations of speakers clearly participate in this variation. This difference between the communities leads to the conclusion that /r/ weakening may have started among suburban middle-class speakers and from this social milieu diffused to traditional inner-city neighbourhoods. The agents of this transmission in Shaghoor are the younger men. Because of the nature of their professions, in particular the need to gain their customers' trust and approval, they were the ones motivated to adopt features of trendy speech.

3.5.10 *Fortition of [j] in Qalʿat Siker, Iraq*

Wisam Alshawi (2020) investigated variation and change in a southern Iraqi dialect spoken by the Mišlab tribe in Qalʿat Siker, 260 km to the southeast of Baghdad. The Mišlab tribe led a nomadic lifestyle until the nineteenth century, when they settled and founded Qalʿat Siker. They then began a gradual pro-cess of sedentarisation, initially as an agrarian community. The community remained fairly isolated from the large cities (the nearest such city is Nasiriyya, 100 km to the south) until the 1960s. It has been transformed, for the most part, into an urban community with a modern economy.

One of the characteristic features of this dialect is [j] as a reflex of /ʤ/, which in Iraq is typical of southern dialects only, e.g. [jɔ:ʕ] 'hunger'.

Figure 3.10 shows Alshawi's findings regarding the rate of usage of the incoming variant [ʤ] across three age groups and two gender groups. We see that male speakers lead in the use of the incoming variant in all age groups and, naturally, for the community as a whole. We do see, however, that men increase their use of [ʤ] only slightly from generation to generation, while women's use rises in larger increments. In the young generation, the gap between women and men is very narrow. This pattern reflects the social change that this community has experienced. Alshawi explains that until recently in this traditional community, men had almost exclusive responsibility over managing the family affairs outside the home, which often entailed coming in contact with members of other communities, in particular Baghdad, where southern features are heavily stigmatised. Additionally, men are conscripted for military service, where they also come into contact for relatively prolonged periods of time with speakers of other dialects. It is therefore not surprising that men should be in the lead in the use of the standard Iraqi form. Another

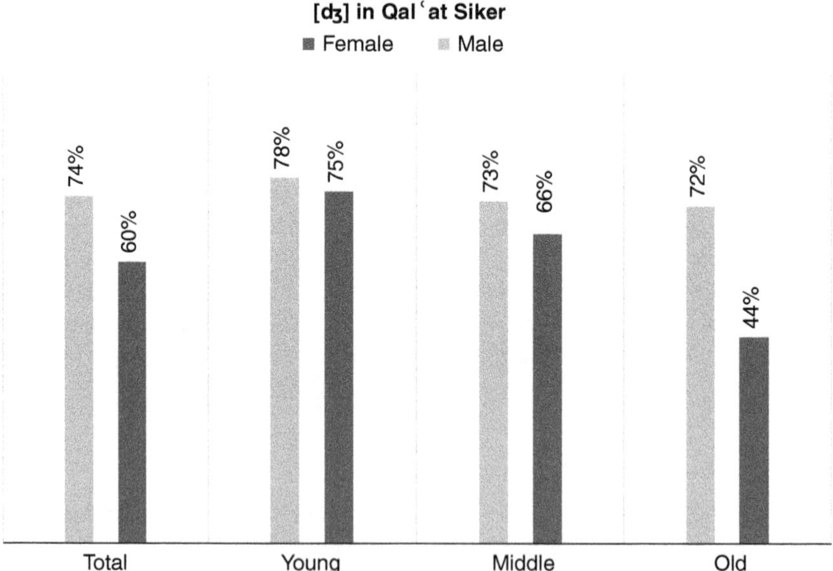

Figure 3.10 Percentage use of [ʤ] in Qalʿat Siker by age and gender (based on Alshawi 2020: 137, Table 4.6)

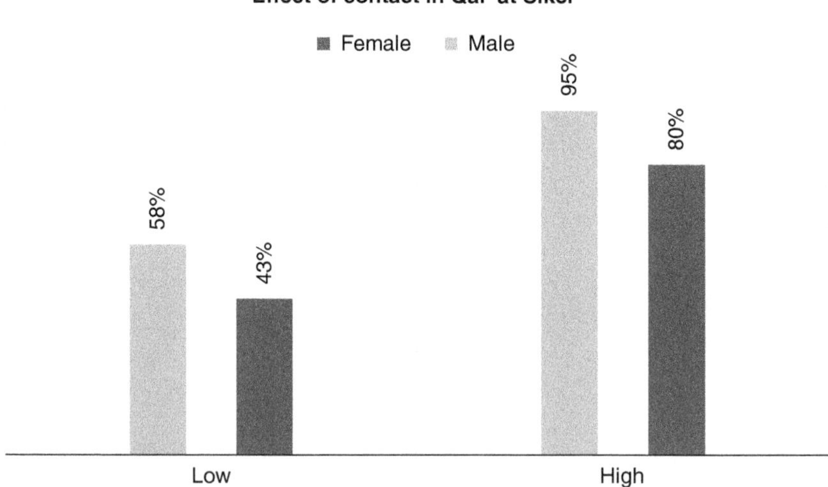

Figure 3.11 Percentage use of [ʤ] in Qalʿat Siker by contact and gender (based on Alshawi 2020: 137, Table 4.5)

route to contact with outsiders is university education. In Alshawi's sample, it is only in the young age group that seeking a university education became a norm for women. Clearly, therefore, intensity and frequency of contact with speakers of dialects that have [ʤ] are catalysts of change which involves adoption of this feature. This is confirmed in Alshawi's study; in addition to age and gender, speakers were classified according to their level of contact with speakers of the Baghdadi dialect. Figure 3.11 shows the percentages of [ʤ] by gender and level of contact (high versus low).

Interestingly, even when contact is factored in, men are in the lead, such that men with both high and low levels of contact use [ʤ] at higher rates than women in the same contact-level category. A plausible explanation for this is that while men have had several avenues to acquiring non-local linguistic features, women's only opportunity to do so has been through higher education – which, as stated above, only became widely available for the youngest generation.

3.5.11 *Fortition of [j] in Dammam*

Another community which has seen comparable changes in circumstances concerning gender roles is the Dōsarī tribe in Dammam, eastern Saudi Arabia. A similar pattern of gender differentiation, with men leading, was found in this dialect by Hind Alaodini (2019). Coincidentally, Alaodini found this pattern

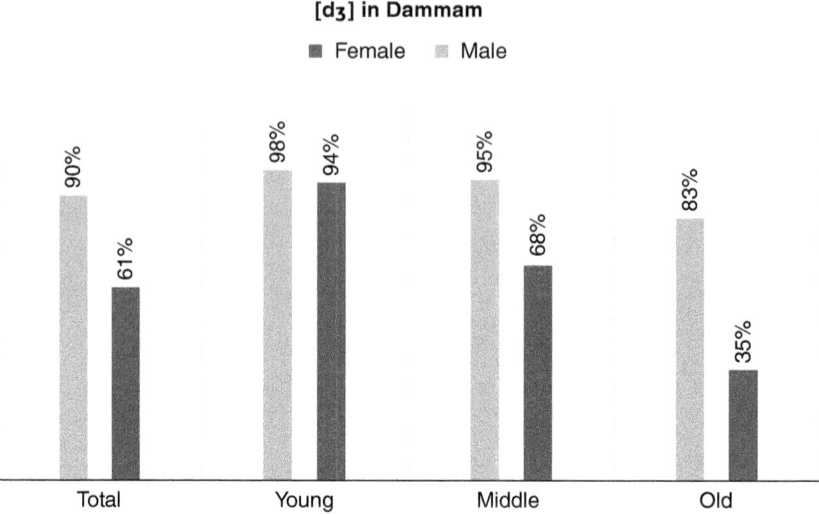

Figure 3.12 Percentage use of [dʒ] in Dammam by age and gender (based on Alaodini 2019: 125, Table 11)

in the same variable, which has the same range of variation in Dammam as it does in Qalʿat Siker (see Section 3.5.10). There are further similarities between the two cases. The first relates to the status of the variant [j] in Iraq and Saudi Arabia, namely that in both countries it is peripheral, localised, and stigmatised. In Iraq, it is considered peculiar to the south of the country, while in Saudi Arabia its stigma is even stronger. Alaodini maintains that outside the group that uses [j] for /dʒ/, people perceive this variant to be 'non-Saudi'. This is in line with the fact that [j] is a characteristic feature of the dominant dialects in Gulf countries (e.g. Kuwait and Bahrain). The second similarity has to do with the traditions of the two communities. In both cases men are considerably more mobile and have more public presence outside the home, and at the same time both communities have undergone change in recent decades which saw younger women increasingly attending universities and furthering their education and careers. Figure 3.12 shows that the change from [j] to [dʒ] in Dammam is now almost complete.

3.5.12 *Summary and Further Remarks*

The cases reviewed in this section demonstrate that either women or men can lead the use of innovative linguistic features in a variety of social circumstances. It is important to keep in mind that social circumstances are not static. In our interpretations of the data, we intentionally looked at gender in conjunction with at least one other social variable. This is because gender roles may vary across generation, social class, or degrees of mobility, to name a few potential social factors. While evaluating the effect of gender on language variation and change for a community at-large is often useful, the data on gender alone may not be sufficient to draw a reliable conclusion as to sociolinguistic patterns. For instance, in the last example provided (see Figure 3.12), in the community as a whole, men appear to use the incoming variant 50 per cent more frequently than women. But when we look at the linguistic behaviour of the young generation, we notice that both gender groups use [dʒ] almost categorically. Who, then, is in the lead of this linguistic change? On the one hand, overall, men use the innovative variant more often than women, but on the other hand, the results from the young age group suggest that women of future generations will no longer lag behind, if only because for both gender groups the change is near completion. Notice as well that in this example, as in several others, women begin the process of change at much lower rates than men. They do, however, within two generations, reach, and sometimes surpass, the rates shown by men. In other words, if we consider acceleration in interpreting the dynamics of the change, the question of 'who leads whom' in language change becomes moot.

A case in point is the gender crossover we saw above in Hussain's study in Medina (Table 3.3; Figure 3.2). In the old generation, women use the incoming fricative [ʒ] nearly half as frequently as men (8% and 15%, respectively), but within three generations their rate of use becomes approximately 50% higher than men's (79% and 53%, respectively). Furthermore, the acceleration rates in women's speech are much higher than in men's. Men increase from 42% to 47% to 53% in the three youngest age groups, while women go from 38% to 56% to 79%. Women are now ahead of men by a whole generation, having lagged behind in the oldest generation.

3.6   Further Reading

Al-Wer (2014) – A chapter in the *Handbook of Language, Gender and Sexuality* summarising research on gender-based variation in Arabic.

Chambers (2009) – This is a textbook of general sociolinguistic theory. The author devotes a chapter to the many facets of sex and gender as they are related to language variation, including a section on data from Arabic.

Eckert (1989) – This is essential reading that introduces a sociocultural interpretation of gender differentiation in language.

Ehrlich and Meyerhoff (2014) – This is a handbook that covers theoretical issues regarding language, gender, and sexuality in general, and also includes chapters that focus on language and gender in specific languages, including a chapter on Arabic by Enam Al-Wer (see above).

Ibrahim (1986) – This is essential reading for understanding the reinterpretation of gender-differentiation patterns in Arabic.

Labov (2001) – This book is essential reading for all students of sociolinguistics. It synthesises findings in research over four decades including cross-linguistic findings regarding gender-differentiated variation.

Miller et al. (2007) – This is a collection of studies that address various themes in Arabic sociolinguistics. In many of these studies, gender plays a significant role in structuring variation.

Sadiqi (2003, 2007) – These two publications (a book and an encyclopaedia entry) discuss gender differentiation in Morocco in relation to space (public and private).

3.7   Exercises for Chapter 3

1. In many communities, there are stereotypes that associate particular pronunciations with gender. For example, in Jordan, many people associate the use of [ʤ] with 'masculinity' and the use of [ʒ] with 'femininity', e.g. [ʤeːbe] ~ [ʒeːbe] 'pocket'. Another example is the perception that 'all speakers of dialect X sound effeminate'. Think of similar stereotypes that you have encountered. Explain the origins of such associations. Are they based on frequency of usage? Are there alternative explanations for sociolinguistic associations of this sort?

2. Several earlier studies have argued that in formal settings, e.g. political discussions in the media, women tend to utilise Classical Arabic features or expressions less frequently than men. To what extent do you think this can be accurately generalised to *all* women and *all* men? Can you think of additional factors that may influence speakers' choice of linguistic features in such settings? Support your answer with examples from the media.

3. Using examples from English, James Milroy and his colleagues reformulated the generalisations concerning gender-differentiated linguistic patterns by suggesting that men tend to use localised linguistic features more frequently than women, who in turn prefer supralocal features. To what extent do you think that this reformulation applies to gender-differentiated patterns in Arabic? How would you distinguish between supralocal and 'Standard' features in Arabic?

4. Recent findings from Arabic-speaking communities show that gender as a sociolinguistic factor interacts with other social factors, such as age. Choose two of the studies presented in this chapter and investigate the interaction between gender and other social variables. Make sure to pay close attention to the idiosyncrasies of different societies; how do these idiosyncrasies help us understand and explain the differences between linguistic patterns?

5. Research by Hachimi (2011, 2012) and Barontini and Ziamari (2009) suggests that certain individuals or groups often challenge popular perceptions of how women 'should' speak. For instance, Barontini and Ziamari analyse the speech of a woman factory worker in Meknes, Morocco, who intentionally adopts discourse strategies which are widely associated with men's speech in order to fend off abuse and harassment by men within the work-place. They also discuss the speech of a peer group of six young women adopting structural features, phonological and syntactic, as well as stylistic devices (e.g. the use of obscenities) which are associated with male speech in the city.

    Think of similar cases that you have encountered where individuals speak in a way that is counter to societal conventions for gender. Provide examples and offer an interpretation of the motives behind these speakers' adoption of such unconventional usages.

6. Al-Wer and Herin (2011) report the following patterns for the use of the variants [g] and [ʔ] of the variable (q) among youth in Amman:
    *   The girls used [ʔ] consistently.
    *   The boys used both variants; their choice depended on interlocutor, style, and dialectal heritage, such that they tended to use [ʔ] when addressing or interacting with girls, [g] in disputes with other boys, and their heritage variant in in-group discussions (e.g. with members of their own ethnic group or their own families).

    What does this distribution tell you about the social meanings associated with the use of the two variants in this community?

7. Al-Rohili (2019) studied de-palatalisation of [gʲ] in Medina among the Ḥarb community and found that it was involved in change in progress towards the standard Medini pronunciation [g], as in *gʲidi:m ~ gidi:m* 'old'.

    The overall results of the study show that women use the [g] variant 82% of the time, and men use it 67% of the time. The table below (Al-Rohili 2019: 92, Table 4.7) shows the cross-tabulation of gender with two additional social variables. The first is age group; the second is level of contact, which measures the degree of exposure to [g], the target variant.

Examine the table below closely. How can the interaction of gender with other variables give us a more accurate understanding of the progression of the change within the various social groups in this community?

High contact	Female	Male	Total
Young	96%	99%	97%
Middle	99%	100%	99%
Old	95%	88%	92%
Total	97%	96%	96%

Low contact	Female	Male	Total
Young	83%	45%	63%
Middle	76%	39%	54%
Old	36%	38%	37%
Total	67%	41%	53%

8. It has been suggested that the increasing participation of women in the public space might have sociolinguistic consequences. For instance, Fatima Sadiqi (2003, 2007) analysed the links between women's involvement in politics and similar male-dominated careers and the adoption of a formal style of speech, which includes the use of Classical Arabic features. With this in mind, conduct a small-scale study that explores the linguistic characteristics of the speech of Arab women in politics (e.g. members of parliament, cabinet ministers). You can expand this study to include other instances of social mobility and their effect on language. Based on your findings, assess the relative role of gender in linguistic patterning; to what extent does it interact with general choice of career? Do particular arenas prescribe linguistic choices regardless of gender?

4   Education

4.1   Introduction

In Arabic sociolinguistics, two social factors have often been used almost interchangeably. These two factors are level of education and social (or socio-economic) class. In this chapter, we focus on education as a social variable and review its significance with respect to Arabic data. A few researchers working within the variationist paradigm have additionally incorporated social class, social network, and life-mode as independent variables, which we discuss in Chapter 5 .

In the general social sciences (e.g. sociology, anthropology, political science), education is typically considered a component in determining one's socio-economic status, rather than serving as a stand-alone metric by which communities are classified and sampled. Ash (2013) explains that the three social factors which are constant in virtually all social scientific studies involving social class are occupation, education, and income. For instance, in Trudgill's (1974) study of Norwich, an 'income' factor was included, alongside education, occupation, locality, and housing type. Trudgill used these criteria to assign each speaker a social-class index score, which he found useful in obtaining objective information about social stratification within the community. For Arabic, Haeri (1994, 1996) devised an index for calculating speakers' social class in Cairo. This index included parents' occupation, type of education, neighbourhood of residence, and speaker's own occupation.

In interpreting some of the gender-differentiated patterns in Chapter 3, we cited the availability of formal education as a means through which speakers are exposed to and gain access to supralocal features. Education also featured as a catalyst for transmission and diffusion of innovative features. In this chapter, we will focus on education as a speaker variable and elaborate on its implementation in sociolinguistic studies of Arabic.

In many studies of Arabic, education was treated as an independent variable, in both sampling and analysis. In a number of early studies in the Middle East (in the 1980s–1990s), researchers relied on 'level of education' to stratify the speakers, almost in the same way as socio-economic class is used to classify speakers in studies in North America and the United Kingdom. The inclusion of education in these studies was a matter of convenience, as it provided researchers with a fairly simple way to categorise speakers. Its relevance to linguistic patterns was unidimensional, in that it was associated with the assumption that educated speakers would use features of Classical Arabic and would lead change in that direction. Results from sociolinguistic studies on a wide range of Arabic dialects show that change in the core grammar (phonology, morphology, syntax) of these dialects is independent of Classical Arabic and its features (see Chapter 3). For instance, studies that examined the interdental fricatives (θ) and (ð) as variables (e.g. Al-Wer 1991, 2007 in Jordan; Alghamdi 2014 in Mecca) show that the change is in fact towards the alveolar stop variants [t] and [d], respectively. This change represents a merger between the interdental phonemes and the stop phonemes, a feature that is radically different from Classical Arabic. Notice also that the variants that are abandoned are identical to the Classical Arabic features [θ] and [ð]. Alghamdi, who studied the speech of migrants from Al-Baha in Mecca, also found that another feature common to the Al-Baha dialects and Classical Arabic, the diphthongs /ai/ and /au/, is changing in the direction of the monophthongs /e:/ and /o:/ among these speakers. The incoming feature in this case is the one typical of the dominant host community's dialect and at the same time divergent from Classical Arabic. In morphology, many Arabic dialects have neutralised grammatical gender in a wide range of plural forms, again representing a departure from a system that was akin to that of Classical Arabic.

In view of the available evidence regarding the relation between education and language change, several scholars have begun examining education as a speaker variable more closely, in order to determine its true relevance to variation and change in spoken Arabic. Al-Wer (2003) re-analysed education as a sociolinguistic variable and proposed that education is a *proxy* variable. We discuss this proposal in detail in the next section.

4.2   Education as a Proxy Variable

Al-Wer's (2003) suggestion regarding the correlation between level of education and language variation in sociolinguistic studies of Arabic is that education may be a proxy variable. In these cases, it acts on behalf of other variables such as contact and speakers' social networks (see Section 5.3).

According to this suggestion, the highly educated individuals and the most mobile individuals are often the same people. In several countries, institutions of higher education are usually located in or around large conurbations. Until recently, members of small-town communities who wished to pursue university education had to leave their home towns and reside in or commute to relatively large and heterogeneous cities for the duration of their education.

Walters (1991) notes that university-educated speakers in his sample from Korba, Tunisia, had all spent several years outside this small town, where they picked up 'Tunis-like' features. This, in turn, had widened their circle of contacts and exposed them to a larger variety of linguistic systems more frequently. Such exposure can occur through increased interactions with speakers who use these features natively or have adopted them as part of a process of koineisation. Within this revised framework, education is a means for speakers to expand their social networks to include a more diverse cohort of friends and acquaintances. In many cases, these diverse groups of speakers may employ speech patterns considered more 'appropriate' in certain domains and contexts, e.g. university, particular workplace settings, military service, or mixed friendship groups. In this sense, then, education is just one criterion for measuring contact.

In studies that detected language change in progress, the highly educated members of the community have consistently been reported to be in the vanguard of change. This can be explained as a consequence of increased access to the target features, not through education per se but through the expansion of their circle of contacts and more frequent exposure to these forms.

Al-Wer (2003) tested the possibility that education is a proxy variable, as explained above, by analysing data from the city of Salt in Jordan where (θ) is a variable undergoing change from local [θ] to supralocal [t]. In this analysis, the speakers were categorised according to their rate of usage of the target feature rather than by their level of education. The results showed the speakers' rate of usage of the incoming variant [t] was aligned with their degrees of contact with speakers of dialects that had the same variant. Another contributing factor to speakers' access to the target variant was their socialisation pattern. Those speakers who attained their university degrees outside of Salt, and in several cases in Damascus – where the dominant variant of (θ) is [t] – used this variant most frequently. On the other hand, speakers whose social networks were concentrated more locally and whose activities, ambitions, and interests were locally oriented maintained the local variant [θ] most often, regardless of their levels of education.

In this community, access to higher education functioned as a conduit of speakers' exposure to certain supralocal linguistic features. Through this exposure, supralocal features were adopted by mobile individuals. Upon their return from university, they introduced these newly adopted features to the local community through their own speech. Subsequently, the rest of the community began to associate the new features with educated speech, leading to an increase in the social evaluation of the forms used by educated members of the community.

Based on the same principle, that education is a proxy variable, Hachimi (2005, 2007) in her study of a group of Fessi (i.e. from Fez) women in

Casablanca asserts that through education this community has become exposed to the speech of non-Fessis. Hachimi maintains that this exposure facilitated 'the fragmentation of a previously tight-knit Fessi network and the development of weak ties with non-Fessis' (Hachimi 2005: 138; see Section 5.3).

4.3   Changes in Educational Opportunities and Experiences

Educational provisions in several Arab countries have significantly increased and diversified since the late 1990s. While in the past, higher education in most countries was available only in the major cities, new universities and colleges have been established in provincial areas as well. Furthermore, investment in higher education has expanded to the private sector, resulting in a further increase in number and type of universities. These include local private universities as well as branches of American and European universities.

The rest of this section is devoted to reviewing notable developments in education and their effect on sociolinguistic configuration.

4.3.1   Localisation of Education in Ha'il

An example of such expansion and diversification of educational opportunities is reviewed by Deema AlAmmar (2017), who studied the community of Ha'il in north-central Saudi Arabia. One of the social factors that she considered, and which was found to be statistically significant ($p < 0.001$), was contact with speakers of non-local dialects. The way AlAmmar measured contact was by devising an index that consisted of five criteria, one of which was education. Since education in this study was a criterion for measuring contact, AlAmmar obtained information for each speaker regarding the place where they attained their education. The choice was between two options: locally (i.e. in Ha'il) or outside the city (including abroad). Her decision to rely on this indicator (local versus non-local education) was motivated by her observations as a member of the community of the sociolinguistic effects of leaving the city for higher education.

AlAmmar explains that from 1934 onwards, education in Ha'il has seen a fundamental transformation. Until that time, education was limited to the traditional *kuttāb*, where children (mostly boys) learned basic literacy skills and religious tenets. A few primary schools were opened in the 1930s, and it was not until 1960 that a school for girls was established. An intermediate college for teacher training became available locally in 1984, and in 1989 the first academic degrees were offered through this college. A fully fledged university began operating in 2007. Until a local university became available, virtually all students who wished to pursue university education had to travel elsewhere for this purpose. The expansion in the availability of education within Ha'il itself has affected the city in several domains. It increased the range of jobs that people could train for locally; it attracted students from other cities and regions to come to Ha'il; and it enabled women to seek employment outside of the traditional sectors (e.g. teaching). All of these domains have contributed to alterations in the linguistic profiles of numerous members of this speech community. So, we see that education is a complex element in one's experience, which is intertwined with other factors, and therefore its sociolinguistic effect must be understood within its local context. This implies that education is just like any other social variable, in that its relation to linguistic variation is constructed locally and acquires social meaning specific to the local community. Merely duplicating a social factor such as education from one community study to another can be misleading. It may well turn out to be the case that multiple communities share a set of values leading to similar sociolinguistic patterns, but this has to be deduced rather than assumed a priori.

The examples in the remainder of this section will demonstrate different types of expansion and changes in educational landscapes in Arabic-speaking communities and the sociolinguistic consequences thereof.

4.3.2   Globalised Education in Amman

If we take Jordan as an additional example to elaborate this point, we can cite the significant expansion of private education, which has led to the creation of a two-tier system in schools and universities. Even though Jordan has always supported both types of school education, state and private, until the early 1980s private schools followed the national curriculum, and their ethos embraced the ideology promoted by the state. Furthermore, most private schools were designated as charities, and even though there were differences among them in prestige and in the fees they levied, most were affordable to a large sector of the middle-class professions. Importantly, even though most of them were affiliated with mainstream Jordanian Orthodox, Catholic, and Protestant churches, these schools were attended by Muslims and Christians alike, more or less reflecting the proportion of the two religions in the country. Also important was the Islamic Scientific College in Amman, which served the same sort of populations. State-school education had been considered efficient, and many state schools ranked very highly academically, providing their graduates with the same degree of access to higher education and the job market as the private schools. Pupils of both types of schools shared the same school-leaving qualifications since the vast majority of graduates of both types sat the national *Tawjihi* exams.

The main changes occurred in the mid-1980s, and their effect was fully evident within a decade. They included liberalisation of educational legislation, which ushered in a new type of private education. New for-profit, international schools emerged and mushroomed across the country, most notably in Amman. These schools offered alternative curricula, often through the medium of English (rather than Arabic), leading to the introduction of British, American, and international forms of examination and accreditation. While the traditional schools, both private and public, encouraged their pupils and prepared them for general higher and professional education, the new private schools began funnelling their graduates to exclusive universities abroad. This inevitably re-stratified Jordanian society, effectively obliterating the middle strata and increasing social distance between the haves and the have-nots. The demand for free state education increased dramatically because of the political instability in the region and the arrival of millions of refugees in Jordan. At the same time, the new private schools have attracted the lion's share of children from affluent backgrounds, and the decline in international aid to Jordan has rendered state schools more vulnerable and less attractive to families of young professionals.

The effect of this almost exclusive education, primarily in Amman, has resulted in a new social configuration among the young, based on the schools in which they were educated. These divisions have been further enhanced by university education. The developments in higher education are also important, as they include the establishment of new private universities and an overall increase in the number of university graduates. Importantly, though, the emergence of private universities has had different societal ramifications. As mentioned above, graduates of the international private secondary schools typically continue their academic studies abroad. The private Jordanian universities, however, cater to graduates of the more traditional schools. While their tuition fees are considerably higher than those of state universities, this is not commensurate with public perceptions regarding the respective qualities of private and state universities. Among the universities that operate in Jordan itself, it is the state universities that attract graduates with higher grades.

Effectively, school graduates from the two polar ends of the education system form separate sub-communities, and thus separate sub-*speech communities*. Research in a city such as Amman can benefit from this re-evaluation of education as a sociolinguistic variable. Assessing the multifaceted role of education in language variation is rewarding, as it leads to a much more elaborate understanding of the true relationship between the educational experience and linguistic behaviour, both at the level of the individual speaker and at the level of the speech community.

4.3.3　Privatisation and Anglicisation in Morocco[1]

Morocco, too, has seen an expansion in private education, beginning in the mid-1980s, although it has not yet reached the same level as that which we see in Jordan and elsewhere in the eastern Arab world. Currently, approximately 7 per cent of higher education students in Morocco and 20 per cent of primary and secondary school pupils attend private institutions. This rate is likely to increase as more private institutions are planned (including British, American, and German universities). Additionally, the ability of private schools and universities to attract high-calibre teachers and follow modern international curricula with state-of-the-art facilities has adversely affected the public education system and increased inequality between students of different socioeconomic backgrounds. Important for sociolinguistic considerations is that these changes and expansions often lead to the creation of an extra dimension of stratification, based on varying educational experiences.

The Moroccan situation is complicated further because alongside the increase in the privatisation of education, English has been introduced as a medium of instruction into a system that had been dominated by French as a second language. The first university to operate entirely in English, Al Akhawayn University in Ifrane, was established in 1993. It is designated an 'independent, public, not-for-profit' institution, with a global outlook, manifested through the adoption of English as its language of instruction and the American model of education and administration. There are clear signs that English is also gaining ground and popularity in businesses and among the young generation of Moroccans. The introduction of English and the likely expansion in its importance can be predicted to have sociolinguistic ramifications. Specifically, it is likely that such changes will result in the emergence of a sub-culture that certain youngsters will ascribe to, thus creating an additional dimension for future sociolinguistic research to consider. In this sense, it is not the mere addition of English that we consider the linguistic outcome of the socio-educational changes mentioned above but rather its potential contribution to the restructuring of Moroccan speech communities. This restructuring is part of the social stratification that may shape specific patterns of language variation and change.

We have thus far addressed educational changes involving privatisation and the increasing importance accorded to English (and to some extent other foreign languages). In the next subsection we discuss the potential sociolinguistic

---

[1] We are extremely grateful to our colleague Moncef Lahlou, former Vice President for Student Affairs at Al Akhawayn University in Ifrane, Morocco, for providing us with invaluable information about the education system in Morocco.

ramifications of changes in language policies at the state level. One such ramification is that certain indigenous languages can be given official status.

4.3.4   *Amazigh in Morocco and Algeria*

Millions of North Africans have a linguistic repertoire that extends beyond local varieties of Arabic and the European languages French, Spanish, and English that have, in recent decades, entered the region. In western Egypt (especially the Siwa oasis), Libya, Tunisia, and most prominently Algeria and Morocco, several varieties of Amazigh are spoken natively.[2] These indigenous North African languages form their own branch of the Afroasiatic language phylum, and only some of them are mutually intelligible. Until recently, they had no official recognition, but their status was elevated to national and, eventually, official languages in Algeria and Morocco. This transition from marginalised languages to languages with state recognition was gradual. In Morocco, the late King Hassan II, in a famous speech in 1994, gave recognition to Amazigh as a language important to Moroccan national identity, alongside Arabic. He also announced for the first time that provisions would be made for including the teaching of Amazigh in the national curriculum. In 2001, the *Institut Royal de la Culture Amazighe* (IRCAM) was founded, and the teaching of Amazigh in primary schools began in 2003. In 2011, Amazigh was declared an official language of Morocco, in addition to Arabic.

In Algeria, the struggle for recognition was accompanied by political activism and public unrest, especially in the 1980s. The 1990s was a turbulent decade in Algeria, marred by militant confrontations in many parts of the country. At some point, the Amazigh question became entangled with decisions taken at the state level. For instance, both Amazigh and French were banned from use in the media, courts, and universities, a decision that was reversed in 1992 by then-president Boudiaf, who was assassinated shortly thereafter. The Bouteflika presidency era (1999–2019) ushered in efforts for national reconciliation and recognition of diversity. Amazigh was initially declared a 'second national language' in 2002, and in 2016 was finally proclaimed an official language (see Rouabah 2020 for details).

These are fundamental developments, whose repercussions are likely to affect not just the educational systems in these two countries but also the sociolinguistic profiles of their respective speech communities. Consider, for instance, the likelihood of an increase in the use of Amazigh as a daily

---

[2] Until recently, the accepted name for the North African Amazigh group of languages was *Berber*, but this label is now considered pejorative by many speakers. In the Amazigh languages themselves, the common name for these varieties is *Tamazight*, but *Amazigh* is often used in the scholarly literature.

language in the public sphere and its probable effect on the components of national identity. A small, but emblematic development that we have recently seen is the inclusion of Amazigh (in its newly codified Neo-Tifinagh orthography) in official logos in Morocco.

As we have demonstrated for education, social categories are not abstract notions but reflect the ever-evolving patterns of human interaction and social change. In light of this, it is important to constantly rethink basic concepts in sociolinguistic methodology and analysis. In the next section we present a different approach to analysing education as a sociolinguistic factor. We include details from two sociolinguistic studies that demonstrate how type of education can be incorporated into a quantitative analysis of language variation. We begin with Haeri's study of Cairo (1994), which was the first to analyse education in combination with social class (see Chapter 5). The second is Horesh's (2014) study of variation in the bilingual Palestinian community of Jaffa, where type of education refers primarily to the medium (i.e. language) of education.

4.4 Type of Education: Two Case Studies

4.4.1 Public and Private Education in Cairo

As in many other sociolinguistic studies, Haeri included level of education as an independent social factor in her study of language variation and change in Cairene Arabic. In addition, she included *type* of education as one of the criteria for determining each speaker's social class, which is the focus of this section. She identified two categories of schools: private schools, whose medium of instruction was languages other than Arabic, and public schools, where the language of instruction was Arabic (Haeri 1994, 1997). Type of education accounted in this study for 25% of the social class index, which additionally included parents' occupations (50%), neighbourhood of residence (15%), and speaker's own occupation (10%).

The results reported by Haeri (1994) regarding palatalisation of alveolar stops (see Chapter 3 for examples) are displayed in Table 4.1.

Table 4.1 *Percentage use of weak and strong palatalisation in Cairo (based on Haeri 1994: 107, Table 12)*

	Weak palatalisation		Strong palatalisation	
	Women	Men	Women	Men
Public school	13%	10%	42%	5%
Private school	28%	13%	15%	4%

In this table, the category 'private' consists of upper middle-class and upper-class speakers. 'Public' includes all other classes, in addition to one upper-middle-class woman and three upper-middle-class men. The results clearly show that for women, type of education is a factor that correlates with this linguistic variable. Public-school-educated women are more likely to use strong palatalisation, whereas private-school-educated women favour weak palatalisation (Haeri reports a p-value of less than 0.001, rendering this distinction statistically significant). Men, however, palatalise considerably less than women, and the distinction between private and public schooling was not found to be significant ($p < 0.10$ for weak palatalisation and $p < 0.20$ for strong palatalisation).

Since the statistics suggest that women are the ones who lead both weak and strong palatalisation, it makes sense to focus on the use of palatalised variants by women, the innovating group. Figure 4.1 shows that for strong palatalisation the higher the social class, the lower the rate of usage. If we compare this finding to the percentages in Table 4.1, we find that there is a correlation between the results for upper-class women and women educated in private schools. Weak palatalisation, however, is used at rates of between 20% and 29% among women of the two highest social classes and drops to 14%–15% for the two lowest social classes. Recall that all privately educated women are in the upper class, and only one upper-middle-class woman was educated in

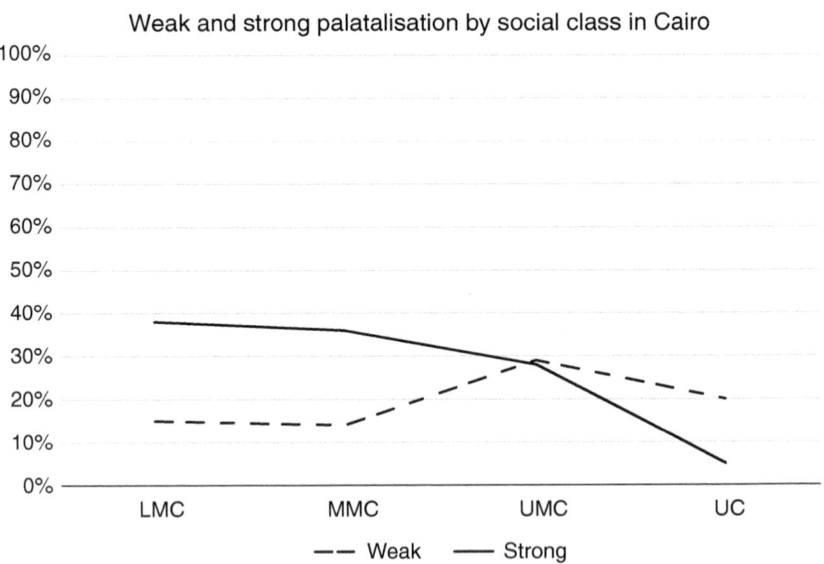

Figure 4.1 Percentage use of weak and strong palatalisation for women in four social classes (based on Haeri 1994: 102, Figure 6)

a public school. From this perspective, then, Haeri explains that considering
correlation with type of education as a sociolinguistic factor 'has some explanatory power in the differentiation of class-based linguistic differences' (106).

4.4.2   *Bilingual Education in Jaffa*

Type of education is not limited to public versus private schools. In a study
of Palestinian speakers in Jaffa, Horesh (2014) investigated the phonological
variable (ʕ), which in this speech community is often lenited (i.e. weakened) or
even deleted. Consider the word /baʕdeːn/ 'later'. This word has been found to
be produced in the following manners:

1. [baʕdeːn]
2. [baʔdeːn]
3. [baːdeːn]
4. [ba.a.deːn]
5. [baØdeːn]

Table 4.2 provides an abridged report of the use of lenited and deleted variants of (ʕ) (variants 2–5) among speakers in Jaffa who have had three types of
educational experience. Some were educated in Arabic-medium schools, some
in Hebrew-medium schools, and others have attended both types of schools.
Note that in this table we use a metric called 'log-odds'. This metric is similar
in the information it conveys to 'centred factor weights' (see Chapter 2) but is
expressed in numbers between $-\infty$ and ∞, such that any positive number indicates favouring of the incoming variant, and negative numbers indicate disfa-
vouring. A log-odd of 0 indicates neutrality (for additional information about
log-odds, see Johnson 2009: 361).

The results above were found to be significant at the $p < 0.05$ level. The
main conclusion that can be drawn from these results is that speakers who were
educated in Hebrew, whether during all of their school years or just a portion
thereof, are more likely to use weakened variants. This pattern is clearly cor-
related with early exposure to and frequent usage of Modern Hebrew. Unlike
Arabic, mainstream Modern Hebrew does not have pharyngeal segments in its
phonemic inventory, and the reflex of proto-Semitic /ʕ/ is either /ʔ/ or Ø. It is

Table 4.2 *Effect of language of education on the
lenition of (ʕ)*

Language of education	Log-odds	Tokens
Mixed	0.306	434
Hebrew	0.188	450
Arabic	−0.494	2,285

likely that lenition in the speech of Palestinians from Jaffa is a feature that was transferred from their Hebrew to their Arabic.

It is important to understand the social meaning of this transfer. In Jaffa, a city that nowadays includes both Arabic-speaking Palestinians and Hebrew-speaking Jewish Israelis, attending Hebrew-medium schools may entail more than just linguistic exposure to Hebrew. For some speakers, immersing oneself in a Hebrew-speaking environment is a way to negotiate one's way into mainstream Israeli society. We see therefore that variation can serve a function; speakers utilise this reality about human language – that it is variable – to maximise gain and minimise loss in social interaction.

4.5   Concluding Remarks

In the American context, sociolinguists have recently looked to refine the analysis of education as a component in the classification of social class. For instance, Prichard and Tamminga (2012) and Prichard (2016) have sampled speakers using a new kind of educational index, which included information about the character and prestige of the colleges and universities attended by the speakers and not just the number of years spent in school.

Parallels can, and should, be drawn between such emergent studies and our intimate knowledge of the educational systems in the Middle East and North Africa. It is important to consider the impact of globalisation, in particular privatisation of formerly state-controlled capital and the creation of new types of employment.

4.6   Further Reading

> Al-Wer (2003, 2013) – The first of these publications lays out the proposal that education in Arabic-speaking communities serves as a proxy variable. The second is a succinct overview of Arabic sociolinguistics focussing on approach and methods, including those related to education.
>
> Haeri (1996) – This book provides details of a sociolinguistic investigation of Cairo Arabic, which includes both level and type of education as social variables.
>
> Horesh (2015); Gafter and Horesh (2020) – These are two studies of variation in the bilingual (Arabic-Hebrew) community in Jaffa, where type of education plays a pivotal role in shaping different patterns of variation, mostly in the domain of phonology.
>
> Meyerhoff (2018) – This is the third edition of a comprehensive introduction to general sociolinguistics, which contains chapters on the social variables covered in this chapter, as well as on theory and methods. Each chapter also includes useful exercises.

Milroy and Gordon (2003) – This is a concise yet comprehensive guide to sociolinguistic methodology, contextualised within questions of theory. Education, including as it is manifest in Arab societies, is highlighted as an important variable which has often been overlooked.

4.7 Exercises for Chapter 4

1. Review the case studies presented in this chapter and write a short essay in which you describe the educational system in a community of your choice. Your aim will be to assess the effect of formal education on the sociolinguistic profile of the community.

   Make sure to address the following aspects in your essay:
   a. What are the educational provisions in this community? How much freedom do members of the community have in choosing schools? What are the constraints on making such choices?
   b. Are graduates of different educational institutions socialised differently, and do they subsequently attain different statuses in the community? Does the level of education and/or type of institution affect one's standing in the community?
   c. How have educational opportunities in the community expanded? For instance, has compulsory primary and secondary education affected the social fabric? Have new institutions of higher education been founded in the community or nearby? Have members of the community begun travelling away to attend university?
   d. What are the linguistic repercussions of the educational stratification in this community? For instance, are there features within one's native language or dialect that are likely to be influenced by the school one attends? Does the type of education individuals attain result in dialect divergence and/or the inclusion of a foreign language in these individuals' repertoire?

2. Consider the following quotation from the Jordanian newspaper *Al-Ghad* and answer the question that follows.

   The idea of establishing universities in smaller towns was for developmental purposes. The goal was to revive the economies of regions far from the capital and to provide job opportunities for the people of those regions. They were also aimed at providing further educational opportunities locally, thus eliminating the need to migrate to other regions.[3]

---

[3] tinyurl.com/jordanuniversities, published July 2011 (accessed 28 July 2021); translated from Arabic by the authors.

What might be the sociolinguistic consequences of establishing new universities in provincial locations? Discuss a case you are familiar with where such a university has been established.

3.   The graph below presents data from three Jordanian cities: Salt, 25 km from Amman, Ajloun, 70 km from Amman, and Karak, 127 km from Amman. It shows the percentage of the use of the variants [t] for variable (θ) and [ʒ] for (dʒ), stratified by speakers' levels of education. Both variants are innovative in the dialects of these cities. In Amman, [t] and [ʒ] are predominant.

Study the graph and answer the following questions:
a.   Describe the pattern for each city and compare the level of usage of the innovative variants across the cities in relation to their respective distances from the capital of Jordan, Amman.
b.   Bearing in mind that the traditional local variants [θ] and [dʒ] are phonetically identical to the pronunciation of these phonemes in Classical Arabic, as used in Jordan, what can you say about the relationship between education and the use of Classical Arabic features? What would be a plausible explanation for the effect of education on choice of variant?

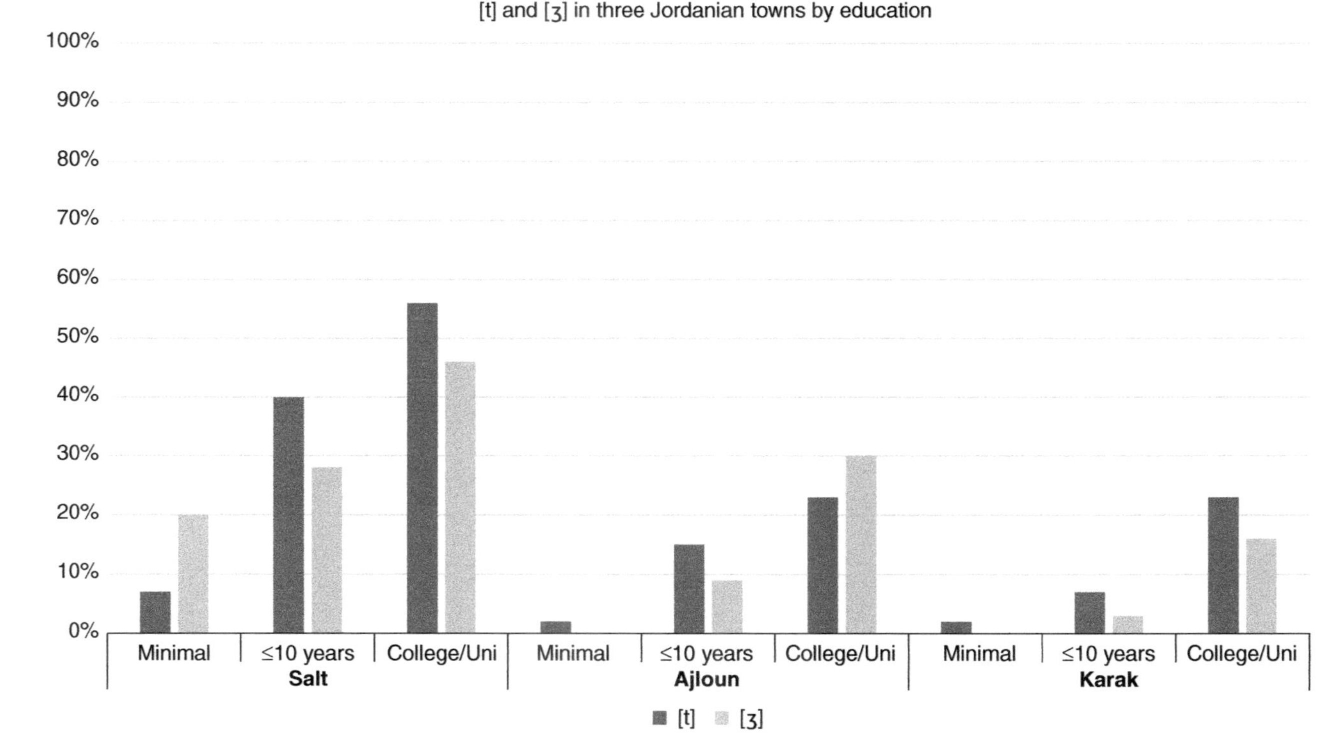

[t] and [ʒ] in three Jordanian towns by education
100%
90%
80%
70%
60%
50%
40%
30%
20%
10%
0%
Minimal
≤10 years
College/Uni
Salt
Minimal
≤10 years
College/Uni
Ajloun
Minimal
≤10 years
College/Uni
Karak
[t]
[ʒ]

5   Social Stratification

5.1   Introduction

Social stratification is a sociological concept that refers to the division of a given society into different 'layers' or groups. All human societies are stratified in one way or another. In modern industrialised societies, stratification is based on a socio-economic hierarchy, commonly known as social class. The economic criteria according to which this hierarchy is determined often translate into and determine social power. In other societies, individuals may differ in economic abilities, but the structure of the society they live in is not necessarily based on the differing wealth of individuals but on factors such as kinship, religion, or ethnicity.

In sociology, as in sociolinguistics, no one set of criteria is used universally for class stratification, but wealth, income, occupation, parents' occupations, educational level, and housing type are among the criteria that many studies have used to determine one's social class. What is clear, however, is that the social class system is a fluid one, such that it is generally possible for individuals to move up and down the scale. This characteristic of the class system, especially as found in industrialised societies, contrasts with the rigidity of stratification systems according to ethnic origin, race, or caste since it is normally not possible to change one's ethnic or racial affiliation.

Similarities in socio-economic status between groups of people are often paralleled by similarities in lifestyle, attitudes, ambitions, and values and lead to differentiation between different classes along these lines. It is also largely the case that people socialise more frequently with others in their own socio-economic class. Trudgill (2000, chapter 2) suggests that this observation leads us to explain the existence of linguistic differentiation according to social class based on frequency of contact. Speakers who belong to the same social class speak similarly because they interact with each other more frequently than they interact with members of other social classes. For the same reason, a linguistic innovation that begins in a certain social stratum is likely to be adopted by members of the same stratum before it affects members of higher or lower strata. Furthermore, certain linguistic features that are characteristic of a particular social class can become so salient that they rise to the status of a symbol of belonging to that social class, leading speakers to embrace and hold on to them to affirm their membership in the class (see Eckert 2012).

Social class is not considered a universal sociolinguistic variable, and not all societies are stratified according to a social class system. In societies which are stratified according to a class system, correlation between class membership and linguistic behaviour has been firmly established. In other societies, linguistic variation may cut across socio-economic differences and not correlate with them. This can be demonstrated by comparing a hierarchical social structure, such as the class system, with an egalitarian tribal system (as in parts of the Levant, Arabia, and North Africa). Not all tribal systems are egalitarian, but in those that are, individuals can differ in wealth but not in social status or prestige as members of the same tribe. This leads to a situation where there are no social barriers between individuals of varying wealth and perhaps, therefore, no linguistic differences according to economic ability.

Since social class is mutable, and thus it is possible for individuals within such a system to move up or down the social scale, we can expect sociolinguistic correlations to alter accordingly. Similarly, the social organisation of a community can alter as a result of changes in the local economy or governance. Tribal systems may gradually transmute, for instance as a result of urbanisation, and adopt a quasi-class-based structure. It is quite likely that such processes are in progress in many Middle Eastern communities, especially those which are experiencing rapid urbanisation, large-scale immigration, and internal migration from countryside to city.

While socio-economic class is still widely used in sociolinguistic analysis, several scholars have over the years worked to improve and refine the classification of speakers on the basis of social stratification. These refinements pertain to sociolinguistic methodology as well as theory. The common thread among them is that they focus on the social meaning of variation as it is constructed by community members in their ordinary daily pursuits. From this perspective, the socio-economic class that community members belong to is an abstract, macro-level organisation. Among the concepts that have been employed in sociolinguistic research are social network, regionality, and lifemode, which are discussed later in this chapter. One advantage of these concepts and the analytical tools associated with them is that they incorporate cultural traits of and within communities in the social stratification of speakers. They therefore capture the behavioural and ideological similarities among members of the same social stratum beyond their economic abilities.

In this chapter, we discuss case studies from research on Arabic which employed various methods of stratification. We begin with Niloofar Haeri's (1994, 1996) study of Cairo, in which the class-based socio-economic stratification is used. We then discuss two studies that applied a social-network analysis to the study of variation: one by Mohamed Jabeur (1987) in a Tunisian town, and the other by Hind Alaodini (2019) in Dammam, Saudi Arabia. We then present studies that for the first time analyse Arabic data in relation to regionality (Alghamdi 2014 in Mecca) and life-mode (Ismail 2007, 2008 in Damascus). Finally, we introduce the community-of-practice construct, which has been widely used in sociolinguistics in general and was introduced into Arabic through the pioneering work of Atiqa Hachimi.

5.2   The Classic Social Class Paradigm

Haeri (1996) shows that in Cairo social class is an important variable which clearly correlates with linguistic variation, blurring differences among the speakers in terms of their ethnic or regional origins. Upon her investigation of the palatalisation of alveolar stops in Cairene Arabic, Haeri discovered two degrees of realisation of this phenomenon. Social class appears to play a somewhat different role in each of these realisations of palatalisation. But first, let us recapitulate what Cairene palatalisation is.

Among many speakers in Cairo, there is a tendency to pronounce alveolar stops with a coarticulated palatal glide, resulting in pronunciations such as /gidiːd/→[gidʲiːd], 'new', and /kitiːr/→[kitʲiːr], 'a lot'. Palatalisation may be 'strong' or 'weak' and is much more common among middle-class women than among men or members of any other socio-economic class. Haeri has compared each of these degrees of palatalisation, among women in Cairo, in four 'styles', or situations:

1. Speakers were asked to read words from a list.
2. They responded to questions.
3. A sample of non-narrative speech was analysed for each speaker.
4. A sample of narrative speech was analysed for each speaker.

Since palatalisation was most common among middle-class women speakers, this group alone was further divided into middle middle class (MMC) and upper middle class (UMC). As can be seen in Figures 5.1 and 5.2, the MMC do not participate much in the process of weak palatalisation. The UMC speakers differ from the MMC considerably in this regard in that they palatalise at rates ranging between 20% and 35% in all styles of speech. In the narrative style, which is assumed to be one of the styles in which speakers are least conscious of their linguistic behaviour (see Labov 1981: 32), the difference between MMC and UMC for weak palatalisation is the greatest.

The situation is dramatically different for strong palatalisation. Here, both MMC and UMC women converge at around 35% for the narrative style but diverge at a 50-percentage-point difference for the word-list style, in which speakers are assumed to pay close attention to the way they speak. In this style,

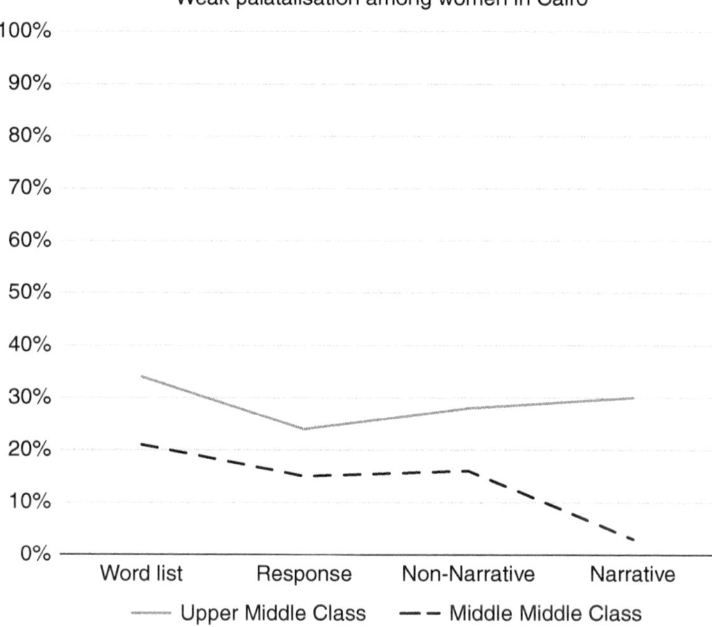

Figure 5.1 Social class and style for weak palatalisation among women (based on Haeri 1996: 80, Graph 7)

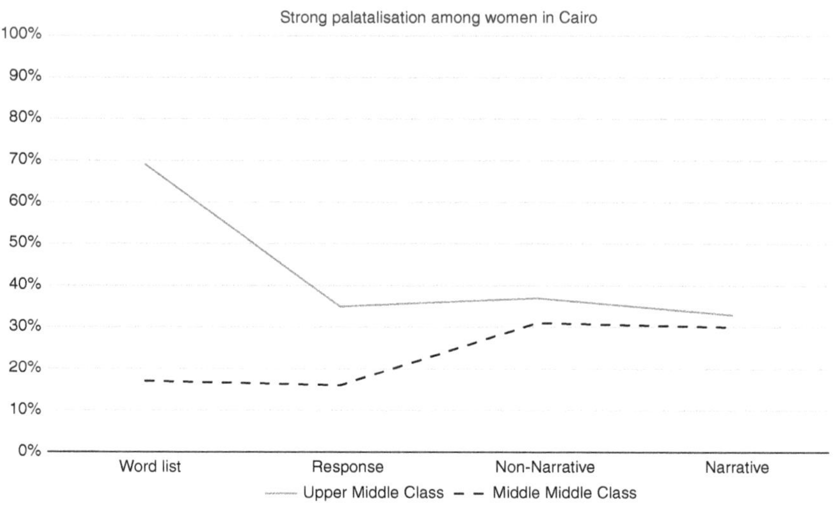

Figure 5.2 Social class and style for strong palatalisation among women (based on Haeri 1996: 80, Graph 8)

UMC speakers produce far more palatalised alveolar stops than non-palatalised ones, whereas MMC speakers do the precise opposite.

5.3   Social Network

The social-network approach to analysing linguistic variation has been used in smaller-scale communities, the most famous of which are the three working-class communities studied by Lesley Milroy (1987) in Belfast. This framework is not meant to replace or compete with the socio-economic-class-based approach. Rather, it allows for a more nuanced understanding of the correlation between linguistic usage and speakers' immediate social contacts. A social network is defined as the sum and nature of relationships that an individual has forged through social contacts and work. The principal idea is that the type of social network that one belongs to affects the way one speaks. A person who belongs to a closed (tight-knit) social network, where their contacts are connected to each other in multiple ways, e.g. kin as well as neighbour and workmate, is under pressure to adhere to the group's norms of social behaviour, including linguistic norms. By contrast, innovations, including linguistic innovations, are much more likely to permeate through open social networks. In such networks, an individual's contacts do not necessarily know each other and are only connected indirectly through that one individual. Maintenance or abandonment of traditional ways of speaking are attributable to the pressure exerted by the social network or the diminution of that pressure, respectively.

A study by Mohamed Jabeur (1987) examined a number of phonological and morphosyntactic features among rural migrants in the Municipality of Rades, a suburb of Tunis, 9 km southeast of the city. He investigated language variation in relation to social network and social change. For this purpose, he devised a social integration index, according to which each speaker was assigned a numerical value to indicate their degree of integration in this urbanising suburban community. The index consisted of five criteria; each criterion comprised between three and five measures, and each speaker's indexical value was calculated as a sum of their points for each criterion.

The five criteria Jabeur considered for assessing social integration were as follows (based on Jabeur 1987: 98–99).

1. Social contacts with rural district and length of visits (5 measures)
2. Social contacts with (rural) relatives in the community of Rades (4 measures)
3. Social contacts with neighbours from the same rural district or from any other rural district in Tunisia (4 measures)
4. Social contacts at work or at school (3 measures)
5 Social contacts outside work (excluding neighbours and relatives) (4 measures)

The scores for each speaker ranged from 0 (lowest integration) to 15 (highest level of integration). Social integration was considered along with seven additional social factors and tested for correlation with linguistic usage. These social factors were age, sex, education level, occupation level, employment, origin, and percentage of lifetime stay in Rades.

The quantitative analysis showed statistically significant correlations between the social integration index and each of the linguistic variables in the study, always at the level of $p < 0.001$. Some of the other social factors were also found to correlate with some of the linguistic variables, though not as consistently and not as strongly as social integration.

Let us consider the results for one of the variables in this study, which Jabeur defines as a morphosyntactic feature and labels (DV1). This variable concerns variation in the endings of defective verbs in the 3rd person plural of the perfective conjugation between the rural form *-u*, as in *mʃu* 'they went' and the urban form *-aːw*, as in *mʃaːw*.

Figure 5.3 shows that speakers who are fully integrated in the urbanising community (social integration index 12–14) do not use the rural forms at all. 'Fully integrated' in this context denotes extremely rare visits to the rural district, low or no contact with rural-origin relatives and neighbours in the city, and school, work, and social contacts predominantly among the urbanites of

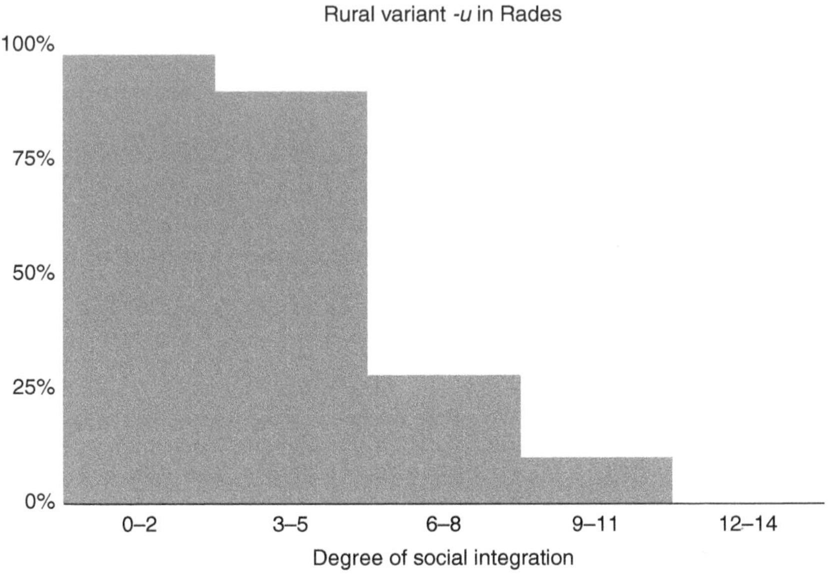

Figure 5.3 Percentage of rural variant *-u* (based on Jabeur 1987: 167, Figure 5.3)

the city. By contrast, the least integrated speakers are only just beginning to adopt the urban features. These are the ones who visit the rural district frequently, maintain frequent social contacts with relatives and neighbours of rural origin in the city, whose schoolmates, work colleagues and friends comprise predominantly fellow ruralites. We thus see that the rate of usage of the rural forms increases as the degree of social integration decreases. In this case, the type of social network that is conducive to the maintenance of the rural dialect is one that consists predominantly of contacts of rural background. As the composition of one's social network becomes more heterogeneous, the pressure to abandon heritage forms increases, leading to linguistic assimilation to the city dialect.

Several researchers have devised indices to quantitatively measure social networks as a means for assessing levels of contact. One such study (Alaodini 2019) in Dammam, Saudi Arabia, investigated variation and change among speakers of the Dōsari dialect in the city. Alaodini focussed on one particular group in the community, who roughly correspond, in Western terms, to the upper middle class, and classified these speakers based on the tightness of their social networks. This social variable was factored into the quantitative analysis alongside gender and age. The social network index she devised consisted of five criteria: marriage, neighbours, friends, place of study, and regularity of attending family gatherings. For the two phonological variables examined in this study, (j) and (a:), all three social factors were found to be statistically significant at least at the $p < 0.05$ level. In both cases, the tighter a speaker's social network, the more likely they are to maintain the traditional Dōsari variants [j] and [ɒ:] versus the supralocal [dʒ] and [ɑ:], which were found to be favoured by speakers with loose social networks.

Alaodini's findings confirm the significant role that the structure and density of social networks can have on the mechanism of language change and demonstrates the importance of selecting potential social factors based on the researcher's knowledge and understanding of the social dynamics of the community under investigation.

5.4   Regionality

Demographic diversity is typical of large cities and metropolitan areas. Part of this diversity can be attributed to large portions of the population having moved into the city from multiple locations and at different times in the city's history. J. K. Chambers tackled this attribute by proposing to incorporate an independent social variable called 'regionality' into the study of language variation in two Canadian conurbations in Ontario and Quebec. In order to operationalise and quantify this variable, he devised a Regionality Index (RI) for measuring 'the subjects' links to the region' (Chambers 2000: 180). By including this variable, he was able to obtain representation of the cities' current populations, without overlooking the nature of the city as a destination for migrants from different places over a long period of time.

Najla Alghamdi (2014) adapted these principles, which Chambers had originally implemented in Canada, and tested them in a different setting, that of the city of Mecca. Mecca has not only been a destination for short-term pilgrimage for Muslims worldwide for centuries but has also become home to a large and diverse array of populations. One such migrant group is the Ghamdi community, who migrated from Al-Baha in the western region of Saudi Arabia in waves, starting around the beginning of the twentieth century. As outlined in Chapter 3, each of these waves had its own characteristics in terms of its gender make-up as well as the degree of integration in the city's social composition. Additionally, once in Mecca, different families settled in different parts of the city, adding a further dimension of diversity within the Ghamdi community of Mecca. Alghamdi explains that residence in relation to the Holy Mosque area is a crucial factor in the socialisation patterns of this community. The population in this area is heterogeneous while further away from the Mosque groups of migrants of shared backgrounds have established more homogenous neighbourhoods. This situation has been complicated further by later movements within the city, mostly away from the city centre.

To account for these differences among the community members, Alghamdi devised a Regionality Index specific to this social context. Borrowing Chambers's terminology, Alghamdi classified the speakers in her sample on a scale ranging from 'Indigenous' to 'Interloper', based on their RI scores. In other words, the RI allowed Alghamdi to assess the degree of indigenousness in relation to the city. Alghamdi's RI is displayed in Table 5.1; note that none of the speakers scored 1 (Indigenous).

As Table 5.1 shows, the classification of speakers along the scale is quite sensitive to the main components that Alghamdi judged to be germane to the question of integration in the Mecca community, which in turn may have linguistic consequences.

The results of the analysis of the five phonological variables included in this study all showed significant correlation between RI score and the use of Mecca-like linguistic variants. This is illustrated in Table 5.2 for the variable (ai), as in /bait/ 'house'. Recall (see Section 3.5.3) that this variable has three variants: the traditional Ghamdi diphthongal form [aɪ], the Mecca monophthong [ɛː], and an intermediate variant [ɛɪ], e.g. *baɪt ~ bɛɪt ~ bɛːt* 'house'.

As the figures in Table 5.2 show, there are three groups of speakers: those with RI scores 2–3, who are closest to Indigenous status, use the Meccan variant nearly categorically. The second group, with RI scores 4–5, use the Meccan form at about 75% on average, and those with the highest RI score, who are the least integrated (or 'Interlopers'), use the Meccan form at a rate of 31%. What

Table 5.1 *Regionality Index among the Ghamdi in Mecca (based on Alghamdi 2014: 56, Table 3.8)*

Status	RI	Profile
Indigenous	1	(Speakers and parents) born, raised in Mecca and settled around the Mosque.
Near-indigenous	2	a. (Speakers) born, raised in Mecca, settled around the Mosque; (parents) born in Al-Baha, settled around the Mosque. b. (Speakers) born, raised in Mecca, settled away from the Mosque; (parents) born in Mecca, settled around the Mosque.
Fairly indigenous	3	(Speakers) born, raised in Mecca, settled around the Mosque; (parents) born in Al-Baha, settled away from the Mosque.
Fairly interloper	4	(Speakers) born in Al-Baha, raised in Mecca, settled around the Mosque; (parents) born in Al-Baha, settled away from the Mosque.
Near-interloper	5	(Speakers) born in Al-Baha, raised in Mecca, settled away from the Mosque; (parents) born in Al-Baha, settled away from the Mosque.
Interloper	6	(Speakers) born, raised in Al-Baha, settled away from the Mosque; (parents) born in Al-Baha, settled away from the Mosque.

Table 5.2 *Monophthongisation of (ai) among the Ghamdi in Mecca (based on Alghamdi 2014: 85, Table 4.9)*

RI	[aɪ] %	[ɛɪ] %	[ɛː] %	N
1	–	–	–	–
2	1	2	97	362
3	4	2	94	176
4	8	23	69	118
5	4	18	78	108
6	37	32	31	227
Wald χ^2	460.670	444.747	541.494	–
Significance	0.001	0.001	0.001	–

distinguishes groups 4–6 is their noticeable use of the intermediate variant [ɛɪ], which is almost non-existent in the speech of the most integrated speakers. Group 6 is further distinguished from the other groups in their relatively high level of maintenance of the traditional Ghamdi diphthong [aɪ]. Alghamdi also reports that the use of Mecca-like monophthongs is higher among younger speakers, suggesting that the dialect spoken by the Ghamdi community in Mecca has been undergoing changes in the direction of the city dialect. During the course of these changes, a third variant emerged which includes phonetic elements that are intermediate between the heritage and target variants. Since the intermediate variant is used across the community, albeit at different rates, we may conclude that the mechanism of change is one of phonetic approximation rather than sudden replacement. Furthermore, we see that this mechanism renders the linguistic system of the Ghamdi dialect as spoken in Mecca more complex, since there is more than one variant to choose from, before it levels out the heritage form and the intermediate form. This levelling out appears to already be in place for certain portions of the community, particularly among young speakers and those of lower RI values.

An identical pattern of progression is also reported by Alghamdi for the variable (aw), as in /lawn/ 'colour'. Here, too, a phonetically intermediate variant, [ɔu], is used across the community, in addition to the heritage diphthong [aʊ] and the Meccan monophthong [ɔː], e.g. *laʊn* ~ *lɔun* ~ *lɔːn* 'colour'. This indicates that the change affecting the diphthongs in this dialect is systemic.

The index used by Alghamdi to measure Regionality is similar in many ways to the social integration index devised by Jabeur (see above). We may therefore consider Regionality, too, a technique for quantifying social network, including contact with and access to target features. Other techniques that have been implemented for this purpose in Arabic-speaking communities include devising appropriate indices for measuring contact with speakers whose dialects include target features. For example, Al-Essa (2008) devised such an index to measure Najdi speakers' contact with speakers of the dialect of Jeddah; Alshawi (2020) did the same for speakers in Qalʿat Siker in relation to contact with the Baghdadi dialect; and AlAmmar (2017), with respect to the Šammar dialect in Haʼil.

5.5 Life-Mode

'Life-mode' is a sociological concept that considers both economic and cultural criteria in the division of societies into social strata. It derives from Marxist theory and has been expanded upon by the ethnologist Thomas Højrup (1983, 2003). Lesley Milroy and James Milroy (1992) have introduced this concept into sociolinguistics as an analytical tool compatible with small units of analysis such as social networks (see above), which in themselves bring the analysis closer to the social frameworks that people form within their immediate communities.

Højrup identified three life-modes (LM), as follows. LM1 is the self-employed; LM2 is ordinary wage earners; LM3 is highly skilled, professional wage earners. In identifying these three modes, Højrup had the typical societal structures of Western Europe in mind, but we shall see that they can be adapted for other scenarios as well.

Hanadi Ismail's (2007, 2008) analysis of variation and change in Damascus makes an important contribution, methodologically and analytically. She focussed on two neighbourhoods: Shaghoor and Dummar. Shaghoor is located in the Old City and is considered one of the oldest quarters of Damascus. Dummar, on the other hand, is a modern suburban residential area, home to professionals, intelligentsia, artists, and writers. The differences between these two neighbourhoods are parallel to those between working-class and middle-class cultures in the European context. Importantly, an index based on socio-economic criteria would fail to capture the social and cultural contrasts between them. For instance, many residents of inner-city Shaghoor are wealthy, as they own and run their own successful businesses, while the majority of the Dummar residents are wage earners. Within the life-mode framework, Shaghoor would be represented by LM1, i.e. the self-employed, for whom work is both a means and an end. In contrast, in Dummar, most residents are wage earners, for whom work is a means to an end. In Ismail's analysis, a major difference between the two communities centres around the separation between work and free time. In LM1, Shaghoor, there is no separation between work and leisure, while in LM2, Dummar, one of the main goals of work is to earn enough money to afford leisurely activities.

In Ismail's analysis of the variable (r) (see Chapter 3), age, gender, and life-mode were found to be statistically significant. Figure 5.4 shows that in Dummar (LM2), all three age groups use the incoming variant, with a slight rise from generation to generation. By contrast, in the Shaghoor community (LM1), the old and middle age groups use the incoming variant at very low rates, while the younger Shaghoor speakers diverge quite considerably from the previous generation, to the point where their use of [ɹ] slightly surpasses that of the young Dummar speakers.

The statistics show that the change started in LM2; the evidence for this is that the feature is already in use by the older generations in Dummar, whereas in Shaghoor, the innovation was picked up primarily by the young generation. Recall that in Chapter 3 we saw different gender patterns across the generations and between the two life-modes. This complex differentiation between the two neighbourhoods reinforces the need for a classification of speakers that goes beyond mere economic considerations. Life-mode, in this case, provides a more nuanced explanation of this specific pattern of variation.

5.6   Community of Practice

Another important departure from larger, abstract groupings of stratification such as social class is the adoption of the concept of 'community of practice'. This approach has not been used much in studies on Arabic – but see Hachimi's study discussed below. The community of practice construct was introduced into sociolinguistics by Penelope Eckert and Sally McConnell-Ginet (1992)

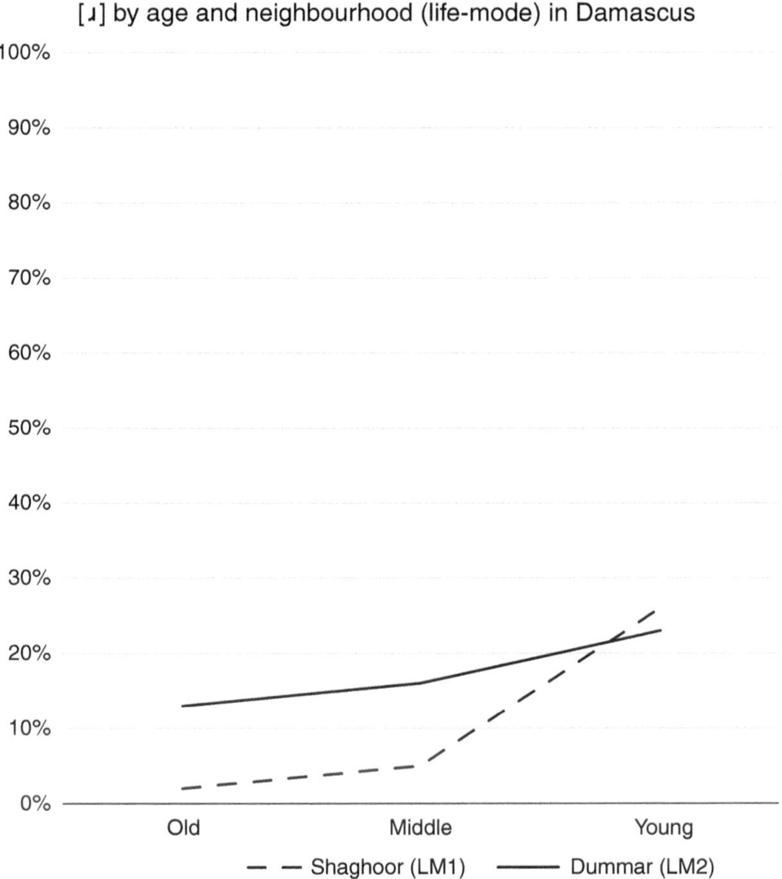

Figure 5.4 Percentage use of [ɹ] by age and life-mode in Damascus (based on Ismail 2007: 207, Figure 9.7)

and used as an analytical tool in Eckert's study of variation and change among high-school students in a suburb of Detroit (Eckert 1989, 2000). According to Eckert (2006: 109): 'A community of practice is a collection of people who engage on an ongoing basis in some common endeavor: a bowling team, a book club, a friendship group, a crack house, a nuclear family, a church congregation.' Communities of practice can also be described as 'a specific kind of social network' (Meyerhoff 2018: 213). In her research in Detroit, Eckert shows that the social meaning of variation is constructed through membership of communities of practice. As far as studies on variation in Arabic are concerned, the construct has been applied in Atiqa Hachimi's study of Fessis in Casablanca (2005, 2007). This approach led Hachimi to identify local and socially meaningful associations of linguistic variation, e.g. the use of localised Casablancan variants by various groups of Fessi migrants in the city. Examples of such practice-based classifications of speakers in Hachimi's study include '*Fwassa-d-kasa* "Fessi-Casablancans"' (Hachimi 2007: 115), whose use of the Casablancan variant [g] of the variable (q) – rather than the old Fessi variant [ʔ] or the contemporary variant [q] – has led to the labelling of their dialect as *ḥərša* 'tough', as opposed to *rṭiṭba* 'soft', which is associated with the traditional Fessi dialect.

5.7   Summary

In this chapter we have explained and demonstrated five ways of conceptualising social stratification. Recall that socio-economic class, the most commonly used conceptualisation in the social sciences, may be determined based on different criteria for different societies. What the four additional approaches (social network, regionality, life-mode, and community of practice) allow us to do is to further refine the stratification by introducing additional criteria that are sensitive to the local circumstances of each community, and even subtracting elements that are central to mainstream social-class divisions, such as wealth.

5.8   Further Reading

> Eckert (2012) – This is a critical review of the so-called three waves of variationist sociolinguistics. Its relevance to the topics discussed in this chapter has to do with the role of what Eckert calls 'macrosociological categories', such as social class, and the more refined classifications, such as the ones we describe above.
>
> Mallinson (2009), Mallinson and Dodsworth (2009) – These two articles explore the connection between sociological and sociolinguistic interpretations of social class.
>
> Milroy and Milroy (1992) – This article presents a novel approach to social stratification as it situates social network analysis within a broader framework, which is based on and compatible with social class, rather than viewing the two approaches as mutually exclusive.
>
> Vitt (2011) – This is a brief discussion of 'class' from a sociological perspective, as presented in *The Concise Encyclopedia of Sociology*.

## 5.9	Exercises for Chapter 5

1. Think of your own community or one with which you are familiar.

    a. Propose two ways to divide the community into social strata. You may choose from among the stratification systems presented in the chapter or suggest some of your own (e.g. family, tribe, wealth).

    b. State the advantages and disadvantages of applying each system to this community.

    c. Explain to what extent they can be combined or whether they are mutually exclusive.

2. It is normal in most societies for individuals to be stratified according to varying levels of wealth and status. But this stratification does not necessarily have linguistic correlates. What may be the reasons for this? To help you answer this question, you may want to think about the social structure of the communities, including such elements as urbanisation, contact, isolation, and the role of tribal systems, where applicable.

6   Religion and Ethnicity

6.1   Introduction

In many speech communities, an important dimension of variation is religious affiliation and ethnicity, which form important components of group identity. The two may be separate from one another or intertwined and overlapping. For example, in the study of African American Vernacular English (AAVE), religion is seldom considered as a sociolinguistic variable, because the speakers often share religious belief systems with white speakers or even belong to the same church. In other cases, religious affiliations also overlap with ethnic divisions, such as the case of some ethnic minorities in Britain. It is often observed that the South Asian ethnic community in Britain is divided into subgroups based on their religious affiliation, e.g. Hindu, Muslim, Sikh. At the same time, Muslims of South Asian descent in Britain share experiences having to do with their religious affiliation with Muslim Arabs, for instance, even though the latter may be ethnically aligned with fellow Arabs who are Christian. In the United States, the Latinx community is ethnically distinct from Anglo-Americans but is further divided based on their specific origins (Puerto Rico, Mexico, Dominican Republic, etc.), while not necessarily differing in religion. There is an infinite number of combinations worldwide for instances of intersectionality of this kind, which renders the task of discerning the possible effects of each component on one's speech quite complex. In order to thoroughly understand and explain such effects, it is crucial to also understand how speakers, as individuals and as members of speech communities, index their multifaceted identities.

The Arabic-speaking countries are generally ethnically and linguistically diverse. The linguistic consequences of this diversity, which varies from place to place, are potentially twofold. At the macro-sociolinguistic level, it presents itself in multilingualism, while at the micro-sociolinguistic level we find cases of linguistic variation within a single language (such as Arabic), which correlate with religious and/or ethnic affiliation. It is important to emphasise that just as there is nothing intrinsic about the effect of gender or age on linguistic variation, the same can be said, in many cases, about religion and ethnicity.

Rather, what seems to be the case is that there are underlying factors that mediate variation according to religion and ethnicity, as will be explained in the course of this chapter.

Given the diversity described above, we must point out that while many descriptions of Arabic varieties that are labelled according to the religious affiliations of their speakers – or, in the case of historical written texts, authors – studies that provide sociolinguistic analyses of potential correlations between linguistic variation in Arabic and religion and ethnicity are few and far between. As we shall see, the sociolinguistically informed studies all point to the general principle that attributes variation in these cases to mediating factors – such as social integration, isolation, and marginalisation – and differences in the histories of the various groups.

Along these lines, the existence of varieties in Arabic which are delineated according to religion can be attributed to one or a combination of two historical factors: differing genealogies and prevalence of social barriers. In this chapter, we discuss several aspects of this level of variation and provide examples from well-documented accounts of such variation. Our first examples are of varieties of Arabic spoken by Jewish communities in North Africa. While many descriptions are available of varieties collectively labelled 'Judaeo-Arabic', pertaining mostly to written attestations of Arabic written in Hebrew letters from mediaeval and early modern times, our focus will be on studies that are based on spoken data and whose analytical approach is compatible with a sociolinguistic framework.

6.2   Jewish Varieties of Arabic

A number of descriptive accounts are available of modern dialects spoken by Jews in North Africa (e.g. Heath 2002 for Morocco, and Behnstedt 1998 for Djerba, Tunisia) and in Iraq (Blanc 1964 for Baghdad). Heath's (2002) study provides a detailed linguistic description of Moroccan Arabic varieties, with dialectological commentary regarding regional and sectarian variation.

Historically, the Jewish community in Morocco includes both an old population that predates the 1492 expulsion from Spain and those Jews who migrated to Morocco following the expulsion. There are two hypotheses regarding the linguistic background of the Jewish influx from Spain and its linguistic consequences. One hypothesis is that the Jews from Spain (known by the Hebrew terms *Sephardim*, lit. 'Spaniards', or *megorashim*, lit. 'expellees') spoke a variety of Andalusian Arabic, which has had a strong effect on the old Jewish Moroccan varieties (that of the *toshavim*, lit. 'residents'). The other hypothesis is that upon arrival in Morocco, the *Sephardim* spoke Judaeo-Spanish and were eventually Arabicised in Morocco, adopting the old Arabic varieties spoken by both the existing Jewish population and the upper-class urbanites.

In addition to the genealogical factor, Heath (2002) highlights the relative homogeneity of the Jewish varieties across the country, compared with other Moroccan varieties which exhibit regular regional variation. In describing the general differences between the Jewish dialects and those spoken by Muslims, Heath explains that in some cities, e.g. Meknes and Fez, the Jewish community was sharply segregated in a separate quarter of the city. Segregation in these cities contributed to the homogeneity of the Jewish varieties and to the preservation of old urban features in these varieties. On the other hand, the Muslim varieties include rural features, due to migration from the countryside into the cities (see Chapter 8).

Similarly, Behnstedt (1998) outlines the situation in the Tunisian island of Djerba, off the southeast coast. The native population of the island comprises three main religious groups, whom Behnstedt refers to as Maliki, Ibadi, and Jewish. The first two groups are named after two of the Islamic schools of thought. The Jewish community represents one of the oldest groups in North Africa, dating, according to some sources, as far back as the first century BCE. According to Behnstedt, the island was formerly Amazigh speaking, and the first Arabic variety that was formed there was probably modelled after the original dialect spoken by the Jewish population. As in Morocco, another layer of Jewish Djerbans date to the 1492 expulsion of Jews and Muslims from Andalusia. At the time of Behnstedt's research, the Jewish population of the island numbered up to 1,500 (out of a total population of approximately 150,000). The Jewish population is primarily concentrated in two neighbourhoods in Houmt Souk, the island's largest city.

In his description, Behnstedt compares phonological and morphological features across the varieties spoken by all three religious groups on the island. Where appropriate, he also compares certain forms spoken in Djerba to those spoken in Tunis. He demonstrates that the three Djerba varieties can be distinguished systematically, while at the same time they share a set of features. For instance, the Jewish dialect of Djerba shares the distribution of variants of /q/ with the standard dialect of Tunis. In both, [q] is the primary reflex of /q/, alongside which there is a lexical set of items that occur invariably with [g]. On the other hand, the Jewish variety diverges from the standard Tunis dialect in the realisation of interdentals. While in Tunis the interdentals are maintained, the Jewish dialect of Djerba has merged them with the corresponding stops. For this feature, it is the Ibadi and Maliki dialects on the island that align with the dialect of Tunis.

Behnstedt's description also shows that certain features are shared among the three religious groups on the island and distinguish island speech from mainland dialects. One such feature is the merger of sibilants /s/ and /ʃ/, with their voiced counterparts /z/ and /ʒ/. The phonetic qualities differ between different groups on the island, with the Jewish variety generally realising the merged phoneme as apical [s̺] and [z̺], and the Ibadi varieties having [s] and [z]. This feature is heavily stigmatised, such that, in interaction with outsiders, Djerba speakers, irrespective of religion, consciously keep these sounds apart.

We see that these differences originate in different genealogies and that they may have been sustained by the social structure among the island communities. Once again, we see that religious affiliation is one factor among many that influence variation in a heterogeneous community. Like other social factors, its effect is subject to change alongside social and political changes in the life of the community.

6.3 Druze Varieties in the Levant

One of the earliest reports of differentiation along religious lines is that of Haim Blanc (1953) in northern Palestine. In this study, Blanc focussed on the phonetics and phonology of the Druze dialects of several villages in the Carmel mountains and the Galilee region. The Druze are a Muslim religious sect, thought to be an offshoot of Ismaili Shi'a. Ethnically, they are an Arabic-speaking Levantine group, whose traditional home is in the Chouf Mountains of Lebanon and the Horan plateau in Syria, where Jabal al-Druze (also known as Jabal al-ʿArab) is located. In addition to Lebanon and Syria, they dwell in northern Palestine and northeast Jordan (the Azraq oasis).

Some of the villages in Palestine where Blanc conducted his research, such as Kufur Yasif, Mghar, and Al-Rameh, are home to more than one religious community, which in some cases includes Christians and/or non-Druze Muslims. Two main features are reported to distinguish Druze speech from the other groups, namely /q/ and the interdental fricatives /θ/, /ð/, and /ðˤ/. All of the traditional Druze dialects have [q] and interdental realisations of /θ/, /ð/, and /ðˤ/. Non-Druze Palestinian speakers in the region have [ʔ] for /q/ and stop realisations of the interdentals: [t], [d], and [dˤ]. Blanc also points out that some variation exists in Druze speech, specifically in villages whose population is predominantly Christian. In these villages, Druze speakers use a combination of traditional Druze and non-Druze features of the phonemes listed above. For example, in the lexical item /θqiːl/ 'heavy', several variants were recorded, including [θqiːl], [tʔiːl], and the mixed forms [θʔiːl] and [tqiːl]. It is worth noting that since the mixed forms are reported for localities whose residents include combinations of religious groups, it is likely that they represent outcomes of dialect contact.

Even earlier, Cantineau (1946) observed that certain features were unique to the Druze dialect in Horan, particularly in Sweda in Jabal al-Druze, the traditional homeland of the Druze community. In his discussion of /q/ in Horan, he points to the pronunciation [q] in *byiqdar* 'he can' as being characteristic 'only of Druze dialects' (127; our translation). Furthermore, in the atlas section of Cantineau's grammar, two of the maps are allocated to delineating the different ethnic and religious groups in Horan, suggesting that he had anticipated the potential relevance of these categories to language variation, on top of the regional variation which was the focus of his research (see Chapter 8). Cantineau (1938) also conducted a study specifically focussing on the Druze dialects of Horan.

In Jordan, the history of the Druze community dates to the beginning of the twentieth century, when several Druze families moved to the oasis of Azraq, where until recently they practised salt mining. Today they number approximately 10,000 people, many of whom continue to dwell in Azraq and the nearby village of Umm al-Quttain. Importantly, they maintain close family links with their home territory in Syria and, for the most part, refrain from marrying outside the group. Ongoing research in Jordan among the Druze community in Azraq reveals stability in many of the core features of the traditional dialect, including maintenance of the interdentals, [q] for /q/, and the fricative realisation [ʒ] of /dʒ/.[1] The presence of interdentals in this dialect is shared with other Horani dialects. But the Azraq Druze's distinct realisations of /q/ and /dʒ/ align them with the traditional Druze dialect spoken in Jabal Al-Druze, as described by Cantineau (1938), and by Blanc (1953) in northern Palestine.

Regardless of country of residence, the most salient features of the traditional Druze dialect are maintained, especially in towns and villages where they constitute the majority group. We can consider the Druze dialect to be a prime example of differentiation along ethno-religious lines. The persistence of this differentiation can be explained by examining historical and contemporary attributes of the Druze in the Levant.

In at least two of the four countries where substantial communities of Druze live, their distinctiveness is also recognised by the state and the surrounding communities. In Lebanon, the Druze form an important and influential part of the prevalent sectarian political system, on a par with, for example, Maronites, Shi'a, and Sunnis, with a traditional, hereditary, and unified political leadership. Another interesting case is the Druze of northern Palestine, who have become citizens of Israel since its establishment in 1948. They are designated by the state as an ethnic group that is separate and distinct from other Palestinians. Importantly, Druze men are conscripted in the Israeli military, aligning them more closely with Israel's Jewish population than with other Palestinians, namely Muslim and Christian citizens, who are exempt from military service. The sociopolitical status of the Druze as distinct communities in these two countries is conducive to the maintenance of group boundaries and, consequently, their linguistic idiosyncrasies.

---

[1] Herin, Al-Wer and Al-Hawamdeh have been collecting and analysing data in Jordan; Horesh has been working on recently recorded data from the northern Palestinian village of Kufur Yasif.

In Syria and Jordan, on the other hand, the Druze are not flagged as a separate group. What preserves the distinctiveness of the Druze in these countries is their in-group social cohesiveness, which is sustained by a multiplicity of practices. An important characteristic of Druze tradition is the strict practice of endogamy, i.e. marriage only within the group. Conversion into and away from the faith is also not permitted. Alongside visible symbols of group boundaries such as dress and cuisine, the leadership is largely unified and commands the consent of the vast majority of the community. The geographical distribution of Druze communities in the Levant is such that they traditionally have kept a territorial base in mountainous areas, which to this day function as their strongholds (the Chouf Mountains in Lebanon, Jabal al-Druze in Syria, as well as the Carmel and Upper Galilee mountain ranges in Palestine). This is not to imply that the Druze in the Levant are insular communities. In fact, some of the acclaimed national heroes in the region, especially during the Ottoman occupation, were Druze. Notable historical figures include Fakhr ad-Dīn II, (c. 1572–1635), who is considered a pioneer in the unification of the Lebanon, and Sulṭān al-Aṭrash, who led a revolt against French rule in Syria in 1925. Rather, they have throughout history maintained a 'living heartland' (see Edwards 1985), which seems to have enabled them to maintain the group's distinctive cultural content, including their distinctive dialect.

6.4   Communal Dialects in Baghdad

The first comprehensive study to focus explicitly on religion-differentiated varieties of Arabic is that of Haim Blanc (1964). In this study, Blanc compares three Baghdadi varieties, which he calls Muslim Baghdadi (M), Christian Baghdadi (C), and Jewish Baghdadi (J). His analysis covers phonology and morphology and, to a lesser extent, syntax and lexicon. It is for this reason that Blanc considers the three varieties separate dialects, each with its own distinctive system. For some linguistic features, there is a three-way distinction between the three Baghdadi communities, while in others he reports that the C and J varieties pattern closely with one another, differentiating them from the M variety. In a small number of cases, features were shared between the M and C varieties, contrasting them with J. With the exception of a number of lexical items that are part of the religious jargon of each community, Blanc does not attribute the emergence of linguistic distinctions along religious lines to religion itself. Rather, he looks into the history of the city, and of Iraq in general, to trace the demographic transformations in the population of Baghdad, which have led to the situation as he recorded it in the 1960s.

Let us look at some of the linguistic features that characterise each of these varieties. In characterising these communal dialects Blanc begins by classifying them according to the now-standard typology of Mesopotamian dialects, namely *qeltu* and *gelet* types. This classification highlights two distinctive features: [q] versus [g] and the inflection of 1st person perfective verb, with either -*u* or Ø (i.e. zero vowel) as its suffix. Under this classification, C and J pattern together as *qeltu* dialects, while M is of the *gelet* type, thus C and J have /qəltu/ and M has /gələt/ 'I said'. This shows that the dialect types are distinct from one another at both the phonological and morphological levels.

As Table 6.1 shows, there are features that are shared between all three Baghdadi varieties and at all linguistic levels. In other cases, however, we see that two of the communal dialects share a feature, which distinguishes them from the third. Blanc demonstrates that C and J share many features that are characteristic of old sedentary Mesopotamian *qeltu* type dialects, while M contains several features that are characteristic of the *gelet* Bedouin dialects of

Table 6.1 *Examples of Christian, Jewish, and Muslim Baghdadi Arabic (data extracted from Blanc 1964)*

Feature	C	J	M	Gloss
/q/	sˤedeq	sˤedeq	sˤudug	'truthfulness'
/r/	qamaɣ	qamaɣ	gumar	'moon'
Interdentals	taqi:l	θqi:l	θegi:l	'heavy'
Affrication	sake:ki:n	skaki:n	stʃa:tʃi:n	'knives'
Vowel raising	sake:ki:n	skaki:n	stʃa:tʃi:n	'knives'
Unstressed long vowel	sake:ki:n	skaki:n	stʃa:tʃi:n	'knives'
Unstressed short vowel	sake:ki:n	sØkaki:n	sØtʃa:tʃi:n	'knives'
Independent pronouns	ana	ana	a:ni	'I'
	neħna	neħna	eħna	'we'
	entem	entem	entu	'you (pl.)'
2sg.f. possessive bound pronouns	be:t-**ki**	be:t-**ek**	be:t-**etʃ**	'your (sg.f.) house'
	abu:-**ki**	abu:-**ki**	abu:-**tʃ**	'your (sg.f.) father'
Postpositional copula	optional: kalebna kelleʃ ze:n **yanu:**	nonexistent	nonexistent	'Our dog is very nice.'
Clitic doubling	ba:ʕ-**u le-l-be:t** (infrequent)	ba:ʕ-**u le-l-be:t** (very frequent)	ba:ʕ-**a le-l-be:t** (rare)	'He sold the house' (lit. 'He sold **it to** the house)'. Note: all three dialects also have the unmarked structure ba:ʕ el-be:t.
Lexicon	ɣada	ɣada	ba:tʃer	'tomorrow'
	kti:ɣ	kθi:ɣ	hwa:ja	'much'
	ʃa:f	ʕa:jan	ʃa:f	'he saw'

southern Iraq. This raises two questions. Firstly, how do we explain the emergence of what appears to be differentiation along the lines of religious affiliation? The second related question is whether the history of Mesopotamia can explain the emergence of this differentiation.

During the last two centuries of the Abbasid Caliphate in Baghdad, urban life was in decline, as was the effectiveness of the central power of the Abbasids, which led to multiple raids on Baghdad, culminating in the catastrophic Mongol raids of 1258 and 1400–1401. As a result, the urban Muslim population of Baghdad and southern Iraq in general suffered severe devastation. As Clive Holes (1995) points out, the Muslim community of Baghdad was later re-established through the migration of Bedouin tribes from neighbouring areas to the west and southwest. This explains the designation of Muslim Baghdadi as a *gelet*, i.e. Bedouin-type, dialect. At the same time, it suggests that the varieties nowadays dubbed Jewish and Christian represent instantiations of the original old sedentary dialects of Iraq, irrespective of religion. Blanc in fact suggests that we may consider the Christian and Jewish dialects of Baghdad to be direct descendants of mediaeval Baghdadi. He further points out that C and J bear much resemblance to the dialects of northern Iraqi cities, e.g. Mosul, which is consonant with the proposal that the original Arabic dialect of Baghdad is a typical sedentary *qeltu*-type dialect. What this suggests, in turn, is that Christian and Jewish Baghdadi are conservative varieties, and that the Muslim variety represents a more recent development that is in essence a Bedouin-type dialect, with a measure of sedentary influence.

In summary, the existence of differentiation along religious lines in Baghdad results from historical circumstances that led to reconfiguration of a traditional Mesopotamian regional dialect in the Middle Ages. There is no evidence that these communities lived in isolation from each other or that they formed three separate speech communities within the city. We will later see how circumstances in a different region, namely Jordan, and at a different point in history seem to be leading to a somewhat similar situation.

6.5 The ʿArab and Baharna Dialects in Bahrain

Blanc's descriptive studies cited above were instrumental in recognising the role of religious affiliation in sociolinguistics, but it was Clive Holes who first approached language variation and change in an Arabic-speaking community from a fully fledged variationist perspective. In his important study of Bahrain, Holes (1987) discusses at length the significant effects of religion on language variation, but crucially, religion is just one of a number of quantifiable social factors included in his analysis. Bahrain is thus the location of the earliest variationist study of an Arabic-speaking community and the first to consider religion as part of a multivariate array of linguistic and social factors.

Additionally, Bahrain is the only site from which we have real-time data in the form of an investigation by Muna Al-Qouz (2009). Al-Qouz's study included several linguistic features that had been analysed by Holes three decades earlier.

The Bahraini community comprises two roughly equally sized Muslim religious sects: Shi'a and Sunna. The ethnic composition of each sect is mixed and includes majority Arabs and minority Persians. Holes focusses his study on the Arabic dialects of the Baharna and 'Arab groups. An important distinction between these two groups is their sectarian affiliation. The Baharna are Shi'a, while the 'Arab are Sunni Muslims.[2] In terms of social and political dominance, the 'Arab group enjoys considerably more power and perhaps prestige. The dialects of the Baharna Shi'a and the 'Arab Sunna descend from two different dialect norms, sedentary and Bedouin, respectively. As in the case of Baghdad, we shall see that the differentiation of dialects in Bahrain along sectarian lines may be explained as an artefact of the different genealogies of these dialects, coupled with historical circumstances.

Unlike the different religious groups in Baghdad, where, as explained above, there is no evidence of physical segregation within the city, the 'Arab and Baharna communities in Bahrain reside in localities that differ in both type and place. In addition to the capital, Manama, the 'Arab live mainly in towns and large villages (e.g. Muharraq and Hidd), while the Baharna mostly reside in a large number of small villages. The population of Manama is similarly segregated, with each ethnic group living in different quarters of the city, with the exception of Madinat 'Isa, a newer neighbourhood, which was deliberately designed to house members of both communities. By and large, physical segregation is conducive to the persistence of group boundaries, and in cases where groups can be distinguished linguistically, it also limits face-to-face interaction and hence linguistic convergence.

The Baharna and 'Arab dialects are distinguished by a range of mostly phonological and morphological features. Some of these differences are listed in Table 6.2.

The bundle of features that characterise the 'Arab dialect of Bahrain are shared with the major dialects in the other Gulf states. On the other hand, the combination of features found in the Baharna dialect described above is peculiar to Bahrain and the eastern province of Saudi Arabia. Some of the Baharna features appear to be ancient features of Arabic, which survive, though usually not all at once, in scattered locations both in the Arabian Peninsula and in some peripheral dialects.

---

[2] *'Arab* /ˤarab/ and *Baharna* /baħa:rna/ are ethnonyms which are used by the groups themselves as well as by outsiders. Note that both groups are ethnically Arab.

Table 6.2 *Examples of ʿArab and Baharna linguistic differences in Bahrain (based on Holes 2019: 75, Table 5.6)*

Feature	ʿArab			Baharna			Examples + gloss
/θ/	[θ]			[f]			θalaːθa – falaːfa 'three'
/dʒ/	[j]			[dʒ]			iji – idʒi 'he comes'
/q/	[g] and [dʒ]			[k] or [kˁ]			gaːl – kaːl 'he said' dʒiriːb – kariːb 'near'
/k/	[k] and [tʃ]			[tʃ]			tʃam – tʃam 'how much' kubur – tʃubr 'size, age'
/ɣ/	[q] and [ɢ]			[ɣ]			qeːr – ɣeːr 'except'
2nd person object pronoun	m -k	f -tʃ	pl -kum	m -tʃ	f -ʃ	pl -tʃim	qanam-ik, qanam-itʃ, qanam-kum – ɣanam-tʃ, ɣanam -š, ɣanam-tʃim 'your sheep'
2nd person independent pronoun	m inta	f intaj	pl intaw	m inta	f intiːn	pl intuːn	'you'
2nd person perfective inflection	m -t	f -taj	pl -taw	m -t	f -tiːn	pl -tuːn	gilt, giltaj, giltaw – kilt, kiltiːn, kiltuːn 'you said'
-*n(n)*- infix in active participle + object pronouns	no			yes			əhijja jaːjbat-ah – hi dʒaːybat-inn-uh 'she has brought it'

By way of illustration, the -*n(n)*- infix that occurs between active participles and object pronouns (see Table 6.2), is 'an extremely old feature of the eastern/south-eastern Arabian dialects', which 'only acquired its saliency as a marker of sect (in Bahrain and nowhere else) very much later' (Holes 2019: 76). The association of the different Bahraini dialects with the two religious sects dates, according to Holes's analysis, to the late eighteenth century, when Najdi tribes migrated to Bahrain and assumed political power. Since the dialects which were spoken by these newcomers did not have many of the characteristic features of the dialects spoken by the Shi'a of Bahrain, specifically the Baharna, these features came to be associated with sect. In other words, what were originally regional dialectal variations – and still are outside of Bahrain – became signifiers of sectarian identity within Bahrain. Holes's research overall showed that the Baharna accommodate to features of the ʿArab dialect in various contexts. On the basis of these findings, Holes predicted that this trend would increase over time, motivated by the dominance of the ʿArab group in Bahraini society.

The research conducted by Al-Qouz (2009) among youth in Manama confirms Holes's prediction. In data that she collected in four Manama schools from pupils belonging to both sects, she found large-scale convergence towards the ʿArab dialect, the socially dominant dialect. A good example of this is the abandonment of the stigmatised and salient Baharna variant [f] for /θ/. An interesting, though not surprising, pattern that emerges from Al-Qouz's study is the tendency for pre-adolescent Baharna children to use their heritage variants more frequently than their teenaged counterparts. In other words, during their years in school, these children acquire the competence to socially evaluate the relative appropriateness of the use of the various linguistic forms that are available in the school environment. Upon starting school, the effect of their parents' speech patterns is strongest, and as they grow older, they become acquainted with the full range of variation in the school and the community it represents, alongside the social meanings attached to the available variants. This in turn leads to a much stronger tendency to diverge from their parents' habits and converge to the school norm.

In this case, the school environment acts as a conduit for community-wide norms. When Al-Qouz tapped into the children's overt evaluation of their linguistic usages, it was revealed that rather than associating the school linguistic norm with a particular sect, the children viewed the variety spoken at school as the unmarked 'Bahraini' dialect. Holes interprets this development as a sign that a Bahraini-wide standard is emerging, based on the ʿArab dialect, which itself is akin to the Gulf-wide regional standard (Holes 2011, 2019). As the Manama community has become less segregated – evinced by shared neighbourhoods, new employment patterns, and, as seen above, a unified educational system – linguistic differentiation along sectarian lines may be diminishing. Clearly, these situations are mutable, and any subsequent sociopolitical escalations or developments have the potential to alter the situation further.

The results of these studies in Bahrain at different points in time provide us with details of the mechanism by which religion emerges as a sociolinguistic factor and survives for a given period of time and eventually tapers off. Each of these phases is shaped by broader social, political, and ecological developments whose connection to religion per se is indirect. In this case, it emerged as a result of demographic changes, which juxtaposed two distinct dialects that happen to have been spoken by members of different religious sects. What sustained it and made it visible in Bahrain is probably the physical segregation fuelled by asymmetrical power relations between the two communities. Finally, new economic and political realities have led to the blurring of religious divisions and the creation of a common national identity.

The linguistic repercussions of this process eventually led to dialect shift at the community level, in favour of the dialect that has been dominant both locally and regionally. In the next section, we look at eastern Saudi Arabia, where a similar mixture of Sunna and Shi'a is involved in processes of language variation and change.

6.6   Sunna and Shi'a in Al-Ahsa

The information and data cited in this section are based on Al-Bohnayyah (2019), a study of variation and change in Al-Ahsa, in eastern Saudi Arabia. While the vast majority of the population of Saudi Arabia are Sunni, in the Al-Ahsa province a sizeable Shi'a community forms about half of the population in various cities, towns, and villages. The distribution of the two sects within this region is not uniform. In some localities (e.g. the city of Mubarraz) the population is split almost evenly between the two groups, while in others (e.g. Hofuf) there is a Sunni majority. Additionally, some small villages are exclusively Shi'a, while some of the larger villages are home to mostly Sunni populations. In cities, the two sects have for many years self-segregated in separate neighbourhoods, but recently, efforts have been made to create heterogeneous neighbourhoods and mixed residential areas in cities as well as villages. According to Al-Bohnayyah, relations between the Sunna and Shi'a have been amicable over the years; Al-Bohnayyah maintains, however, that the tension that resulted from recent political developments in the region as a whole has had sociolinguistic repercussions. In particular, media representation of Shi'a as being connected with Iran, has caused social anxiety among mixed-sect communities in Saudi Arabia, as well as elsewhere. Consequently, it has become vital to accentuate national identity over sectarian divides.

Unlike Bahrain, the Shi'a and Sunni communities of Al-Ahsa speak the same traditional dialect. The dialects of eastern Saudi Arabia share a good number of features with the dialects of the Gulf states, e.g. [j] for /ʤ/ and a rounded realisation of /aː/. Research findings show that where there is differentiation according to sect in this region, it manifests itself in proportion of use of individual features, rather than exclusive use of any feature by one community or the other. In this sense, the linguistic situation found in Al-Ahsa is a classic case of variation that is constrained by social factors which apply to the whole community. Recall that in Chapter 3 we noted that Al-Bohnayyah's statistical analysis found sect to be a significant predictor of change, alongside age and gender. In the analysis of the unrounding of /aː/, we commented on the overt social stigmatisation of the rounded variant [ɒː], which is also seen as a stereotype of Shi'a speech within the greater Saudi community. We pointed out that this stereotype is based on an inaccurate impression and that both communities share this variant as a traditional local feature. Similarly, this variable is undergoing change in both communities, with the Sunna leading the Shi'a in the adoption of the Saudi supralocal unrounded form [ɑː]. Let us look at the results of a different variable that Al-Bohnayyah investigated, namely the feminine ending. Traditionally in eastern Saudi Arabia, the feminine ending -*a* is raised across the board to /e/, whereas the major city dialects of the country, e.g. Riyadh and Jeddah, do not raise this morpheme at all. In Al-Ahsa, Al-Bohnayyah found that this feature is variable and involved in a change in progress, such that the use of the lowered variant [a] in lieu of traditional [e] is increasing. This change was found to be constrained by both linguistic and social factors, including sect, as seen in Table 6.3.

Important for the current discussion is the difference between the two sects, which was found to be statistically significant at $p < 0.001$. We notice that in this case, the Shi'a lead the Sunna in the change towards the lowered variant. In his interpretation of the results for both variables, Al-Bohnayyah notes that while both Sunni and Shi'a speakers converge to the supralocal variants, unrounded [ɑː] and unraised feminine ending [a], each group is subject to different types of pressure. The popular (albeit inaccurate) association of the variant [ɒː] with 'Shi'a speech' motivates Sunni speakers to avoid using this variant, lest they themselves be misconstrued as being members of the Shi'a community. On their part, the Shi'a are under pressure to assert a Saudi identity over sectarian affinity, which explains their convergence to the pan-Saudi

Table 6.3 *Percentage use of lowering of the feminine ending in Al-Ahsa by linguistic and social factors (based on Al-Bohnayyah 2019: 170, Table 5.6)*

Factor	N	%[a]
Preceding consonant		
Pharyngeal	181	75%
Labial	227	37%
[j]	265	22%
Coronal	669	16%
Age		
Young	660	38%
Old	682	19%
Sect		
Shi'a	**680**	**36%**
Sunni	**662**	**21%**
Gender		
Female	656	34%
Male	686	23%

norm of the low variant of the feminine ending. If this trend continues, one might expect the public perception of such linguistic variables as symbols of sectarian affiliation to eventually cease to exist.

Al-Bohnayyah points to an important difference in the social meaning indexed by each of the two variables. While a rounded realisation of /aː/, e.g. [banɒːt] 'girls' is widely stigmatised in Saudi Arabia, no such stigma is attached to the use of a raised variant in the feminine ending. Importantly, there is no public perception of sectarian association in the case of the feminine-ending variable. These observations explain the relatively slower rate of change among the Sunni community for this variable. The Shi'a, on the other hand, as a minority group in the country, are likely to be particularly susceptible to public scrutiny, compelling them to be meticulous in expressing their national identity. One of the ways in which minority groups in such situations can put themselves beyond reproach is by aligning with national norms of social behaviour, including linguistic norms.

In the next section we review the case of religion emerging as a sociolinguistic factor in Jordan, where the linguistic differences between religious groups are much more subtle than the cases reviewed so far.

6.7   Christians and Muslims in Jordan

The cases reviewed above have long been known to involve dialects that vary according to religious affiliation. The Baghdad and Bahrain cases, in particular, are often cited as the exemplars of such a demarcation. Jordan, on the other hand, was first mentioned as a case where religion plays a role in sociolinguistic stratification in 2015, in a study by Al-Wer, Horesh, Herin, and Fanis. In none of the previous dialectological and sociolinguistic studies on Jordanian dialects had religion been mentioned as a factor. It is therefore a particularly interesting case because it can potentially provide information about the early stages of the emergence of sociolinguistic variables, in this case religious affiliation. It can also shed additional light on the underlying causes of sociolinguistic re-stratification in line with sociopolitical and demographic change. Such understanding of social histories is instrumental in shifting the discussion away from simplistic notions which ascribe variation to religion per se. In this sense, religion is not unlike gender in that there is nothing inherent about any social category that dictates such variation. Rather, it is the manifestation of social dynamics.

Modern Jordanian society is currently predominantly Muslim. Until the beginning of the twentieth century, Christian Jordanians formed approximately a quarter of the indigenous population. Since then, the percentage of Christians in the country's population has been decreasing steadily, reaching about 4–6 per cent in the second decade of the twenty-first century. This decrease is not so much due to the Christian Jordanian community shrinking in size as to the massive increase in the number of Muslim incomers into Jordan, primarily as a result of political turbulence in the region. In other words, what has changed is the concentration of Christians relative to the total population. This numerical increase of Muslims in the population of Jordan coincided with the rise of fundamentalist religious ideologies, which in turn has brought religious differentiation in the country to the forefront. In addition to the population at large becoming more conscious of religion, the arrival of millions of refugees and other migrants, mostly from Palestine and more recently from other countries as well (e.g. Iraq and Syria), increased public consciousness of ethnic differences and intensified tensions. While these developments affected all sectors of Jordanian society, it was Christian Jordanians who became doubly marginalised, once as ethnic Jordanians and once as a much smaller religious minority than they ever were. It is important to mention that Muslims and Christians in Jordan do not normally intermarry, while marriage across ethnic lines (e.g. Jordanian and Palestinian, Jordanian and Syrian) within the same religious group is commonplace. Bearing in mind the profile of the majority of the newcomers to Jordan as outlined above (mostly Muslims), these traditions mean that the Christian Jordanian community has remained more homogenous ethnically than the Muslim Jordanian community. This, in turn, leads to a situation where Christian children in Jordan, especially in their formative years, continue to be exposed predominantly to the traditional Jordanian norms of speech more consistently. Muslim children, on the other hand, are more likely to be exposed to a mixture of dialects from early childhood, rendering them prone to acquiring a koineised linguistic system. With this background in mind, let us now look at some data.

Al-Wer et al. (2015) examined data collected between 1987 and 2012 from central Jordan and, for the first time, documented and analysed patterns of variation that show a certain degree of linguistic conservatism on the part of the Christian speakers in that region. By 'conservatism' we refer to adherence to traditional and older Jordanian linguistic features, which by and large have subsided and given way to koineised forms that are the outcome of contact between Jordanian and Palestinian dialects. We shall now present a few examples of the features that were found to be used more consistently by Christians.

6.7.1   *u/i Alternation*

Traditional central and northern Jordanian dialects have /u/ in the following lexical items, which in the koineised dialects in the region have /i/: /dʒubne/ 'cheese', /zubde/ 'butter', /dunja/ 'world', /ʕulba/ 'box', /gusˤsˤa/ 'story', /ʕubi/ 'traditional men's gown', /dʒumʕa/ 'Friday', /juktub/ 'he writes', /tudʒaːra/ 'trade'.

Al-Wer et al. report that many of the /u/ items, i.e. the older forms, appear exclusively in the speech of Christians, and several /i/ forms are used exclusively by Muslims. Even when variation is documented within each group, there are no /u/ items that are used only by Muslims or /i/ items that are only found in the speech of Christians.

6.7.2   Resyllabification

a. Traditional Jordanian dialects have the nominal template CaCi:C in words such as /zabi:b/ 'raisins', /mali:ħ/ 'good', /sani:n/ 'years'. This pattern is resyllabified in the modern koineised dialects to CCi:C, thus /zbi:b/, /mli:ħ/, /sni:n/. There is change in progress towards the innovative pattern CCi:C, and where the traditional pattern CaCi:C is maintained, it occurs more consistently in the speech of Christians.

b. Traditional Jordanian dialects have an /a/ vowel in verbal forms of the type CiCCaCi(C), e.g. in /jiħtafil/ '(that) he celebrates', /btistaħi/ 'she is shy,' /jistawi/ '(that) it cooks/ripens'. This pattern is stable in these traditional dialects. However, two innovative patterns are found in the data reported by Al-Wer et al.: CiCCiCi(C), where traditional /a/ is replaced by /i/, as in /jiħtifil/, /btistiħi/, /jistiwi/; and CiCCCiC, whereby /a/ is elided altogether. The latter pattern occurs frequently in the conjugation of the imperfective form of the verb /jisʃtaɣil/ 'he works'. Examples include /aʃtɣil/ '(that) I work', /jiʃtɣil/ '(that) he works', /tiʃtɣil/ '(that) you/she work(s)', /biʃtɣil/ 'he works'. Both of these incoming patterns, CiCCiCi(C) and CiCCCiC, are typical of urban Palestinian dialects, and in the data from central Jordan were only used by Muslim speakers while Christian speakers all used the older forms.

These data suggest that, overall, the Christians preserve older forms more consistently. This situation was in the first place predicated upon the nature of the demographic changes outlined earlier and the marriage traditions. What began as a case of koineisation has developed into stratification along religious lines. If the salience of religion as an element of group identification continues to rise in Jordan, as we have been witnessing elsewhere in the region, we can predict that these subtle linguistic differences will become emblematic of ethnic identity for Christian Jordanians. While there still exists a stratum of Muslim Jordanians outside the large heterogeneous cities, who preserve the traditional features (some of which are mentioned above), it is the Christians who nowadays are most consistent in preserving these features in the country overall. In the speech of most Jordanians, these features are increasingly being levelled out, and so awareness that they simply represent continuity and maintenance of traditional Jordanian dialects is likely to erode. As a result, it is quite likely that in the long run such traditional linguistic features will end up being associated with Christian speech rather than with Jordanian speech.

6.8   'Izbat Basili, Upper Egypt

In his classification of Upper Egyptian dialects (in the southern region of Egypt), Manfred Woidich (1996) provides brief but theoretically valuable comments on the dialect spoken in the Coptic-Christian village of 'Izbat Basili, located on the west bank of the Nile, in the Governorate of Luxor. Woidich reports that the dialect in this village differs from the dialect spoken by Muslims in the same region of the west bank but is identical typologically to the dialect of the east bank. Woidich proposes two possible explanations for the existence of an eastern linguistic enclave on the west bank. The first is that the Muslims in the area surrounding 'Izbat Basili had mixed with Bedouin newcomers to the region and, as a result of dialect contact, their dialect diverged from the original local dialect. Within this scenario, the dialect spoken by the Copts represents the older local norm. Alternatively, the Copts of 'Izbat Basili may have originated on the west bank and relocated to the east bank around the nineteenth century to serve the ancient monastery nearby. Either way, it appears that the Coptic population in the area preserves local dialectal norms, whereas the dialects of the Muslims on this side of the river diverged from local norms because of historical dialect mixture.

We see, therefore, that in this case as well, what appears to be dialect differentiation according to religious affiliation is in fact attributable to historical events that led one group to come into close contact with speakers of a non-local dialect. In this specific case, contact between local Muslims and Muslim newcomers led to the emergence of a new dialect type.

6.9   Ethnicity, Religion, and Language Shift

6.9.1   The Ajam Group in Kuwait

In a unique study of a small, yet ethnically and religiously diverse community, Batoul Hassan (2009) investigated the relationship between language shift and ethnicity in Kuwait City, within the framework of Bourdieu's (1977) Theory of Practice. Kuwaiti society includes two main religious sects and two main ethnic communities. As far as religion is concerned, the Kuwaiti population is divided mostly between the Sunni majority and a sizeable Shi'a minority. Precise statistics regarding the ratio between the two sects vary across sources, but an estimate of roughly 30 per cent Shi'a is probably reasonable. Ethnically, the two major groups are Arab and Ajam. The latter originally migrated from southwestern Iran during the nineteenth and twentieth centuries. Both ethnicities include adherents of both Sunna and Shi'a, and thus there is a four-way distinction across religious and ethnic lines: Sunni Arab, Shi'a Arab, Shi'a Ajam, and Sunni Ajam. Linguistically, the Ajam are originally speakers of several, mutually intelligible, dialects of Persian. In Kuwait, their language is referred to collectively as 'ʕAjami' (pronounced /ʕiːmi/ in Kuwaiti Arabic and often spelt Eimi in English). Hassan focussed her research on the Shi'a Ajam, partly because the small Sunni Ajam community tend not to consider themselves as part of the same group.

The Ajam community used to be concentrated in two of the oldest neighbourhoods of Kuwait City, Šarq and Qibla, which constituted a linguistic enclave of Eimi within the city. This linguistic enclave was disrupted following the discovery of oil in 1937, after which these areas were demolished to make way for industrial and commercial facilities. According to Hassan, this enclave had functioned as an important territorial base and a heartland for continued use of the heritage language, Eimi. Once its population dispersed to various areas around the city, it lost a vital domain for the use of Eimi.

Other important historical events that Hassan factored into her research design and analysis are the Iranian Revolution of 1977–1979, the Iran–Iraq War of 1980–1988, the Iraqi invasion of Kuwait in 1990, and the subsequent Western-led liberation of Kuwait in 1991. Firstly, she divided the sample of speakers into three age groups, each of which was hypothesised to have been affected differently by these events. Thus, the oldest age group (ages 40–70), who grew up in the predominantly Eimi-speaking enclave, witnessed the Iranian Revolution first hand, and lived through the Iran–Iraq War. The middle group (23–39) bore witness to the invasion of Kuwait in the early 1990s, and some of them sought refuge in Iran during the crisis. The youngest group (12–22) lived in Kuwait itself, outside the enclave (which by now had been demolished) and experienced a heightened sense of local Kuwaiti nationalism in the aftermath of the invasion by Iraq.

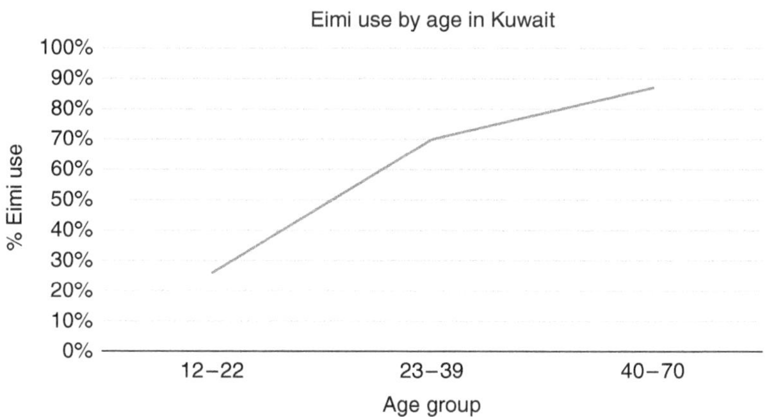

Figure 6.1 Eimi language use across age groups (based on Hassan 2009: 134, Table 3.7 and Figure 3.8)

The results regarding the degree of maintenance of Eimi as an in-group language of communication across the three age groups give credence to the age grouping adopted in this research project. As seen in Figure 6.1, the use of Eimi declines from generation to generation, and most drastically so for the youngest age group. This group of young Kuwaiti Ajam, born between 1983 and 1993, lived most of their lives after the Iran–Iraq War, the youngest within this group having been born and raised after the liberation that followed the Iraqi invasion. Hassan explains that the sharp decline seen in the youngest generation is directly related to two main factors, both of which point in the same direction. The first is the diminished exposure to Eimi – both at home and in the community – and its lack of communicative utility. The other is the ideological shift in Kuwait in reaction to the occupation and the consequent emphasis on taking pride in Kuwaiti identity. Hassan explicitly discussed this latter point with the speakers she interviewed. It was common for speakers to express the view that speaking Kuwaiti Arabic was a major component in shaping their 'Kuwaitiness', which Hassan also associates with their disillusionment with pan-Arab nationalism.

Equally interesting are the figures for proficiency in Eimi, which Hassan reports are highest amongst the middle age group, even higher than those reported for their parents. Hassan explains this directly in relation to the period of time when their families relocated to Iran in the 1990s, requiring them to attend Iranian schools, where they were formally educated and immersed in Persian-speaking communities. This high level of proficiency in Persian in the 23–39-year-old group has facilitated increased use of Eimi (recall that Eimi is an umbrella term for a number of local dialects of Persian).

Over the course of the events outlined above, the Shi'a Ajam community's interests came to be aligned with those of the dominant group in the country, namely the Sunni Arabs, mostly as a result of the invasion of Kuwait by Iraq and its aftermath. The Ajam's identity as Kuwaitis necessitated reducing differences between themselves and the dominant group, leading to sacrificing the language that had helped identify them as a distinct community to begin with. In Hassan's study, we see linguistic convergence in the form of language shift, i.e. abandonment of a heritage language, as a means to reduce differences and unite around a common national cause.

In a separate study of the Kuwaiti community, Taqi (2010) examined phonological variation and change, with ethnicity as a social factor. She sampled both ethnically Ajam and Arab speakers. One of the linguistic variables she investigated was (ʤ). In the mainstream Kuwaiti dialect, the phoneme /ʤ/ is realised as [j], whereas the Ajam community traditionally use [ʤ]. Figure 6.2 illustrates that here, too, younger speakers tend more than their elders to converge towards the mainstream Kuwaiti dialect. Similarly to Hassan's analysis, Taqi evokes the Iraqi invasion as a powerful force that united Kuwaitis of all

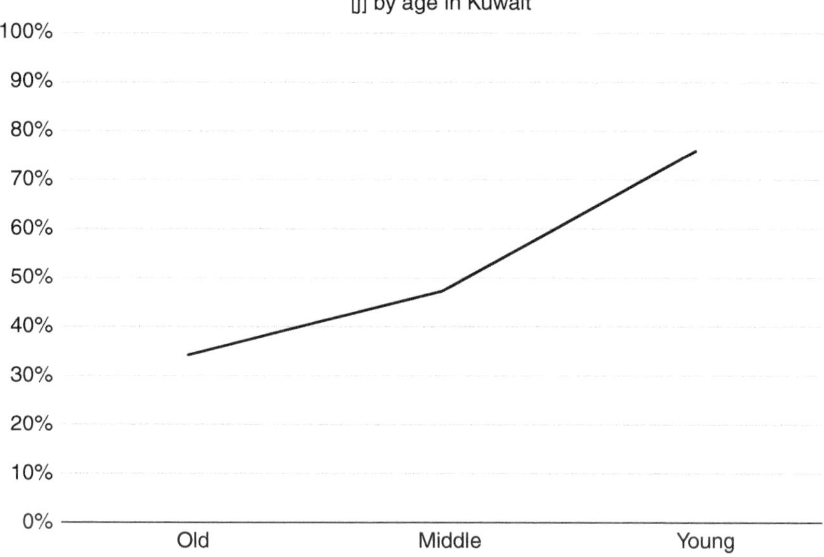

Figure 6.2 Realisation of (dʒ) as [dʒ] by age for the Ajam community in Kuwait (based on Taqi 2010: 140, Table 4.6)

ethnicities. In Taqi's study, the linguistic manifestation of this evolving unity is dialectal convergence.

The findings by Hassan and Taqi complement one another and in fact are indicative of two interrelated processes. Hassan shows that the Ajam group, for the most part, shift their everyday linguistic practice, such that Arabic is replacing Eimi as the main language of communication. Taqi's results indicate that the Arabic variety adopted by the Ajam is increasingly similar to that which is spoken by the dominant ethnic group in Kuwait. The combination of results from these two studies, one at the macro level and the other at the micro level, demonstrates rather neatly that language shift – in the case reported by Hassan, from Eimi to Arabic – is a form of language change. Taqi reports on change at the structural level, and Hassan on shift from one language to another, but we see that the two processes involve a similar set of dynamics.

6.9.2 Circassians and Chechens in Jordan

Two additional cases of minority groups undergoing language shift from their heritage languages towards Arabic are the Circassians and the Chechens in Jordan, who are originally from the North Caucasus. Like the majority of Jordanians, they are Sunni Muslim but constitute distinctive ethnic groups. In this section we review these cases to further illustrate that language shift as a form of language change is intertwined with community-specific histories and trends. We shall see that in these cases, the Circassians and Chechens in Jordan differ substantially in these respects from the Ajam in Kuwait, leading to different community-internal dynamics and subsequently perhaps also to different linguistic outcomes.

The destinies of much of the population of the North Caucasus were determined by the policies of the superpowers in the seventeenth to nineteenth centuries, namely the Ottoman and Russian empires. As a direct result of these policies, large groups of various local ethnic communities were forced to leave their homeland. They were transported to various parts of the Ottoman Empire, including the Levant. Between 1876 and 1911, several waves of Circassians and Chechens were settled in Jordan, mostly in the central region. The majority of the originally Circassian and Chechen settlements have been integrated into the urban sprawl of Amman and Zarqa, and to some extent Jerash. Today, only two originally Chechen villages remain, Sukhna and South Azraq, while all originally Circassian settlements have dissolved. The number of Circassians currently living in Jordan is estimated at 80,000–100,000; Chechens are estimated at between 15,000 and 20,000.

Upon arrival in Jordan, the Circassians and the Chechens were monolingual in their respective languages, which are classified as North Caucasian, Circassian being North-West Caucasian and Chechen being North-East Caucasian. The two languages are mutually unintelligible. Both groups gradually acquired the Arabic dialects of the groups they interacted with. Arabic began to spread more rapidly among Caucasian Jordanians through formal education, beginning in the 1920s. Al-Wer (1999) reports that there has been a steady decline in the use of Circassian, and only 16 per cent of the Circassian population under the age of twenty spoke the language at the time. In contrast, all of the Chechens sampled were bilingual in Arabic and Chechen. In other words, while both communities initially experienced additive language change, i.e. they moved from being monolingual in their respective heritage languages to becoming bilingual, the Circassian case can be construed as a more advanced case of this change, which eventually led to the replacement of their heritage language by Arabic. The Chechens, on the other hand (at the time of Al-Wer's research) demonstrated a case of stable bilingualism. This is despite the fact that Circassian, but not Chechen, has been supported by some degree of schooling at the community level, including a secondary school (Prince Hamza School) where Circassian is taught as a subject.

Bearing in mind the many obvious similarities in the backgrounds and histories of these two ethnic groups, the differences in linguistic outcomes are all the more interesting. How can these opposing results be explained? Al-Wer identifies several factors, which, combined, offer a plausible explanation.

The original Circassian settlements in Jordan were all located in Amman and in its immediate vicinity. The growth and diversification of Amman as the commercial and political capital of Jordan led to the rapid dispersal of the all-Circassian neighbourhoods. The Circassian community thus lost a vital space where their heritage language was consistently used in as well as outside the home, within the Circassian neighbourhoods. The growth of Amman and the development of suburban areas also contributed to members of the Circassian community who had owned property and resided in downtown Amman relocating to new, heterogenous residential areas around the city. This process of urbanisation, accompanied by mass arrival of war refugees and internal migration into Amman and neighbouring Zarqa, inevitably led to the dilution of the Circassian communities. Consequently, the instrumentality of Circassian as a communicative language eroded, and Arabic began to replace Circassian, not only in the public domain but in family settings as well.

Since the establishment of Jordan as a separate political entity in 1921, the Circassian community have proactively participated in the building of the Jordanian state. This has been reflected in their advancement to high ranks in civil service, in government and in the armed forces, including the appointment of a Circassian, Sa'id al-Mufti, as prime minister, an office he occupied four times, and several other high-ranking ministers and army officers. Over the years the Circassian community came to be admired and trusted as an integral part of Jordanian society and its state institutions. The central roles that were played by key members of the community, as well as the desire of the community to contribute to the national project, necessitated high degrees of competence in Arabic. Circassian was thus gradually relegated to narrower domains, serving mostly as a cultural symbol, on a par with other symbols, such as music, wedding and funeral traditions, and cuisine. This combination of physical dispersal and social integration within Jordan's mainstream society has reduced the utility of Circassian as a communicative language. This particular aspect of bilingualism, the loss of communicative function of the heritage language, is usually taken as a strong sign of imminent language shift. Commenting on language shift and its potential effects on group identity, John Edwards writes: 'Perhaps the most common adaptation, however, is communicative language shift, accompanied by some "symbolic" retention. That is, the forces acting upon a minority-language community may be such that a shift to the overarching variety becomes inevitable' (Edwards 2010: 6). The Chechen community, too, has experienced social integration and participated in the development of state institutions. In the general public perception, Jordanian Chechens and Circassians are considered to be the same community. The Chechens are also counted with the Circassians for the purpose of allocating seats in the Jordanian parliament. At the same time, all of the Chechen settlements are outside central Amman. Two of these settlements had a similar fate to that of the Circassians. Importantly, though, the two remaining villages, South Azraq and Sukhna, have remained rural and continue to have a strong Chechen character. These villages act as a 'linguistic heartland', which seems to have slowed down or delayed the shift from Chechen to Arabic. In other words, there still exists a physical domain where Chechen continues to be transmitted naturally from parent to child and used for ordinary everyday communication by members of the community. The preservation of a linguistic heartland is vital to the maintenance of endangered languages. This principle is corroborated by research in the field of language maintenance and shift the world over. It is for this reason, for instance, that in the Republic of Ireland, the government protects the last remaining enclave where Irish Gaelic, the indigenous language of the island, is spoken (see Edwards 2010 for an extensive discussion of the Irish situation). Indeed, in the Chechen villages mentioned above, at the time of Al-Wer's research, when Chechen children started primary school, most of them could only speak Chechen. This is evidence that these children were still acquiring Chechen naturally at the home.

Another crucial difference between the Circassian and Chechen communities discussed by Al-Wer concerns their respective social structures. The Circassian society has traditionally been organised hierarchically within each extended family, with princes ranking on top down to bondmen. According to Shami (1982: 24): 'Although there was a total disruption of Circassian social organisation with the emigration from the Caucasus, in Jordan the ideology of the hierarchy was maintained until the 1950s.' In the context outside their historical homeland, this system could not be sustained, and importantly, it inevitably led to the weakening of 'ethnic corporation' among the Circassians. By contrast, the Chechens have remained united as an ethnic group, most probably due to their social structure being 'egalitarian, unstratified and classless' (Nichols 1996: 7). In other words, the Circassians and Chechens eventually found themselves in very different predicaments. The former have largely fragmented as an ethnic group while the latter have remained a united group. Al-Wer concluded that the combination of the factors outlined above explains the disparity in the degree of maintenance of the two languages in the Jordanian setting.

It is very likely that the ongoing language shift among the Circassian community will progress towards monolingualism in Arabic. It is plausible to expect that the Chechen case, too, will change. Even though Chechen displays a high degree of maintenance, we must remember that this is a relatively small ethnic group in a predominantly Arabic-speaking environment. Indeed, the Chechens are not monolingual in their heritage language but bilingual in both Arabic and Chechen. Research on communities in cases like this has found that bilingualism is often an unstable, temporary situation, and that monolingualism in the majority language may be underway. This does not necessarily mean that *ethnic* identity – for either the Chechen or Circassian communities – will erode alongside their languages. What usually happens in these situations is that a distinctive language becomes less essential in defining ethnic group boundaries. By way of illustration, Irish has been shifted in favour of English in the formerly Irish-speaking territories on the island of Ireland. This has not led, however, to the erosion of a distinctive ethnic Irish identity. The same can be said about Scotland, where English has replaced Scottish Gaelic, yet most Scots do not identify as ethnically English.

6.10   Further Reading

Edwards (2009, 2010) – These two books provide a theoretical framework for the study of language and identity from multiple perspectives and are rich in data and case studies of minority languages.

Germanos and Miller (2015) – This article surveys a large number of studies on religion as a potential sociolinguistic factor across the Middle East and North Africa.

Hoffman (2007) – This highly readable ethnography of the Sous Valley and Anti-Atlas Mountains of southwest Morocco, where Amazigh is widely spoken, tackles issues of ethnicity and gender in relation to minority languages from a linguistic anthropological perspective.

Holes (2000, 2005, 2016) – These three volumes present the culmination of Clive Holes's decades-long research on dialect, culture, and society in eastern Arabia. The first volume is an extensive glossary; the second includes ethnographic texts; and the third deals with linguistic variation in phonology, morphology, syntax, and style.

Rouabah (2020) – This is a doctoral thesis in sociolinguistics which investigates language shift and maintenance among the Chaouias, an Amazigh community in eastern Algeria, based on carefully collected and analysed empirical data.

6.11   Exercises for Chapter 6

1. The examples discussed in this chapter have demonstrated that, for the most part, linguistic differentiation along religious lines was not motivated by religion per se but was linked to the historical and social circumstances that each religious group has experienced. Can you think of parallel examples where different religious or ethnic groups are involved? How does society react to these different religious or ethnic groups' differential speech patterns?

2. In most cases, people are affiliated with their family's religion from birth. This, however, is not equivalent to religiosity, i.e. the degree to which individuals adhere to the doctrines of their nominal religions.

   a. How important do you think this distinction is when exploring the relation between religion and language variation?

   b. In soap operas, the religiosity of certain characters is conveyed to the audience both visually (e.g. beards, crosses, attire) and linguistically. Research the use of such linguistic symbols in the media. Describe the ways in which religiosity is symbolised and explain the choice of symbols (e.g. the varieties of language used, vocabulary, phonological features). To what extent is this portrayal realistic?

3. Consider the following quotation from a study of greetings in Beirut. Marie-Aimée Germanos discusses people's reactions to the use of the phrase *as-salāmu ʿalaykum*, lit. 'peace be upon you'.

   only two informants said they would use *as-salāmu ʿalaykum* themselves. Christians consider it a 'Muslim' greeting, or a 'non Lebanese' greeting (used by 'Arabs' from Gulf States); and Muslim informants added a nuance to that statement, saying it was used among practicing Muslims. *as-salāmu ʿalaykum* is also the expression to which the biggest number of informants reacted negatively. (Germanos 2007: 152)

   What does this quotation reveal about the politics of religion and the intersection of religion and ethnicity in this community?

7　Language Change

7.1　Introduction

Variation and change are the two areas of study that concern sociolinguistics most. They reflect two facts about natural language. The first fact is that language is variable, and as we have seen, this variation is governed by linguistic, social, and situational factors. The second fact about language is that it changes over time. That languages change is self-evident and not in itself a matter of controversy. It is easy to see from a distance in time that a language has changed by looking at earlier records of that language. English, for instance, has changed from the time of Chaucer (fourteenth century) to Shakespeare (sixteenth century) and through to modern times; and just as English has changed in the past, it continues to change in the present. The same truism holds for every living language that has native speakers.

It is not possible to give examples for Arabic by comparing written texts from different periods that would be analogous to the English example cited above. This is because the Arabic written variety has been strictly normativised for centuries and thus has not reflected the changes that have occurred in the native varieties of the authors. We do, however, have detailed linguistic descriptions by mediaeval grammarians (most notably, Sibawayh, 760–796; see, for example, the 1988 published edition of his *Al-Kitāb*) that include information about the phonetic values of Arabic sounds, including variation where it was observed.

One of the sounds that has changed in almost all varieties of Arabic is the phoneme represented in writing by the letter ض (*ḍād*). Sibawayh described it phonetically as an emphatic lateral fricative ([ɮˁ] or something similar). Incidentally this description enables us to dispel a myth about Arabic. Arabic is commonly referred to in popular discourse as *luġat al-ḍād* 'the language of *ḍād*', implying that the sound is unique to Arabic, and that its phonetic value has always been [dˁ], as in contemporary varieties. The student of linguistics should be aware that both assumptions connoted by *luġat al-ḍād* are incorrect. As we described above, the original phonetic value of this phoneme was quite different from the modern realisation, and while lateral fricatives are rare in the world's languages, it is by no means unique to Arabic.

131

This phoneme has undergone significant changes both phonetically and phonologically in various Arabic varieties, including the modern Standard. In the latter, it is realised as a voiced emphatic stop [dˁ] and is phonemically distinct from the voiced emphatic interdental [ðˁ]. In most of the spoken dialects it merged with /ðˁ/ and is realised as [dˁ] in some dialects and [ðˁ] in others. Other phonemes that have changed quite dramatically are the interdentals /θ/ and /ð/. In many dialects the interdental sounds completely disappeared. In most of them they merged with the stops /t/ and /d/, and in several other dialects (e.g. Sason) with sibilants /s/ and /z/. In yet a third type of dialects (e.g. Bahrain), /θ/ merged with /f/, and /ð/ was fronted to [v] in others (e.g. Siirt in current-day southern Turkey).[1]

Another form of documentation of spoken Arabic, which has been used by contemporary linguists as evidence of language change, is reports by European travellers from the sixteenth century onwards. Such are the accounts by Niebuhr, who travelled with a Danish expedition in the eighteenth century and whose reports include transcribed word lists from Egypt. These suggest that [g] as a reflex of /dʒ/ was more widely distributed along the western Delta than it is today. Woidich and Zack (2009) use the data reported by Niebuhr as evidence that the well-known Cairene feature, [g] for /dʒ/, represents a case of retention rather than innovation.[2]

A further source for information about earlier spoken varieties of Arabic are the ancient inscriptions, e.g. the Nabatean and Safaitic inscriptions.[3] Al-Jallad (2015), for instance, shows that in inscriptions written in the Safaitic script, comparison with parallel inscriptions in Aramaic and Greek offers clues as to the pronunciation of Arabic sounds at the time of writing. Thus, the phoneme /dʒ/ is typically written with the Greek letter <γ>, leading once again to the conclusion that a velar pronunciation (i.e. [g] or the like) was prevalent at the time these inscriptions were written.

7.2   Historical Linguistics

The study of language change is the subject matter of a discipline in linguistics known as 'historical (or diachronic) linguistics'. Historical linguistics studies language change over time by analysing the outcome of language change after it has already occurred. In order to do this, historical linguists use a technique

---

[1] Sason is an Anatolian variety, see Akkuş and Benmamoun (2016).

[2] It is well established that modern Arabic /dʒ/ descends from *g (possibly with variants such as [gʲ] and [dʲ]. The old realisation [g] is also mentioned by Sibawayh (see Zaborski 2007 for details).

[3] Safaitic refers to the earliest surviving form of written Arabic, dating from the end of the first millennium BCE to the fourth century CE (see Al-Jallad 2015), concentrated in the Ḥarra region (northeast Jordan).

known as 'the comparative method' to reconstruct the original forms, i.e. the forms that were prevalent before change had occurred.

One of the most important achievements of historical linguists is the discovery that languages can be classified into 'language families', and that the languages in each family are related to one another via a parent language. Thus a language family includes a parent and offspring, by analogy with a regular genealogical family. Some languages which appeared to be very diverse were found to share a number of common structural features and to show systematic sound correspondences. To account for the similarities, historical linguists proposed that these languages descended from one parent language, a common ancestor, which they called a 'proto-language' (from Greek *protos*, i.e. 'ancestral' or 'original'). Using the comparative method, historical linguists were able to show, for instance, that languages such as Greek, Latin, Sanskrit, Russian, Persian, and English are all descendants of a common ancestral language. In this case, the reconstructed parent language is called 'Proto-Indo-European', and the languages in this family are referred to collectively as the 'Indo-European language family'.

Arabic is a member of the Semitic language family, which itself is a member of a larger family known as Afroasiatic. Other members of the Semitic family include living languages – i.e. languages still spoken today – such as Amharic (the majority language of Ethiopia), Aramaic (spoken in some parts of the Levant, Iraq, and Central Asia), Hebrew, and Modern South Arabian languages; as well as languages considered 'dead', which include Akkadian (an ancient Mesopotamian language), Ugaritic (in present-day Syria), Phoenician (on the east Mediterranean coast and parts of North Africa), and Ge'ez (also known as Classical Ethiopic).

By way of illustration, consider the following correspondences among members of the Semitic language family.

(1)   The word for 'land':
        a.   Arabic (Classical and some vernaculars) /ʔardˤ/ or (vernacular) /ʔarðˤ/
        b.   Aramaic /ʔarʕa/
        c.   Hebrew (Classical) /ʔɛrɛsˤ/; (Modern) /eʁets/

In this Semitic root we notice that the final consonant varies from language to language. This consonant is /dˤ/ or /ðˤ/ in Arabic varieties, /ʕ/ in Aramaic, and /sˤ/ or /ts/ in Hebrew. In order to illustrate that this is a *regular* correspondence, let us look at another word that contains this sound, this time at the beginning of its root.

(2)   The word for 'small cattle, sheep and goats':
        a.   Arabic /dˤaːn/ or /ðˤaːn/
        b.   Aramaic: /ʕɔnɔ/
        c.   Hebrew /sˤɔn/ or /tson/

We see that in this word, too, Arabic /dˤ/ or /ðˤ/ corresponds to Aramaic /ʕ/ and Hebrew /sˤ/ or /ts/. It has been found, by examining numerous words and roots across these languages, that this correspondence applies across the board, leading to the conclusion that all of these language-specific sounds descend from a single Proto-Semitic sound.

Through the comparative method of linguistic reconstruction undertaken by historical linguists over many decades, it has been possible to identify some 250–300 language families around the world.[4] These methods have also yielded a number of important generalisations particularly in relation to the study of sound change. By examining trends in the direction of sound change and frequency of attestation of similar changes in different languages, we are able to argue that some changes are possible or plausible while others are unlikely or less likely to happen. For example, a change from /s/ to /h/ is frequently attested in the world's languages, whereas a change in the opposite direction, /h/ > /s/, is extremely rare. The change /s/ > /h/ can be exemplified by Spanish: in Standard Spanish /disko/ 'disk' is rendered as /dihko/ in many non-Standard dialects in Spain and in Latin America. Such generalisations have played a central role in the formulation of principles of language change.

A common sound change in Arabic is the palatalisation and affrication of /k/ and /g/ to [tʃ]~[ts] and [dʒ]~[dz], respectively, in the environment of high-front vowels. For example, in the dialect of Horan (northern Jordan and southern Syria), the word /keːf/ 'how' is systematically pronounced [tʃeːf]. In the dialect of the Bani Ḥasan in Jordan, the noun /gidir/ '(large) pot' is pronounced [dʒidir]. In central Najdi (e.g. in Qasim, Saudi Arabia), the same words become [tseːf] and [dzidir]. This process of affrication of velar stops in the vicinity of front and high vowels is not unique to Arabic. Consider the Italian words *cento* /tʃento/ 'hundred' and *canto* /kanto/ 'I sing'. In these examples, we notice that the phoneme represented by the grapheme <c>, historically a /k/ sound, is affricated in the environment of a front vowel /e/ (also before /i/, as in *cinque* / tʃinkwe/ 'five') and remains a stop elsewhere.

Despite the many achievements of historical linguistics, its methods of analyses provided little information about the *mechanism* of language change: why does it happen? How does it start? How does it diffuse? In fact, until the advent of sociolinguistics, it was widely believed that language change cannot be observed. The famous quotation by Bloomfield (1933: 347) reflects

---

[4] The exact number of language families depends on the method of classification. Some languages have no known relatives, such as Basque, Ainu, Burushaski, Etruscan, and Sumerian. Languages which have no known relatives are called 'isolates' (see Campbell 2004: 187). There are also special categories for constructed languages (Esperanto), creoles, and sign languages. A list of language families, the languages they contain and where they are/were spoken can be found at www.ethnologue.com/family_index.asp (accessed 14 August 2021).

this belief. He wrote, 'The process of linguistic change has never been directly observed; we shall see that such observation, with our present facilities, is inconceivable.'

The methods developed by William Labov in the 1960s added an important dimension to the study of language change, emphasising the fact that language is not an object that changes of its own accord. Rather, human agency and the interaction between language and society are the primary instigators of language change. We have thus been able to respond with more confidence to questions such as, How does a change start? Why does it start? and, importantly, How does it diffuse and spread? In the rest of this chapter, we turn our attention to these questions, which lie at the core of sociolinguistic investigation.

7.3 The Relationship between Variation and Change

Language change is always preceded by a stage of variation. In other words, variation can be said to be a *prerequisite* to change. A change from Form A to Form B prototypically proceeds in the following manner: in the earliest stage, the original feature, Form A, occurs more frequently than the new feature, Form B. As the change progresses, Form B occurs gradually more frequently at the expense of the old form. At an advanced stage of the change, the new feature appears more frequently than the old feature, and thus Form B becomes dominant. If the change is total and completed, ultimately Form A gives way to Form B. We can illustrate this process in the abstract schema in Figure 7.1, which depicts six stages of progression, from the earliest (lowest) to the most advanced (highest).

The progression of the change from A to B as depicted in Figure 7.1 applies to the speech of individuals as well as to the community as a whole. Individual speakers adopt a linguistic innovation (i.e. a new feature) gradually in the manner described earlier, and the sum of the linguistic behaviour of all individuals represents the behaviour of the community. It would be unlikely for a linguistic

Figure 7.1 Progression of a hypothetical change from Form A to Form B

change to affect all individuals simultaneously and in equal measure. More realistically, the change starts with a few speakers, who may use it in limited cases to begin with. They then extend their usage of it in their own speech to a wider range of contexts and transmit it to other individuals within their circle of contacts, who, in their turn, transmit it further until it reaches most or all members of the community. We would not expect any single individual to replace the old form with the new form in their speech without going through a stage where they use both forms, alternating their use of A and B. For some individuals, the alternation happens in the same context, and for others the ratio of occurrence of A or B may depend on a range of factors (context, style, interlocutors, age, gender, etc.). What we are describing here are instances of variation, which are present in language at any point in time.

A linguistic change typically starts very slowly, later gathers momentum and takes off within a relatively short span of time, and finally slows down until the change is complete. This process, when plotted on a graph, often yields an 'S' shape, as in Figure 7.2. The S-curve model of linguistic diffusion was introduced as part of the theory of 'lexical diffusion', developed by William

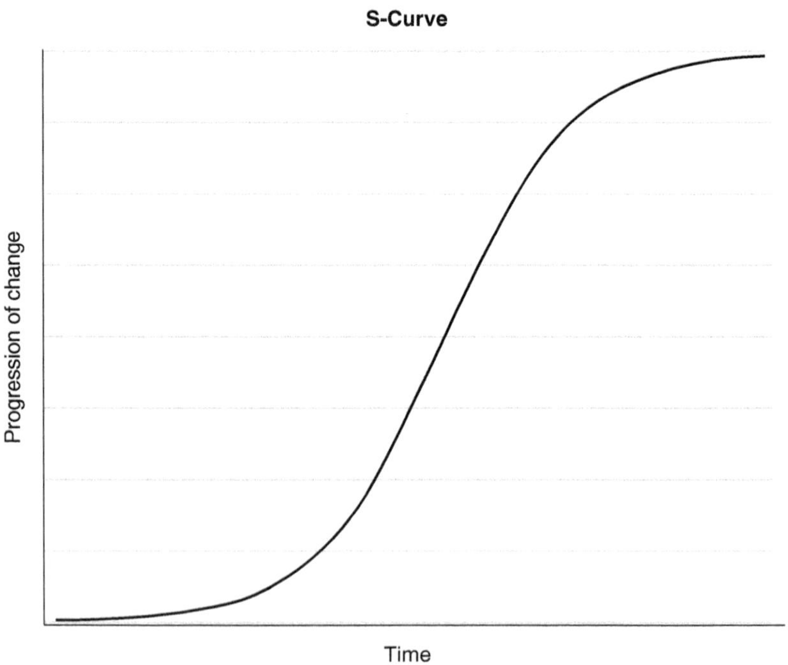

Figure 7.2 The S-curve

Wang and his collaborators in the 1970s.[5] The theory postulates that sound change affects one or a few words in a lexical set, then spreads gradually to other words in the set until it affects all or most of the words in that set. The S-curve model has since been found to recur in very many types of change and is considered to represent a prototype of the mechanism of diffusion of linguistic change.[6]

Variation then is a necessary stage for linguistic change to occur. Therefore, the more we know about the intermediate stages in the progression from A to B (i.e. the more we understand the structure of variation), the more likely we are to understand the change itself. Look at the diagram in Figure 7.1 and imagine that the information about the variable stages (where both shades appear on the line) were unavailable. In such a situation, significant details concerning the progress of change would be lost. In order to understand how A became B, we need to know as much as possible about the ways in which the use of A and B were distributed in the speech of the individual and the community as a whole.

A concrete example of a feature undergoing change in progress is the (q) variable in the Jordanian capital Amman. This variable has two competing forms that occur in natural speech: [g] and [?]. The former is associated with ethnic Jordanians, and the latter, historically, with urban Palestinian dialects. Many Jordanian children who grew up with the velar variant [g], begin encountering the glottal variant [?] upon entering the school system. Some of them accommodate to their peers by switching the majority of their instances of (q) from [g] to [?]. There is a stage during which these children alternate between the two variants, based on the social setting in which they happen to be. Thus, these children may use [?] in school with their friends but revert to [g] when they return home to their families. For a portion of the population, this intra-speaker variation remains stable. Others go a step further and adopt the glottal stop in virtually all social contexts and essentially abandon their native voiced velar stop variant.

A more nuanced understanding of the *social meaning* of variation in this variable requires us to delve further into the social reality in which variation – and ultimately, potential change – occurs. One possibility is to consider some of the dimensions of variation introduced in the previous chapters. A more accurate and complete picture may be arrived at if, for instance, we explore possible effects of gender on the variation in the use of the two variants of (q). While what we described earlier may reflect a general trend among Ammani youngsters, we have evidence that girls and boys often behave differently in their choice of variants. Alongside the axis of ethnicity (Jordanian

---

[5] See Wang (1969); Chen and Wang (1975); Cheng and Wang (1977).
[6] See Charles Bailey (1973).

and Palestinian), the female–male axis of gender is also at play. It has been observed that many Ammani boys prefer the [g] variant of (q), especially when their very masculinity is on the line, e.g. when participating in fights. 'Fighting with [ʔ]' would often be considered unconscionable, as it can be construed as a sign of weakness. It is thus our duty as analysts of variation and change to be aware of all possible predictors of change, lest we end up with an oversimplified account of the forces that drive language change.

In Sections 7.4 and 7.5 we focus on the question of how we study language change within the sociolinguistic paradigm.

7.4   Studying Change in Real Time

The most reliable way to verify that a linguistic feature has changed in a given language is to obtain data at two points in time sufficiently separated and then compare the state of language at the two points. The differences we find, if any, are evidence that change has taken place. This method of investigation is called the 'real-time method'.

There are two sources of linguistic comparisons in real time. The first source is historical records of the language under investigation, which contain information about the state of the language at an earlier point in time. Historical records include earlier descriptions of the dialect under investigation and linguistic atlases (see Section 8.3). There are a number of limitations to this method. The most obvious difficulty is the unavailability of earlier records. In cases where such records are available, the information they contain may be presented in such a way that it does not allow us to make direct and reliable comparisons with data collected and compiled later. Historical records of dialects do not normally include quantification of data, and therefore the comparisons that can be made are qualitative only. Until the invention of the tape recorder, fieldworkers had to rely on their skill at noting down their observations instantaneously, and there was no way to double check the accuracy of descriptions. Despite these limitations, historical records of dialects remain an important and valuable resource in sociolinguistic research.

We should also bear in mind that while written records can offer us a window into language usage at the time they were written, they can also give the false impression that the authors of these texts actually wrote them in the same language variety that was spoken in the region. We know that this is often not the case. In most languages, it is easy to distinguish between spoken and written registers of language, the former being less formal than the latter. In the case of Arabic, this is amplified by the convention of writing in Standard Arabic rather than in the local vernaculars. In this context, we caution against assuming that written records of Standard Arabic, old or modern, represent historical evidence for any spoken variety of Arabic. Therefore, what we mean when we say, 'earlier descriptions of the dialect under investigation' are works based on spoken empirical data, whose aim was to document contemporary dialectological material. Such texts, unlike Standard Arabic texts, are precisely the kind of source one can use when discerning the details of language change.

Several Arabic dialects were studied and documented in various forms as early as the beginning of the twentieth century, e.g. Bergsträsser's 1915 linguistic atlas of Syria and Palestine, and Cantineau's series of grammars and texts from various Levantine dialects published in the 1930s–1950s, as well as Brunot's 1930 description of the urban Moroccan dialect of Rabat. A number of examples of how such early records were used can be seen in Cotter's 2013 sociolinguistic study of the Palestinian dialect of Gaza, for which Bergsträsser's atlas served as a source of comparison; Al-Wer et al.'s 2015 study of religious affiliation as a social factor, which employed Cantineau's studies of Horani dialects; and Messaoudi's 2019 overview of variation in North Africa, in which Brunot is featured as one of the earliest dialectologists of the region.

More recent dialectological studies (e.g. Prochazka 1988 for Saudi Arabian dialects, De Jong's two volumes [2000; 2011] on the Sinai Peninsula, and Behnstedt's series of atlases of the dialects of Syria, Egypt [with Woidich], Morocco, Yemen, and Palestine [with Geva-Kleinberger]), are also invaluable resources for current-day sociolinguists wishing to trace language change. Even a twenty- or thirty-year time depth can be sufficient for documenting changes across a generation or two, and the breadth of coverage in linguistic atlases is also immensely helpful for this purpose.

The second source of real-time studies involves returning to the community to replicate an earlier investigation. This procedure was used for the first time by Eduard Hermann in 1929 in the Swiss village of Charmay, which was studied by Louis Gauchat in 1899 (published in 1905). More recently, the procedure was followed in a number of studies, replicating as closely as possible the early sociolinguistic investigations of the 1960s and 1970s. This includes re-studies of Labov's 1963 famous department store study in New York (Fowler 1986) and his 1962 Martha's Vineyard study (Blake and Josey 2003). For Arabic, Al-Qouz (2009) is, in part, a re-study of Holes's (1987) study of Bahrain (see Chapter 6).

7.4.1   Trend and Panel Studies

There are two types of re-studies: *trend* and *panel* studies. In trend studies (also called 'cross-sectional' research), the investigator replicates the original study, after a number of years, in every detail: the methods of drawing a representative sample of the population and the methods of collecting the data, recording, and analysing of the data. For such studies to yield reliable data in real time, changes that may have affected the community in the intervening years have to be taken into account. For instance, the community could have experienced radical demographic changes through migration. Many of the re-studies conducted so far, including the studies mentioned above, are of this type.

Panel studies (also called 'longitudinal studies') use the original sample by locating the same individuals who participated in the first study. The participants are re-interviewed, and changes in their linguistic behaviour in the intervening period are monitored. The obvious difficulty in this sort of study is that some of the original speakers may no longer be alive, others may have moved, and so on, which would result in a much-reduced number of participants. Another way in which panel studies can be conducted is to record particular groups of speakers regularly over a period of time, thereby obtaining periodic recordings of their speech.

Many studies in real time use a combination of trend and panel methods. For example, the original study on Finnish in Helsinki in the 1970s included ninety-six speakers. In the re-study conducted by Heikki Paunonen in 1996 only twenty-nine speakers from the original sample were re-interviewed, and sixteen new speakers were added. A similar mixture of methods was used in the Montreal project, which is a three-stage re-study of the original research by Henrietta Cedergren, David Sankoff, and Gillian Sankoff.[7] By combining the two methods, researchers are able to compensate for some of the shortcomings associated with these methods.

As mentioned by Holes (2016: 469), not many longitudinal studies of change in Arabic dialects have been carried out, but Al-Qouz's (2009) study of Manama, the capital of Bahrain, is partially longitudinal. She anchored her findings on Holes's 1970s research (Holes 1987). She investigates several features covered in Holes's research, as well as a number of new variables. Notably, unlike Holes, who had studied variation and change across Bahrain, Al-Qouz focussed on schoolchildren in the Manama area only. Therefore, while not strictly a trend study, Al-Qouz's conclusions are in line with what might be expected in a real-time study. What she found was that the trends detected in Holes's study roughly thirty years before hers have continued to advance.

Studies in real time are obviously rewarding since they are capable of yielding direct empirical data about the mechanism of change. They also provide us with a tool to check the validity of inferences made on the basis of observations in apparent time (see Section 7.5). At the same time, however, studying language change in real time is time-consuming and can be very costly. For these

---

[7] See G. Sankoff (2019) for details about the studies cited in this section and for further details about trend and panel studies.

reasons, most studies of change in sociolinguistics follow the *apparent-time method*, which provides immediate results, as will be explained in Section 7.5.

7.5 Studying Change in Apparent Time

The apparent-time method of investigating language change takes a snapshot of language in a particular community at a particular time. In this method, age is used as a 'surrogate' for real time (see Chambers 2008). The assumption is that the behaviour of different age groups represents different stages of development in the language itself. Thus, if the sample includes speakers whose ages range between, say, ten and seventy, the oldest age group is assumed to represent the state of language some six decades earlier while the speech of the ten-year-olds is assumed to represent the current state of the language. Therefore, the hypothesis is that linguistic differences across different generations (i.e. apparent-time differences) reflect actual diachronic developments in the language (i.e. real-time changes). Because in this method the 'time' element is absent, i.e. no waiting for a certain number of years is involved, it compensates for time by drawing a sample of speakers from different age cohorts.

Age is considered the most important variable in the apparent-time method, but other social and stylistic variables, as well as the interaction between all variables, are also important since they, too, correlate with linguistic usage and can show patterns that are indicative of language change, as we will see later. The apparent-time method, like the real-time method, has advantages as well as limitations and pitfalls. One of the advantages is that it provides immediate results without the need to wait twenty or more years; it is thus a practical method, which also guarantees consistency in the circumstances under which the data are collected.

One limitation of the apparent-time method concerns the implied assumption that adults do not change their ways of speaking in the course of their lives. This issue has been investigated in longitudinal studies that analysed multiple recordings of the same speakers at different intervals in their adult lives. Overall, the investigations provide support for the initial assumption that adults do not change their vernacular during adult life. Exceptions do exist, however. Sankoff (2019) summarises decades of research on language change across the lifespan, especially among the Francophone speech community of Montreal. In this summary, three types of trajectories are presented:

1. Adults who retain variation patterns that they acquired in their childhoods.
2. Adults who continue to receive input from the younger speakers and change in the direction of these youngsters' speech.
3. Ageing speakers who become more conservative ('retrograde lifespan change') as a reaction to younger speakers changing their speech away from the older norms.

Contrary to the relative stability typical of adults (the latter two trajectories notwithstanding), the vernacular of adolescents and older teenagers is not stable, and therefore, we cannot reliably assume that the vernacular of the teenage cohort is indicative of their later speech as adults.

All three trajectories proposed by Sankoff can be exemplified through data from the newly formed dialect of Amman. This dialect is the outcome of contact between speakers of Jordanian and Palestinian dialects. In the first generation of Ammanis, the typical linguistic behaviour is one of retention of the traditional features characteristic of each heritage dialect. Speakers of Jordanian heritage usually use traditional Jordanian variants, while speakers of urban Palestinian heritage use the variants that originate in their Palestinian dialects.

One set of features that illustrates these trajectories nicely is the pronominal suffixes. For the 3rd person plural suffix, two variants are in use: *-hum*, typical of traditional Jordanian dialects, and *-hon*, typical of urban Palestinian dialects (e.g. *bēt-hum* ~ *bēt-hon* 'their house'). For the 2nd person plural, the possible variants are traditional Jordanian *-ku*, urban Palestinian *-kon*, and the new Ammani variant *-kum* (*baḥibb-ku* ~ *baḥibb-kon* ~ *baḥibb-kum* 'I like/love you (pl.)). This latter variant is used consistently by the third generation, regardless of dialectal heritage. In other words, third-generation speakers have replaced their inherited variants, viz. *-ku* or *-kon*, with *-kum*.

Second-generation Ammanis consist of speakers who either arrived in Amman at an early age or were born in the city to parents who spoke the traditional dialects of the towns or villages from which they migrated. The parents use these suffixes in a manner consistent with their respective traditional forms. In other words, first-generation Jordanians use *-hum* and *-ku*, and first-generation Palestinians use *-hon* and *-kon*. Interestingly, several of the second-generation speakers have added *-kum* to their repertoire for the second person suffix, which we interpret as increasing alignment later in life with the linguistic behaviour of the third generation, namely, consistent usage of *-kum*.

However, the second-generation speakers exhibit variation, along the lines of the taxonomy laid out by Sankoff. Some speakers of this generation actually retain certain heritage features. Most prominent is the retention among some second-generation speakers of the suffix variants that end in /n/, viz. *-hon* and *-kon*. These variants are socially marked in Jordan; they are not part of the linguistic repertoire of either traditional Jordanian dialects or the newly formed dialect of Amman, both of which have suffixes ending in /m/. The /n/-final suffixes are typical of urban Palestinian dialects, as well as several other dialects of the Levant, most notably those of Beirut and Damascus.[8]

---

[8] In traditional Jordanian dialects, *-in* forms are used for feminine plural only, e.g. *bēt-hin* 'their (f) house', *bēt-kin* 'your (f.pl.) house', while in the city dialects of the Levant, the forms with /n/ are common (i.e. unmarked for gender).

Table 7.1 *Pronominal suffixes in Amman across generations*

Generation	Linguistic behaviour	Examples
1	Relative stability in respective heritage features	(Jordanian heritage) *-hum, -ku* (Palestinian heritage) *-hon, -kon*
2	Trajectory 1: Retention of heritage features Trajectory 2: Input from and change towards Generation 3 Trajectory 3: Retrograde change	(Jordanian heritage) *-hum, -ku* (Palestinian heritage) *-hon, -kon* *-hum, -kum* (regardless of heritage) (Jordanian heritage) Initially *-ku > -kum ~ -kon* In old age: *-kum ~ -kon > -ku*
3	Relative stability in new dialectal features	*-hum, -kum* (regardless of heritage)

Similarly, we have evidence of second-generation Ammanis who had adopted the incoming features of the Ammani dialect but later in life reverted to traditional features. Using the 2nd person suffixes as an example, there are second-generation Ammani women of Jordanian heritage who have been known to use *-kon* during most of their lifetimes (having adopted this pan-Levantine variant) and later in life shifted to *-ku*. What we are unable to say for certain at this stage is whether these *-kon* to *-ku* shifters are exhibiting a conscious alignment with their ancestral dialect or naturally reverting to their native dialect.

Table 7.1 provides a schematic view of the linguistic behaviours and changes of trajectory described above.

The other important challenge presented in the apparent time method is *age-grading*, explained in Chapter 2.

7.6   Variation without Change

Although every linguistic change involves variability, not every instance of variation necessarily means that change is taking place. Occasionally, some features show variation across age groups but are not involved in language change.

This means that although the younger speakers can be found to use innovative linguistic features and thus appear to be initiating change, the generational difference is repeated in every generation in more or less the same proportion. We referred to this phenomenon as *age-grading* (see Chapter 2). In other cases, we may find variation, but the generational differences are non-significant. A good example of such a finding concerns the dropping of /h/ in pronominal suffixes in Damascus, studied by Hanadi Ismail (2007). In this case, although there was variation, the difference in *h*-dropping rates between the oldest generation and the youngest did not exceed five percentage points, ranging from 94% to 99%. Statistical testing did not find this difference to be significant. This pattern, where a feature exhibits variation across the community according to various social and linguistic factors but without a significant age effect, is typical of *stable variation* without change (see Section 9.6.1).

7.7   Variation Indicating Change in Progress

In contrast to the small differences across age groups found in cases of stable variation, where there is a change in progress, we typically find incremental increase across age groups; the younger generation use the new feature considerably more frequently than the older generation. Change in progress can also be indicated by a disruption in the expected pattern. Thus, instead of the neat pattern of correlation, which we saw above in cases of stable variation, in change in progress, the pattern may be disrupted by a crossover. To illustrate these points let us look at some research data.

Another variable studied by Ismail in Damascus is (r), which concerns the phonetic property of the consonant /r/. This consonant is undergoing a process of lenition (or weakening). Ismail identified five possible pronunciations in her data ranging from apical trill [r], which is the old traditional way of pronouncing this sound in the dialect of Damascus, to approximant [ɹ], which is the new innovative sound. The data were analysed in relation to age, gender, and life-mode (see Chapter 5). Most of the sampled speakers used a range of variants, but for statistical purposes Ismail counted all innovations as tokens of the new approximant variant [ɹ]. The most striking generational differences were found in the inner-city community of Shaghoor. Here, the oldest speakers barely show any variation, as they use the innovative variant only 2% of the time, whereas the youngest speakers use it 26% of the time. This difference was found to be statistically significant.

Another clue that the generational difference represents change in progress is in the pattern of correlation between age and life-mode. Figure 7.3 (also presented and discussed in Section 5.5) shows that, unlike the older generation in inner-city Shaghoor, the older generation in the suburban community of Dummar had already begun adopting the innovative variant, the approximant realisation of /r/. The overall increase in the use of this variant in Dummar occurs in almost equal increments from each generation to the next. In Shaghoor, however, the old and middle generations barely use this variant, while the younger generation's usage is markedly higher than that of the middle generation in the same community and even surpasses the highest rate among the young Dummar speakers. An obvious conclusion we can draw from this is that the young Shaghoor speakers did not acquire this feature from

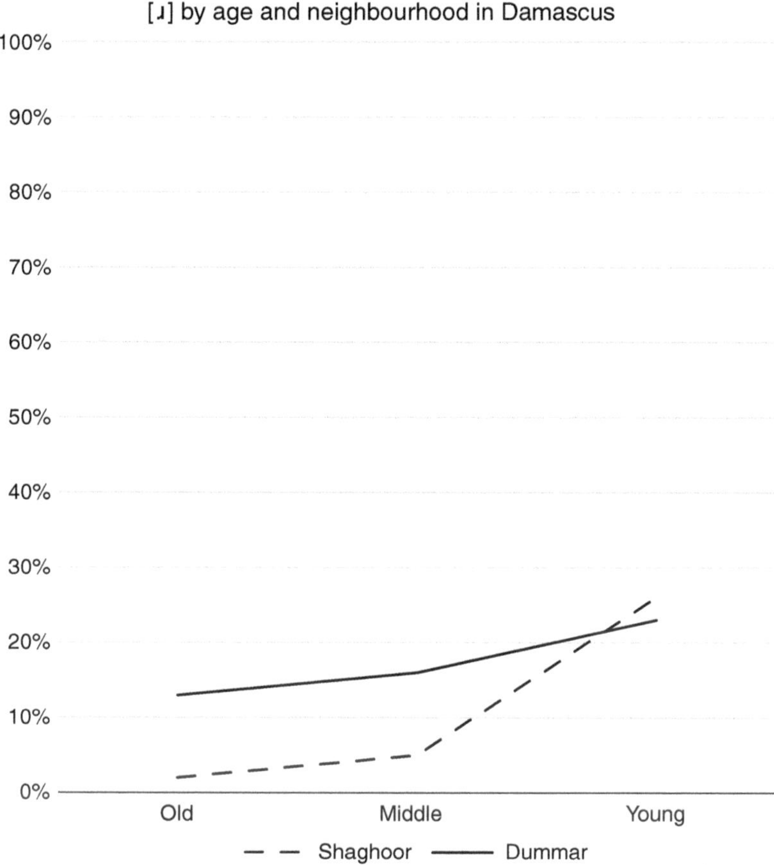

Figure 7.3 Percentage use of [ɹ] by age and neighbourhood in Damascus (based on Ismail 2007: 207, Figure 9.7)

their immediate environment (e.g. their parents) but rather borrowed it from the speech of a prestigious community within the city, namely the suburban community of Dummar. This 'exaggerated' usage is the cause of the crossover we see in Figure 7.3. The crossover can be described as a disruption to a hypothetical scenario of progression of the change across the Damascus community: seeing as the change must have started in the suburban community, the younger Dummar speakers might have been expected to lead the change overall. The behaviour of the young generation in Shaghoor constitutes a disruption to the expected pattern, which is one indication that a given feature is undergoing linguistic change in progress.

In Section 7.8 we will make a distinction between two types of change, and we will see how this distinction further elucidates the manner in which change is introduced and diffused in the language system and the speech community.

7.8   Types of Change

Labov (1966) distinguishes between two types of linguistic change: change from above and change from below. The distinction is primarily made on the basis of the level of *social awareness* associated with each type of change and the *socioeconomic position* of the innovating group, as explained below.

7.8.1   Change from Above

Change from above is introduced by a dominant social class and often with full public awareness, *above the level of social consciousness*. The innovative linguistic feature normally represents a borrowing from other speech communities (or other varieties) that are judged by the innovating high-status group as having higher prestige. As borrowings, changes from above do not immediately manifest in the casual speech (the vernacular) of the dominant class or other classes in the community but appear first in careful speech, i.e. when speakers are fully aware of and monitoring their speech. Because changes from above are, to begin with, borrowings from other linguistic systems, integrating them into the structure (the grammar) of the recipient variety may require changes in other features. According to Labov (1994: 78) such complications 'may prevent the change from above from being integrated with the rest of system and the borrowed element with its associated changes may form a separate subsystem for many generations'. To further illustrate these issues, we cite the following example from Aziza Al-Essa's (2008) research in Jeddah, western Saudi Arabia.

One of the features investigated by Al-Essa concerns the de-affrication of /ts/ in the dialect of a sub-group in the city, the Najdis, who had originally migrated into the city from the Najd province in central Saudi Arabia. The Najdi dialect is characterised by the use of an affricate sound [ts] mainly in the vicinity of front and high vowels, whereas the mainstream dialect in Jeddah has [k]. The affricate [ts] for /k/ is a stereotype of the Najdi dialect and is generally stigmatised by speakers of other dialects. It is the result of a very old historical sound change that affected a number of Arabic dialects in central Arabia.[9] In Jeddah

---

[9] For an account of the history of affrication in Arabian dialects, see Johnstone (1963).

Table 7.2 *Examples of affrication in the stem and the suffix among the Najdis in Jeddah (from Al-Essa 2009)*

In the stem:

/mika:n/ > /mitsa:n/ 'place'
/jakwu:n/ > /jatswu:n/ 'they iron'
/ke:f/ > /tse:f/ 'how'
/kin/ > /tsin/ 'as if'

In the suffix –*ik*:

/ʔumm-ik/ > /ʔumm-its/ mother-your (sg.f.) 'your mother'
/xall-ik/ > /xall-its/ stay-you (sg.f.) 'stay!'
/kta:b-ik/ > /kta:b-its/ book-your (sg.f.) 'your book'

and among the native speakers of the Najdi dialect, this historical change, /k/ > [ts] in the vicinity of front and high vowels, is being reversed, i.e. [ts] is going through a process of de-affrication. The change from [ts] to [k] is a typical type of change from above. In this case the incoming variant [k] is borrowed from the dialect of the majority and is generally considered a feature of the local standard dialect of the city of Jeddah.

In the Najdi dialect, i.e. the native dialect of the immigrant group, affrication affects /k/ in the stem of the word as well as /k/ in the 2nd person singular feminine suffix –*ik*, as illustrated in Table 7.2.

The two types of /k/, in the stem and in the suffix, were analysed by Al-Essa separately. The results show that de-affrication of [ts] to [k] in the stem is a change nearing completion. The affricate sound [ts] was used in only 6% of a total of 668 tokens. This phonetic change is straightforward replacement of one sound by another without any further grammatical complications. On the other hand, the same phonetic change in the suffix -*ik* has ramifications on the syntax, specifically in terms of gender agreement, as illustrated below.

> *Najdi*

> /ʔumm-its/ 'your (f) mother' *versus* /ʔumm-ik/ 'your (m) mother'

In the forms above, the vowel in the feminine and masculine forms is identical (phonetically [ə]). The gender distinction in the 2nd person suffix is signalled by using two different consonants (affricate for feminine and velar for masculine).

By contrast, in the standard (and target) Jeddah dialect the grammatical information concerning gender (masculine versus feminine) is signalled by a change in the vowel:

> *Jeddah*

> /ʔumm-ik/ 'your (f) mother' *versus* /ʔumm-ak/ 'your (m) mother'

Therefore, for speakers of the Najdi dialect, adopting the target feature [k] in place of their traditional form [ts] in the suffix requires not only de-affrication of [ts] but also adoption of a vocalic distinction between the masculine and the feminine forms (*-ak* or *-ik*, respectively), whereas no such readjustment is involved in the case of the change from [ts] to [k] in the stem. This difference in complexity is reflected in the quantitative results reported by Al-Essa. The traditional Nadji form *–its* was found to occur in the suffix 22% of the time (out of 1,247 tokens), i.e. almost four times as frequently as in the stem (6%).

Note that maintenance of grammatical distinctions does not always act as a deterrent to language change. For instance, many varieties of Arabic have lost gender distinctions in the 2nd and 3rd person plural pronouns and suffixes and many others are in the process of losing these distinctions. In fact there are more cases of sound change that lead to loss of distinctions than change in the opposite direction. The point of the example from Najdis in Jeddah is that it presents a neat illustration of the complexity involved in the integration of a change from above in the linguistic system and the effect it has on the progress of change.

7.8.2   Change from Below

Change from below is the basic type of linguistic change that operates within the system. Unlike change from above, which is introduced consciously by a dominant social class and modelled on linguistic features that are characteristic of the speech of a higher-status group, change from below operates below the level of conscious awareness. Typically, phonological chain shifts tend to be changes from within the system, i.e. changes from below. Consider for example the historical consonant chain shift in rural Palestinian dialects:

(1) q > k, e.g. /qalb/ > /kalb/ 'heart'
(2) k > ʧ, e.g. /kalb/ > /ʧalb/ 'dog'

These same rural Palestinian dialects are currently in a state of variation. Alongside the affricate [ʧ], a growing number of speakers use [k] instead. This development is not a reversal of the historical shift, as each of the two phonemes that were involved in the chain shift is nowadays changing in its own direction, under social pressure, in a manner consistent with change from above. For instance, the dialects of Bethlehem, Ramallah, and Beit Jala are traditionally typical rural Palestinian dialects, in which /q/ was realised as [k] and /k/ as [ʧ]. As a result of changes in their demography and status (they became cities, and in the case of Ramallah, the seat of the Palestinian government), their dialects began to change. In principle, the trajectory of change aligns them with the dialects of established Palestinian cities, e.g. Jerusalem, in which /q/ is realised as [ʔ] and /k/ as [k].

A more complex case is the process of change that has affected the interdental fricatives in Arabic dialects: /θ/, /ð/, /ðˤ/. Contemporary Arabic dialects can be divided into two types:

a. Dialects that have interdental fricative phonemes, which are distinct from their dental plosive counterparts, e.g. traditional Jordanian dialects, rural Palestinian, Tunis, some Libyan and Iraqi, and most Arabian dialects.

b. Dialects that do not contain interdental phonemes but merge them with the stops /t/, /d/, /dˤ/, or sibilants /s/, /z/, /zˤ/, e.g. Beirut, Damascus, Cairo, Rabat, some Algerian and Iraqi dialects, and Maltese, as well as the dialects of the following cities in Saudi Arabia: Mecca, Medina and Jeddah.

The change in type (b) dialects ended up being systemic, i.e. in these dialects none of the interdentals have survived. Dialects of this type are nowadays found throughout the Arabic-speaking world. This does not necessarily mean that the change originated in some dialects and spread to the rest. In fact, it is more likely to be the case that the shift in each region arose independently. This is because shifts from interdentals to stops are widely attested cross-linguistically; in languages that do have interdentals these sounds are among the last to be acquired by children. It is therefore not surprising that interdentals are uncommon in human languages. We do not know the exact mechanism by which the change from interdental to stop occurred historically, but it is safe to assume that a shift of this sort happened as a change from below, at least to begin with.

Similar shifts from interdental to stop are currently operative in several Arabic dialects. These contemporary shifts are undoubtedly changes from above, motivated primarily by social factors. Al-Wer (1991) found that change from interdental to stop was already very widespread in the speech of women in provincial cities in Jordan. In a follow-up study in 1997 of one of these cities, Salt, the change was beginning to show in men's speech as well. In her study of the formation of the Amman dialect (Al-Wer 2007), she reports that the stop variants are predominant in the speech of the younger generation. Similar results were obtained from Irbid, the largest city in the north of Jordan (Al-Khatib 1988; Al-Tamimi 2001).

For Palestine, data from Gaza, whose traditional dialect does not have interdentals, show that refugees from elsewhere in Palestine who do have interdentals in their heritage dialects gradually accommodate to the speech of the local dialect and adopt the stop variants (Al-Shareef 2002; further supported by Cotter 2016). Ongoing research by Uri Horesh among speakers of rural central Palestinian dialects, which traditionally have interdentals, suggests that as a result of social upward mobility and urbanisation, these dialects are now in a state of variation between the interdental and stop variants.

In Saudi Arabia, a number of studies included the interdentals as variables. In Al-Jehani's (1985) study in Mecca, he found that the Bedouin sector of the community abandoned the interdentals in favour of the stop variants, which are a hallmark of the speech of urban Meccans. By contrast, three studies of migrant groups in Mecca and Jeddah found only low rates of variation for the interdental variables, with the use of stops not exceeding 10%.[10] These researchers emphasise the fact that the stop variants are associated with strong stereotypes as urban Hijazi features, especially for speakers from outside the region (where the interdentals are intact). Al-Essa (2008: 102) summarises the effect of this stereotyping on the low rate of occurrence of the stop variants among the Najdi speakers in Jeddah as follows: 'The socio-psychological factors related to strong stereotyping and negative attitude may have played the central role in the rejection of the incoming urban Hijazi variants for the majority of speakers.'

In the case of the interdentals, we see very clearly how powerful social factors can be in directing the trajectory of change. In Jordan, Palestine, and the Levant in general, absence of the interdentals is the norm in the regional standard. Despite the fact that Levantine dialects which maintain the distinction between interdental and stop are numerous and distributed throughout the region, their influence in directing language change is hindered by the social stigmas attributed to them. It is therefore not surprising that the interdentals in these dialects are gradually being abandoned. In this particular case of change (from interdental to stop), the social and linguistic motivations coalesce. The social pressures to eliminate the interdentals coincide with a change that is common from a linguistic perspective.

In Saudi Arabia the situation is markedly different. Firstly, the dialects that do not have interdentals are much more confined than in the Levant; they are concentrated in the Hijazi cities of Jeddah, Mecca, and Medina. The stop variants are therefore extremely salient as markers of the speech of these cities, which seems to inhibit their adoption by migrant groups. In this case, a linguistically motivated development is hampered by social stereotyping.

7.9   Concluding Remarks

We began this chapter by observing that historical linguistics is concerned mainly with long-term changes which have already occurred, while sociolinguistics zooms in on ongoing changes and their dynamics as they disseminate through the community. Some of these innovations may be short-lived, but others may have a profound long-term impact on the language system.

Sociolinguistics has in fact revolutionised the methods of studying language and analysing change and has ultimately led to a better understanding of the mechanism by which Form A changes to Form B. Sociolinguistics has

---

[10] For details, see Al-Shehri (1993) and Al-Essa (2008) on Jeddah; Alghamdi (2014) on Mecca.

also systematised the inclusion of social factors as integral to the process of language change. After all, languages do not change of their own accord. It is speakers who change them, and they do so within their specific communities and social contexts.

On a final note, it is important to remember that when we conduct research on language change in Arabic, we must do two things: we must not only examine the empirical data in relation to established knowledge in the field of sociolinguistics but, crucially, also interrogate generalisations and engage in theoretical formulations.

7.10   Further Reading

7.10.1   Resources in Historical Linguistics

Campbell (2004) – This is a comprehensive and accessible textbook about historical linguistics and its methods with many illustrations of the comparative method.

Hock (1986) – This is a classic introduction to historical linguistics.

Lass (1997) – This is a critical survey of the foundations of historical linguistics and its interaction with language change.

Owens (2006) – In this groundbreaking book, Owens presents an account of the history of Arabic, basing his analysis on a large corpus of data drawn from varieties of Arabic of all time periods and across a wide geographical distribution.

7.10.2   Resources in Sociolinguistics

Al-Wer and Herin (2011) – This article analyses the emergence of (q) as a variable in Jordan and further developments in its social meanings.

Chambers (2008) –This is a textbook of general sociolinguistic theory. Chapter 4 focusses on phonological change from a variationist perspective.

Cukor-Avila and Bailey (2013) – This chapter provides a succinct coverage and appraisal of the real- and apparent-time methods.

Labov (1994) – This is the first in a trilogy entitled *Principles of Linguistic Change*; this volume deals specifically with language-internal constraints.

Meyerhoff (2018) – This is the third edition of a comprehensive introduction to general sociolinguistics, which contains extended coverage of several topics pertaining to the study of language change in a sociolinguistic framework.

Al-Wer et al. (2022) – This article probes language change in several Arabic vernaculars, highlighting the pivotal role played by social factors in directing language change.

7.11   Exercises for Chapter 7

1. Consider the following data (based on work in progress by Uri Horesh) from a rural Palestinian dialect, showing variable deaffrication of [ʧ], which is a change in progress (see details in Section 7.8). Comment on these data, keeping in mind the following questions:

    a. How are the two variants distributed (e.g. by linguistic environment, grammatical categories, lexicon)?

    b. Are there are any patterns? If so, describe them.

    c. Are there exceptions to these patterns? Describe what they are and how they can be interpreted in the context of language change?

[ʧ]		[k]	
he:ʧ	'like this'	he:k	'like this'
ʧe:f	'how'	ke:f	'how
ʧθi:r	'much, many'	kti:r	'much' many'
fi:ʧ	'in you (f)'	fi:k (m)	'in you (m)'
ʔabu:ʧ	'your (f) father'	ʔabu:k (m)	'your (m) father'
xalli:ʧ	'stay! remain! (f)'	xalli:k	'stay! remain! (m)'
ʃiʧel	'shape'	kull	'all'
kullha	'all of it (f)'	kullo	'all of it (m)'
jimʧin	'maybe'	ħuku:me	'government'
ʧilmithom	'their word'	kahraba	'electricity'
ʧilme	'word'	kundˤarˤa	'shoes'
ħa:liʧ	'yourself' (f)	ha:lak	'yourself' (m)
ʧbi:re	'large (f)'	hna:k	'there'
		jo:klu	'they eat'
		ʔakam	'how many'
		maʃa:kil	'problems'
		maʃkile	'problem'
		sakkir	'close!'
		biʕkis	'he reflects, shows'

2. Consider the following data from Amman (based on work in progress by Enam Al-Wer), which show change in real time in the conjugation of the verb *ʔakal* 'to eat' in the imperfective.

    a. Firstly, examine Graphs 1 and 2, bearing in mind the following background information:

   i. For 1st and 2nd persons, there are two competing forms: /oː/ vs /aː/, as in *btoːkol ~ btaːkol* 'she eats / you (sg.m.) eat'.

   ii. The forms with /a/ are the incoming (innovative) forms.

b. Secondly, examine Graph 3, which focusses on the 3rd person conjugations. Here, in addition to the /oː/ ~ /aː/ variation, there is variation in the presence or absence of a /j/ glide following the initial *b-* prefix, for example: *boːkol ~ baːkol ~ bjoːkol ~ bjaːkol* 'he eats'.

Your task is to write a commentary on these data. Make sure to comment on the progress of this change across the paradigm. How do you think the presence of four possible forms in the 3rd person complicates the picture?

Graph 1: 'AKAL 2014 in Amman

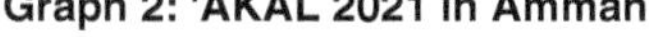

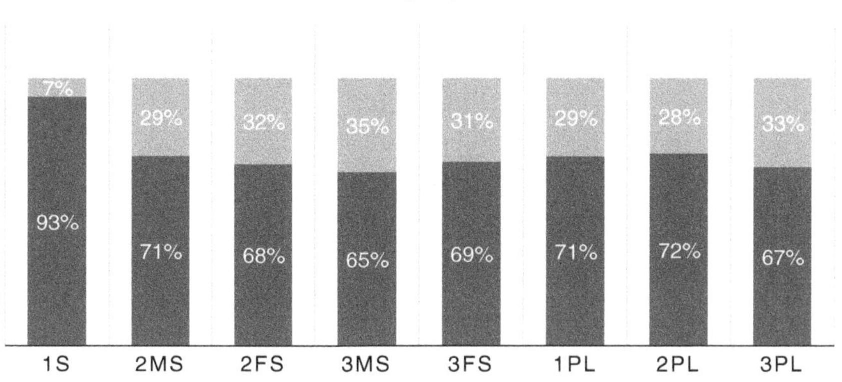

Graph 2: 'AKAL 2021 in Amman

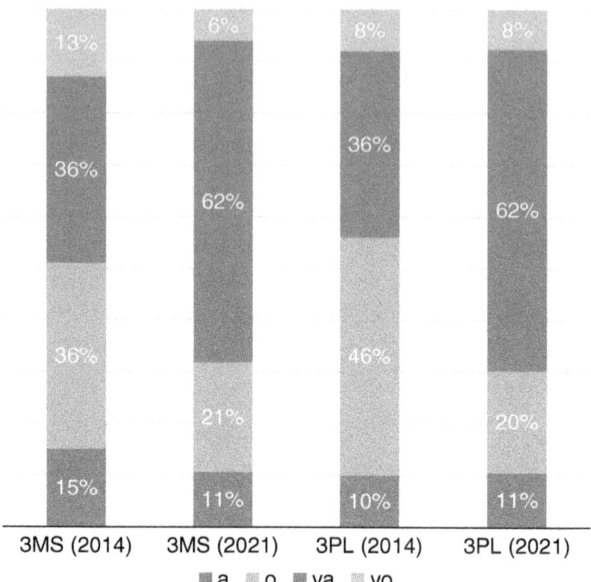

3. In the traditional dialect of Ha'il, Saudi Arabia, the feminine ending is realised as [ɛ]. Variation in this feature involves lowering of this traditional [ɛ] to the innovative [a], which for these speakers is a feature of the supralocal variety spoken in Riyadh. The table under (a) (based on AlAmmar 2017) provides the results of a quantitative analysis of this feature, displaying three social factors that were found to be statistically significant in the realisation of this feature. Based on these results, discuss the following points:

a. These data include speakers from three age groups, making it possible to examine the results from an apparent-time perspective. Do the data suggest that this feature is undergoing change in progress? Why do you think so?

Factor	N	%[a]
Age Young	686	56%
Middle	588	37%
Old	817	3%
Gender Female	981	29%
Male	1,110	31%

b. How can the cross-tabulation (see below) of age and gender refine our hypothesis about change in progress?

	Female	Male
Old	4%	2%
Middle	34%	39%
Young	59%	54%

8   Spatial Variation

8.1   Introduction

So far in this book we have been taking a close-up view of variation and change, focussing on inter-dialectal variation and the diffusion of linguistic change among speakers of the same dialect living in the same community. However, linguistic features do not necessarily remain within the boundaries of one dialect and one speech community but can break these boundaries and diffuse horizontally, spreading to other dialects and other geographical locations.

In this chapter we shall look at the effect of natural barriers on linguistic configuration and diffusion. We begin with an overview of some general observations about the relationship between linguistic differentiation and the physical environment.

8.2   Language and Geography

Language can vary in accordance with the physical environment. This is because geographical features, such as rivers, marshes, mountains, and valleys, can form natural barriers to communication. The more physical barriers there are between communities, the more likely it will be that the dialects or languages spoken on either side will develop in different ways, and innovations which occur in one dialect will be less likely to diffuse to the other. A good illustration of the effect of physical barriers on dialect differentiation in Arabic comes from the Sinai Peninsula in Egypt. De Jong (2000, 2011) shows that dialect classification into different groups in Sinai coincides with geological features of the landscape. In particular, he points to the role of the southern escarpment of the Tīh plateau. In Figure 8.1 (p. 170), an aerial photo of the Sinai Peninsula, the escarpment is clearly visible as the nearly horizontal boundary between the lighter and darker shades of grey. The dialects north of this escarpment share a significant number of linguistic features, such that they form one group of dialects. South of this escarpment, the dialects spoken are of distinct types (see Map 8.6). The escarpment is a clear geological

156

feature capable of preventing intensive dialect contact. Not all geological features are the same, however. Rivers, for instance, can often be crucial in enabling dialect contact (e.g. cross-river trade), as we discuss below. To the south of the escarpment in Sinai, there are clear examples of dialects which have typologically converged. One dramatic example is that of the tribe of Jbāliyya, who had arrived in the area as non-Arabic speakers in the sixth century from Wallachia (in the south of present-day Romania) to serve and protect St Catherine's Monastery. They developed similar characteristics of speech to those of the Arab tribes that settled in the area later, through regular face-to-face contact. The dialect of the Jbāliyya nowadays is very much like dialects spoken by their surrounding Bedouin neighbours. Speakers of the dialects to the north of the escarpment were historically in very limited contact with speakers of tribes to the south of it. We shall return to the Sinai case in Section 8.4.1.

Some natural geographical barriers hamper communication more seriously than others. Rugged mountain ranges, for instance, are normally more difficult to cross than rivers, and therefore people living on different sides of a mountainous terrain are unlikely to have frequent or regular interactions.[1] A very good example of this comes from the ʿAsīr province in the southwest of Saudi Arabia. This area was studied by Khairia Alqahtani (2015). The province comprises three kinds of topography:

1. The highlands, which include the rugged *al-Sarāh* mountains, rising up to 2,200 metres above sea level and extending into Yemen
2. Steep valleys
3. The Tihāma (lit. 'lowlands'), which lies along the plateau of the Red Sea coast down to the border with Yemen.

Owing to its isolation and difficult topography, this area has preserved a unique linguistic character, for instance a lateral realisation [ɮˤ] of the phoneme /dˤ/ and an archaic form of the definite article, which in the local dialect is *m-*, e.g. *m-ɮˤaif* 'the guest'. In the vast majority of Arabic dialects, these features do not exist. Rather, the realisation of /dˤ/ is typically either [dˤ] or [ðˤ], and the definite article is *l-*.

Furthermore, the effect of the topographical variation within the province, ranging from very high mountains to steep valleys and a coastal plateau, is manifested in the diffusion of modern innovations within the region. Alqahtani (2015) investigated the linguistic situation in two villages: al-Jawwa in the highlands (on a mountain slope, approximately 3,000 metres above sea level) and al-Farša in the lowlands, at the foot of the same mountain. The villages are a mere 31 km apart from each other and connected by a rugged mountainous

---

[1] See Chambers and Trudgill (1980, chapter 11); and Trudgill (2000, chapter 8).

road. Al-Jawwa is easily accessed via a fast road to Abha, the capital of the province and the nearest city, some 98 km away. These differences in location and accessibility have led to differences in the way each community adapts its dialect towards the general Saudi linguistic norm. The more isolated village, al-Farša, is slower in shifting from its traditional features to the ones more typical of the country as a whole. In other words, both villages have begun gradually adopting [ðˤ] as a realisation of /dˤ/ and *l-* as the definite article, but al-Jawwa has been doing so more rapidly than al-Farša. The ʿAsīr example provides evidence of how effective physical barriers can be in configuring the linguistic profile of regions as well as shaping ongoing linguistic developments, even over very short distances.

In many cases around the world, topographical boundaries and linguistic boundaries coincide, affecting not only dialects of the same language – as in the case of ʿAsīr – but also altogether distinct languages. In the Middle East and North Africa, we know of cases where Arabic is spoken alongside other languages. For instance, in Syria, where Arabic is the dominant language, there are individual communities that speak predominantly dialects of Neo-Aramaic, in mountainous areas in the Qalamūn. In Iraq, Iran, and Turkey, the Zagros mountain range forms a natural barrier between Kurdish, on the one hand, and Arabic, Persian, and Turkish, on the other. In North Africa, where several Amazigh (also known as Berber) languages are spoken alongside Arabic, there appears to be a tendency for these languages to be concentrated in mountainous areas (e.g. the Atlas Mountains in Morocco). Even in places where Amazigh languages are traditionally spoken in plains and valleys – such as the Sous Valley, in central Morocco – the adjacent mountainous areas are often more conservative regarding language maintenance, while the lower regions are more exposed to the influence of Arabic, as well as Arab culture more generally (see Hoffman 2007, esp. chapter 6).

Elsewhere in the world, this phenomenon can be exemplified by the linguistic situation in the French province of Alsace, which has remained German-speaking despite being part of France for most of its history since the seventeenth century. Dialect geographers believe that one of the main reasons that the province has historically survived as a German-speaking enclave is its geographical location. It is separated from the rest of France by the Vosges Mountains, which seem to have functioned as a barrier to communication with the French-speaking provinces on the western side. On the other hand, the River Rhine, which separates the province from Germany, has functioned as a channel of communication, facilitating contact with other German-speaking areas on the eastern side. In this case, we can consider the mountains to have functioned as a barrier, resulting in the geographical isolation of Alsace, thus preserving a peculiar linguistic character vis-à-vis the French-speaking localities to the west.

8.3 Linguistic Atlases: An Overview

Much of the data about geographical dialect differentiation come from research in dialectology and dialect geography, which goes back to the second half of the nineteenth century in Germany and France, where the first large-scale dialect surveys were carried out. Behnstedt and Woidich (2013) provide valuable information on the history and development of Arabic dialectology, which began to thrive in parallel to the dialectological scholarship in western Europe. The aim of traditional dialectology, according to Behnstedt and Woidich (2013: 301), is 'the collection of linguistic features in a given geographic area and the study of these features with regard to their distribution in this area in order to establish dialectal border lines, transitional areas, core areas, and dialectal continua'.

In dialectological surveys, the data gathered are first organised into separate tables containing all the forms recorded for each linguistic feature and the localities in which these forms were recorded. The content of each table is then plotted on a map of the region, and the boundary of each linguistic form is delimited with a line representing what is called an *isogloss*, or the border between different linguistic forms.

8.3.1 Bergsträsser's Atlas

The first linguistic atlas of an Arabic-speaking region was the *Sprachatlas von Syrien und Palästina* by Gotthelf Bergsträsser (1915). In this atlas, Bergsträsser covers areas that fall within the borders of four modern states: Syria, Lebanon, Jordan, and Palestine. Bergsträsser included data from sixty-eight primary locations, supplemented by thirty additional locations, based on previously studied areas. The atlas covers features that Bergsträsser identified as variable in the region's dialects. They are presented according to four levels of linguistic analysis: phonology, morphology, particles, and lexicon.

His treatment of the phonological level of analysis follows the standard method for dialect description by classifying the linguistic features under the following categories: consonants, vowels, syllables, and stress. This is followed by the morphology of pronouns, nouns, and verbs. His third category, which he calls 'particles', is divided into six sub-categories that include such things as verbal particles, negative particles, and prepositions.

The category devoted to lexicon is a complex one. It includes words whose stems derive from completely different roots across dialects, e.g. f.l.ħ. ~ ħ.r.θ. 'to plough', as well as words that exhibit differences in pronunciation, e.g. θoːr ~ tˤoːr 'bull', and other cases where the same root is used in all areas, but in different verbal templates. An example of this is tˤallaʕ (CaCCaC) ~ ʔatˤlaʕ (ʔaCCaC) ~ tˤailaʕ (CaiCaC) 'to take out, to make one leave'. We see, therefore, that for Bergsträsser, what counts as lexical variation overlaps in some cases with phonological and morphological variation.

While we are accustomed to talking about levels of linguistic analysis (phonology, morphology, syntax, lexicon, etc.) as if they are independent of one another, the reality of language variation is that these different levels overlap. Therefore, it is normal to find two dialects that differ in the pronunciation of specific sounds and at the same time use different lexemes for the same referent. This interaction between dialect geography and variationist sociolinguistics is what has led sociolinguists not to abandon the methods followed and the wisdom gained by the study of traditional dialectology. For instance, in their editorial foreword to the *Journal of Linguistic Geography*, William Labov and Dennis Preston note that lexical variation is quite often related to structural variation, and that the cartographic representation of lexical variation may very well be intertwined with what they call 'competing and complementary forms' (Labov and Preston 2013: 1).

8.3.2   Cantineau's Atlas

It was not until twenty-five years later that another dialect atlas of Arabic was published. Jean Cantineau produced his atlas (1940) entitled *Les parlers Arabes du Ḥōrân: Atlas* (The Arabic dialects of Horan: Atlas). Horan refers to the area, roughly from south of Damascus to the Balqāʾ region in central Jordan. The atlas itself covers selected locations in present-day Syria, Lebanon, and Jordan and deals with phonological and lexical variation in the region's dialects. In conjunction with the atlas, Cantineau also published an extensive grammar of Horani Arabic (1946).

8.3.3   Recent Atlases

Starting in 1985, several atlases were produced in projects led by two prominent scholars in Arabic dialectology, Manfred Woidich and Peter Behnstedt. These atlases covered Egypt (Behnstedt and Woidich 1985–1999), North-Yemen and adjacent areas (Behnstedt 1985; revised edition 2016), Syria (Arnold and Behnstedt 1993; Behnstedt 1997), and most recently, Palestine (Geva-Kleinberger and Behnstedt 2019). Additionally, Behnstedt and Woidich have published a four-volume lexical atlas of Arabic throughout the Arab world (2010–2021).

Another addition to the dialectal cartography of Arabic was made by Rudolf de Jong. His grammars of northern Sinai (2000) and central and southern Sinai (2011) include appendices comprising eighty-eight maps of the Sinai Peninsula, which provide a fine-grained account of many linguistic features that are variable across the region, as well as a final map that represents the classification of dialects in Sinai into eight groups.

8.4   Atlases as a Source of Data

8.4.1   *Dialectological Data*

Let us now look at samples of maps from these atlases. Map 8.1 comes from the oldest atlas (Bergsträsser 1915) and depicts the distribution of the variants of the phoneme /k/ in the dialects of the Levant. The first thing we should turn our attention to is the legend. In it we see that the author divides the pool of data into two main groups, namely *sedentary* (in German: Ansässige) and *Bedouin* (in German: Beduinen). In Arabic dialectology, the term *sedentary* refers to both rural and urban communities. *Bedouin* refers to communities whose dialects are akin to the Bedouin norm, regardless of current lifestyle.

Each one of these groups displays a number of possible variants. In the sedentary group, we see two such variants: *k* [k] and *č* [ʧ]. In the Bedouin group, there are three variants: the same two as for the sedentary group, in addition to *ts* [ts]. Consider the word /iħki/ 'speak!' (imperative). The three possible pronunciations reflected in this map are [iħki], [iħʧi], and [iħtsi]. Note that in each group the variants are numbered differently. Sedentary variants are marked with Roman numerals, and Bedouin ones are marked with capital letters. By dividing the data according to the type of dialects they represent (sedentary and Bedouin), the map provides some social information in addition to the linguistic components. This is essential for analysing the data from a sociolinguistic perspective; as we have seen in Chapters 2–6: variation in language is sensitive to both linguistic and social factors. We shall see later that other maps in other atlases occasionally provide even more information on the social make-up of the speakers in their samples (e.g. gender and religion).

Instead of the usual names of cities and villages on the map itself, each locality from which data were gathered is represented by a number. A key that lists which number corresponds to which village or city is provided in the commentary section of the atlas (not visible here). For example, in the key, the number 5 refers to Damascus, 15 to Jerusalem, and 66 to Beirut. The lines we see on the map are of two types, solid and dotted. We call these lines *isoglosses*, which, as mentioned previously, represent the geographical boundaries between areas with different manifestations of linguistic features. In the case of this particular map, the solid line represents linguistic boundaries (isoglosses) within the sedentary group, while the dotted line represents boundaries within the Bedouin group.

Let us try and read some information on this map. We immediately notice that the distribution is not simple. Thus, we find the two major variants, [k] and [ʧ], in all locations and used in both types of dialects. In the south, for instance, the pronunciation [k] is shared by both sedentary and Bedouin dialects. The former are marked by 'I', and the latter by 'A'. However, in the east,

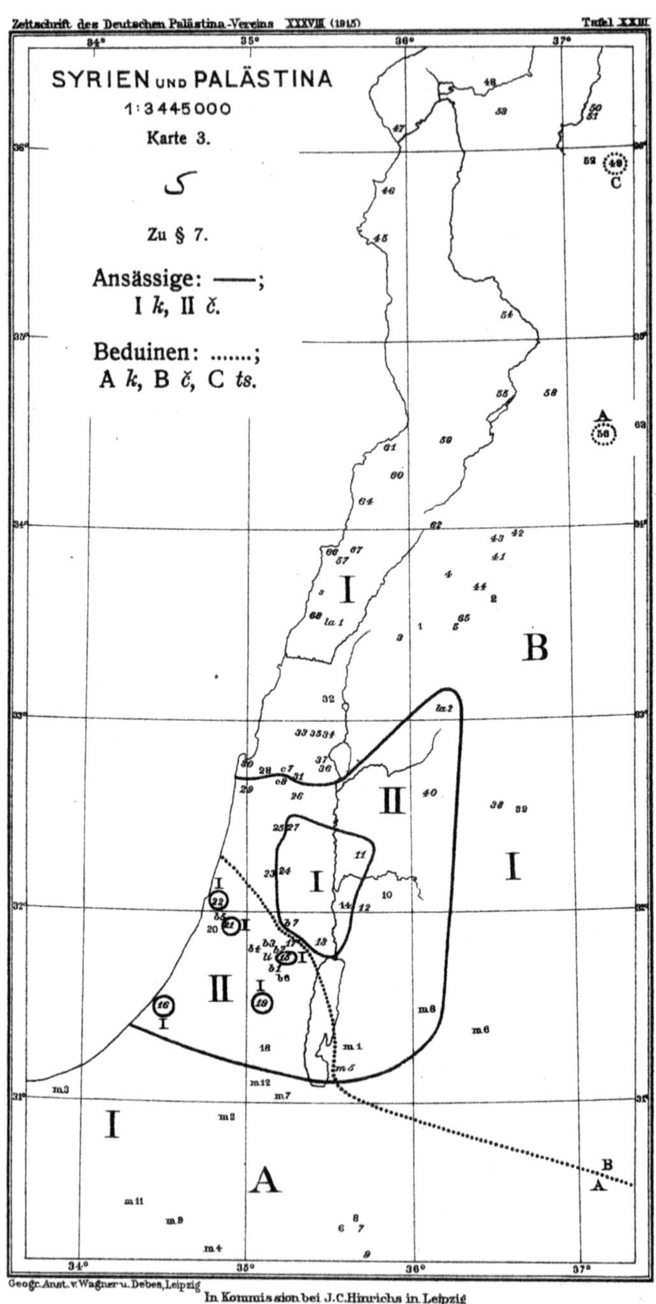

Map 8.1 Reflexes of /k/ (Bergsträsser 1915)

we see that the sedentary dialects have [k], marked on the map by 'I', while the Bedouin dialects have [ʧ], marked by 'B'. Regarding the isoglosses, we see on the map, the dotted line that divides the Bedouin group into 'A' and 'B' runs east to west, through the Jordanian town of Kerak (m5 on the map), and then northwest, just north of Jerusalem (15) and onwards to the Mediterranean shore, north of Jaffa (22). Note that there are two additional dotted lines, in the form of small circles surrounding locations 49 and 56, both of which are tribal territories in Syria.[2] In fact, location 49 is the only place on the map where the pronunciation [ts] is recorded (marked by 'C').

The isoglosses that divide the sedentary dialects – recall that this category includes both urban (city) and rural (village) dialects – are considerably more intricate: while sedentary dialects in most of the Levant are marked by 'I' – indicating a [k] variant for the phoneme /k/ – in the area that includes the western part of Jordan and the central and southern parts of Palestine, the more geographically widespread variant is [ʧ]. However, within this large 'box', delineated by a solid line and marked by 'II', we see a number of enclaves marked by 'I', indicating a [k] pronunciation. These include the Palestinian cities of Gaza (16), Jaffa (22), Jerusalem (15), and Ramle (21), as well as a larger enclave north of Jerusalem, which contains the Palestinian cities of Nablus, Jericho, and Jenin and the Jordanian village of Kufrenǧe.

Our second example, Map 8.2, is from a much newer atlas, that of North-Yemen and adjacent areas (viz., parts of southwest Saudi Arabia), originally published in 1985 by Peter Behnstedt and later revised and translated from German into English in 2016.

Map 8.2 shows variation in the use of lexical items equivalent to English 'money'. Rather than using lines to mark isoglosses, Behnstedt uses colours and shapes to mark the areas where each variant is used. Within each area marked by a coloured shading, the default word used for 'money' is the one that appears in the legend for that colour. For instance, for the area shaded in light grey, unless otherwise indicated, the word used is /zalatˤ/, but if on top of this shading there is a shape, such as the circle that stands for the word /guːʃ/, the specific location indicated by the shape differs from the norm in the region. The principle in Behnstedt's maps is the same as in Bergsträsser's; both authors provide an areal view of the distribution of the different forms of linguistic features, and highlight regional norms (be it through lines or shaded areas), as well as exceptions to the norms in individual communities. For example, in this map, we can describe /bjas/ (marked by dark grey shading) as the norm in the southwestern region and /zalatˤ/ (light grey shading) as the norm in and around Sanaa. The benefit of these systems of representing

---

[2] Bergsträsser identifies location 49 as (the tribe) ʿEneze, whereas location 56 is simply described as 'Bedouins of the region between Homs and Palmyra'.

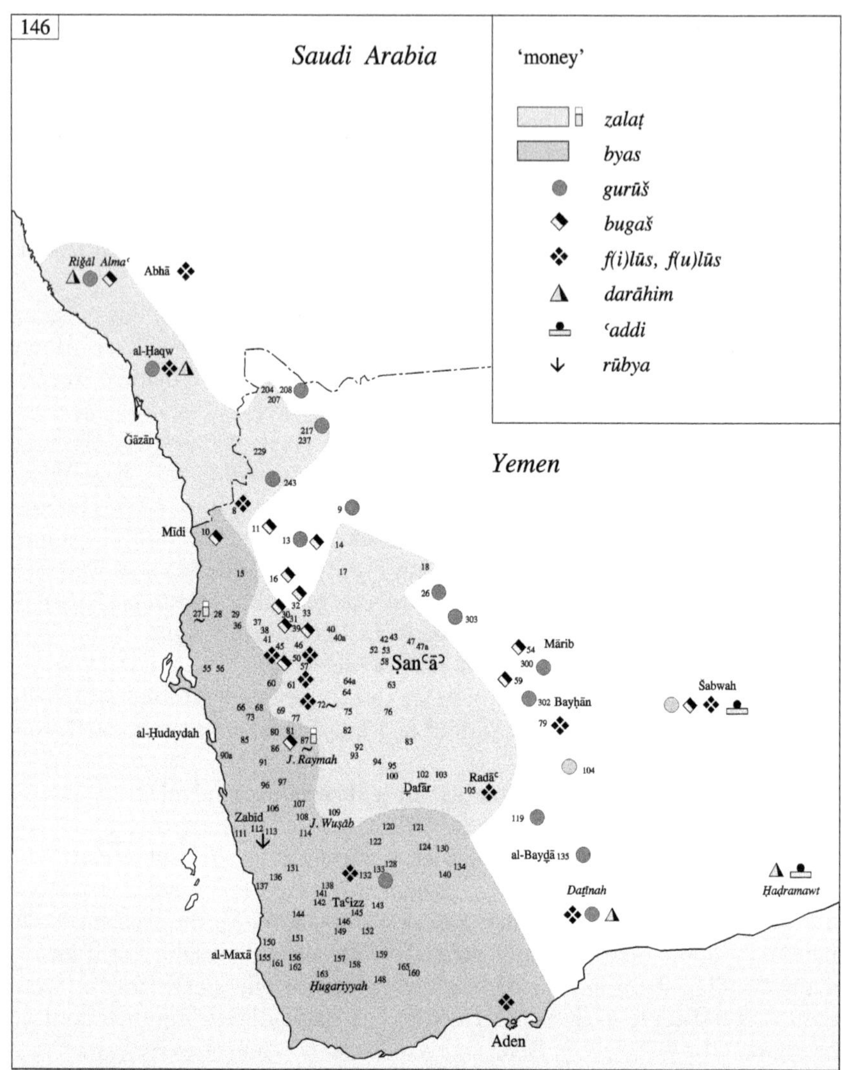

Map 8.2 Words for 'money' (Behnstedt 2016: 366)

regional distribution is that it allows us to identify patterns and norms, without losing sight of variability within.

Our third example comes from the work of Rudolf de Jong (2000, 2011, 2013). Recall that De Jong's work is first and foremost a very detailed grammar of the dialects spoken in different parts of the Sinai Peninsula in eastern Egypt. The very rich appendices at the end of both of his volumes (2000,

2011), as well as the maps in his 2013 article, serve as a crucial means of illustrating the areal distribution of linguistic features, as well as dialect groups. A novel aspect of De Jong's maps is the integration of the sociohistorical dimension into the linguistic generalisations represented in these maps.

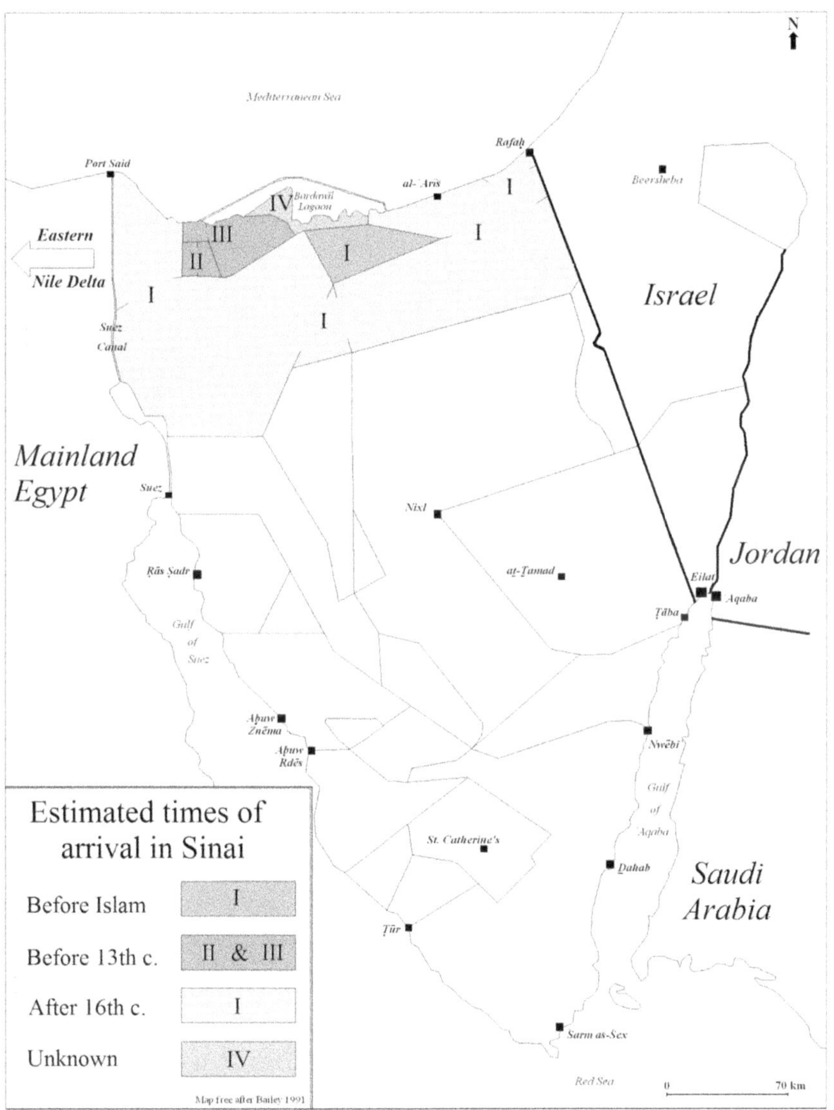

Map 8.3 Estimated dates of arrival of tribes in Sinai (De Jong 2013: 219)

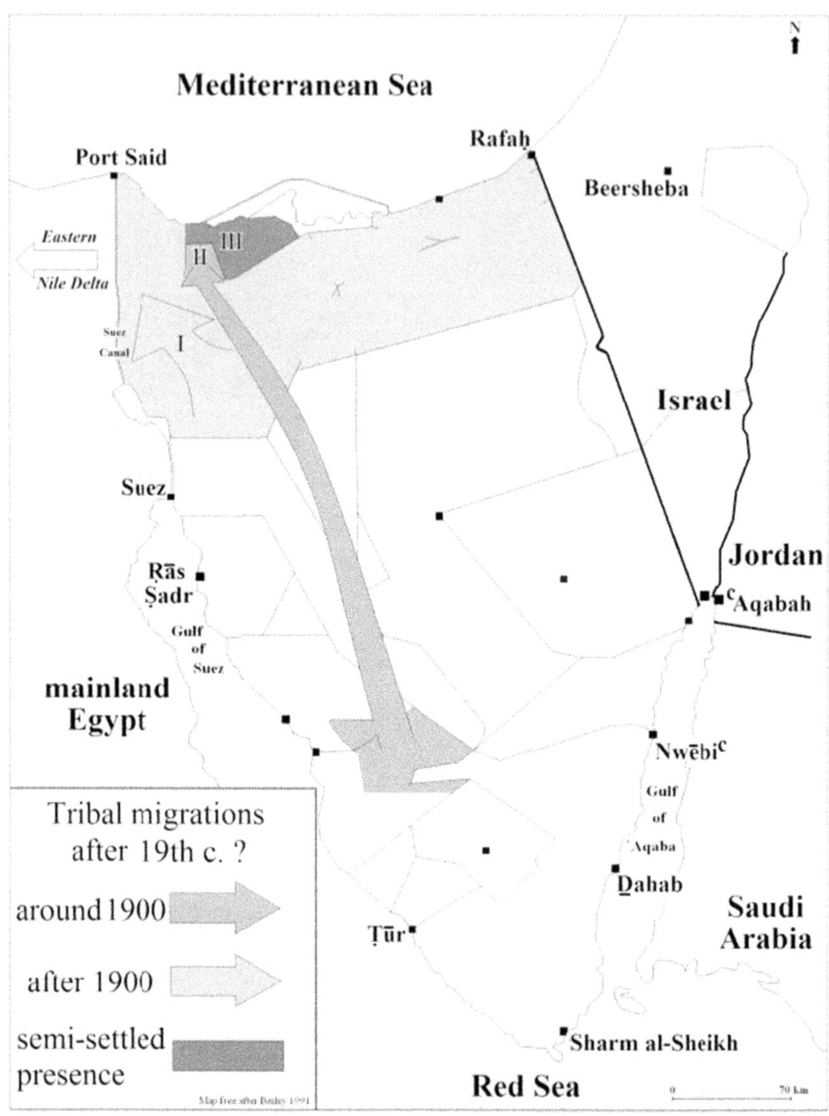

Map 8.4 Tribal migration in Sinai (De Jong 2013: 220)

Maps 8.3 and 8.4 set the stage historically by mapping the estimated times of arrival of the various Bedouin tribes to the northern portion of the Sinai Peninsula and their patterns of migration within the Peninsula. As we know, communities, in particular traditionally nomadic tribes, tend to move from place to place, but this does not mean that they abandon their social and linguistic behaviours. Rather, what can happen is that they leave linguistic traces in the places they inhabited formerly. Another potential outcome of nomadic settlement patterns is the acquisition of new linguistic patterns through contact with the communities in the new places of dwelling. A third, almost obvious, corollary of population mobility is that linguistic features are transported by the speakers to new places where they might not have existed before. These possibilities – linguistic traces, acquisition of new patterns, and transportation of linguistic features to new places – are not mutually exclusive. In other words, we can expect more than one of them to occur for any given community.

An interesting case encountered in Sinai involves the Samāʿna tribe, currently resident in the Gaṭyah oasis in the northwest Sinai littoral. De Jong (2011: 315–316) reports that in the older generation, a pronominal suffix for the 2nd person masculine singular is used, viz. -^{u}ḵ (ḵ here indicates a retracted [k]), which is not found amongst other groups in this region. This feature seems to have been acquired by members of the tribe prior to their migration in the late nineteenth and early twentieth centuries from Al-Ṭūr, in the southwest of Sinai, where this form is prevalent. The younger generation, while aware of the existence of the southern feature -^{u}ḵ amongst their elders, do not use it themselves. In their current location, the Samāʿna were exposed to the typical northern form -ak. This contact situation resulted in the emergence of an intermediate form -aḵ, which is used by the Samāʿna. In this example, we see a trace of the tribe's dialect in its original location, the retracted ḵ, combined with the morphological pattern they acquired in the new location, in which this suffix had an *a* vowel rather than a very short *u*. In Chapter 9 we will see that forms such as this are common in dialect contact situations.

These historical data, in conjunction with the comparison of almost a hundred linguistic features, have not only led to the identification of individual dialects across Sinai but also allowed the classification of the dialects of the Sinai Peninsula into eight distinct groups. These dialect groups and the internal divisions into dialects within each group are represented in Map 8.6.

8.4.2 *Atlases as a Resource for Sociolinguists*

Using linguistic atlases in contemporary sociolinguistics has been an important component in many foundational works in the field.[3] In this section, we shall highlight the value of dialectological atlas data for discerning linguistic variables that have prevailed for long periods of time and for tracing language change through time and space. We discuss the dialects of Horan as an example

---

[3] See, for instance, Labov's (1963) study of vowel centralisation in Martha's Vineyard and subsequent studies, e.g. Britain's work on the Fens in eastern England (Britain 2002, 2012).

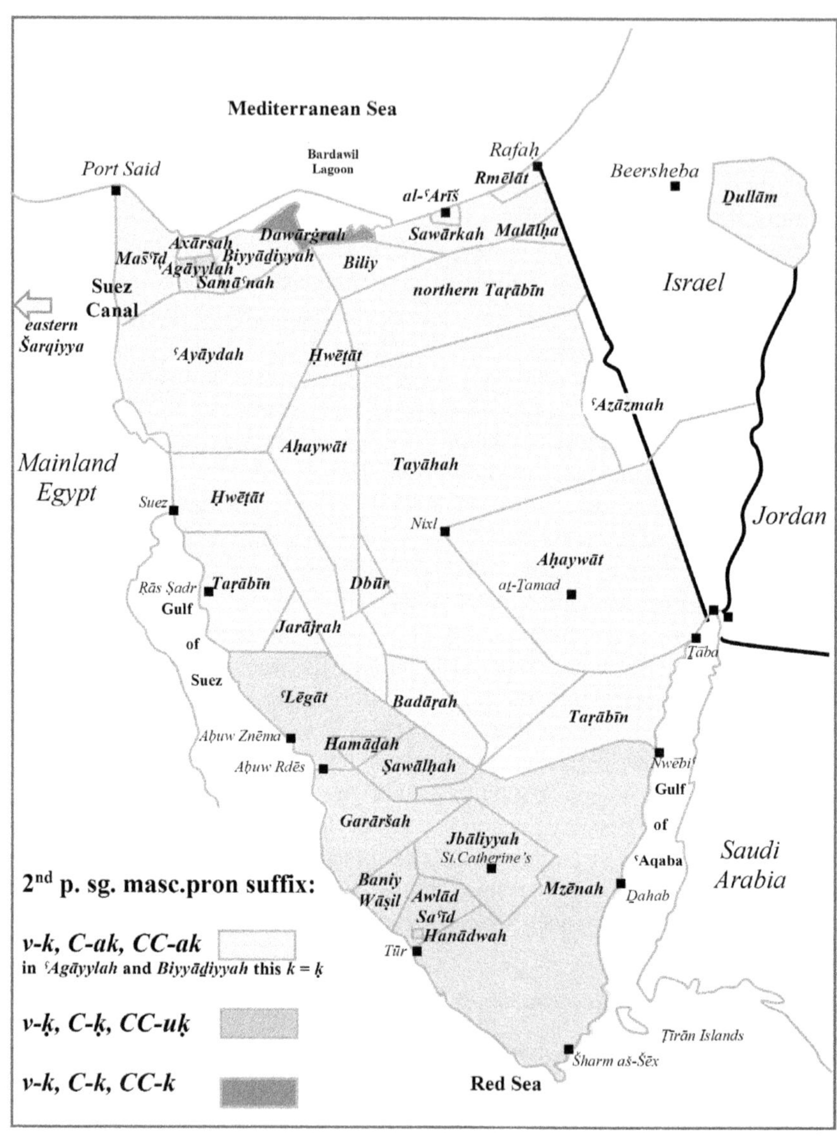

Map 8.5 Mixed forms in Sinai (based on De Jong 2011: 404, Map 36, courtesy of Michael A. Jones)

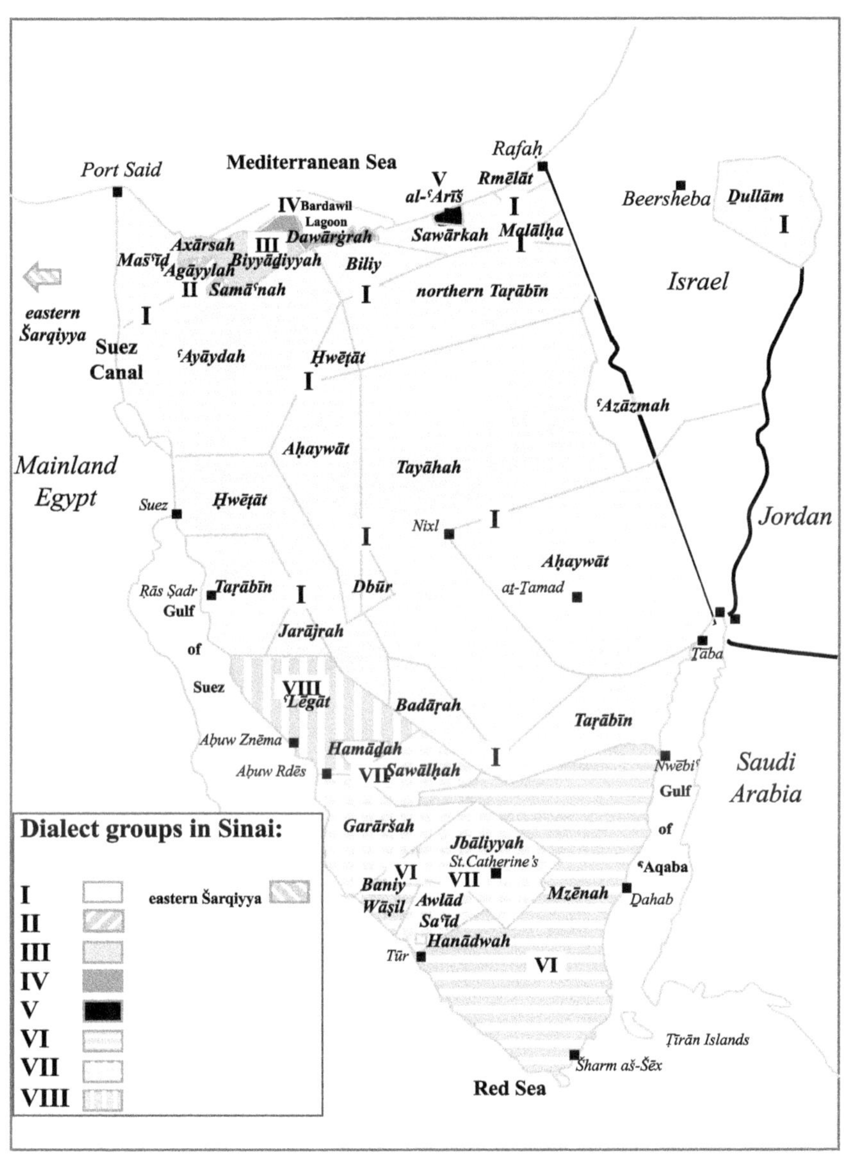

Map 8.6 Dialect groups in Sinai (based on De Jong 2011: 440, Map 88, courtesy of Michael A. Jones)

Figure 8.1 Aerial view of the Sinai Peninsula (Apollo 7 crew, 1968, Public domain, via Wikimedia Commons)

of dialect homogeneity due to the absence of physical barriers to communication, in contrast to the case of ʿAsīr, where the existence of such barriers resulted in different patterns of linguistic development in geographically adjacent areas (see Section 8.2).

The plains of Horan stretch from the outskirts of Damascus in Syria to central Jordan, roughly. These plains comprise a vast stretch of fertile volcanic land approximately 200 km long (north to south) and 100 km wide (east to west). They sit at an altitude of approximately 600 metres above sea level, with elevations at Jabal al-Druze rising up to 1,803 metres and in Jaydur up to 1,096 metres. They are home to hundreds of historically agrarian communities whose basic social structure is tribal. Until the second decade of the twentieth century, Horan had been an uninterrupted swath of land. The division of the Fertile

Crescent by the British and French colonial powers in the aftermath of World War I led to Horan being split between two countries. The splitting of the Horan region between Syria and Jordan has also split several of the largest local tribes, and thus we find the same clans on both sides of the border. In other words, members of some communities have become Syrian citizens while others have become Jordanian citizens. Their political identity has therefore been altered such that their national loyalties have become divergent. These divergent loyalties were apparent particularly during political and military tensions between Syria and Jordan. Later we will see the effect of this redrawing of political borders on linguistic developments in the region. For now, let us look at examples that demonstrate the relatively high degree of homogeneity – due to lack of physical barriers – across the dialects of the Horan plains.

For information on Horani dialects, we are fortunate to have detailed linguistic maps from 1940 and a grammar from 1946 by Jean Cantineau. We shall look at the distribution of a few phonological features throughout the region.

Map 8.7 provides a good example of a Horani feature, which is almost uniform, regardless of the political division. It concerns the realisation of the phoneme /l/ in words such as /baɣla/ 'mule'. In Horan, the traditional

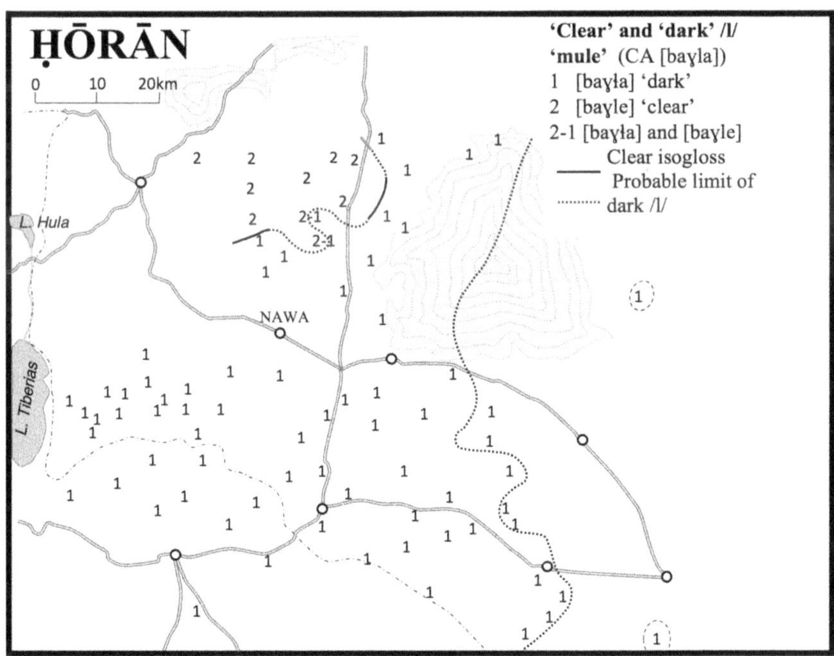

Map 8.7 Clear and dark /l/ in Horan (based on Cantineau 1940, courtesy of Michael A. Jones)

pronunciation includes an emphaticised variant of /l/, viz. [ł] (also known as 'dark /l/'). As we see on the map, this pronunciation, [bayła], is consistent in all of the localities that were surveyed on both the Jordanian and Syrian sides, with the exception of localities at the periphery of Horan, in the north, nearer to Damascus (whose dialect does not have the emphatic variant).

Map 8.8, which shows the distribution of the phoneme /ʤ/, displays what we might now, eighty years later, interpret as an incipient change. As in Map 8.7, here, too, we see a uniform pronunciation of this phoneme, as an affricate [ʤ], in the whole of Horan ('1' on the map). We also see enclaves where this phoneme is realised as a fricative [ʒ] ('2' on the map), in the word /ʃaʤara/ 'tree'. Cantineau (1946: 104–106) commented on this pronunciation, saying that the affricate pronunciation [ʤ] is the norm throughout Horan. He further explains that the fricative [ʒ] pronunciation, which is a hallmark of prestigious urbanite speech in the Syro-Palestinian region as a whole, particularly in Damascus and Beirut, and among the Druze population, was sometimes used by particular informants. The primary example Cantineau cites is from a Horani speaker who had studied in Beirut and pronounced several words

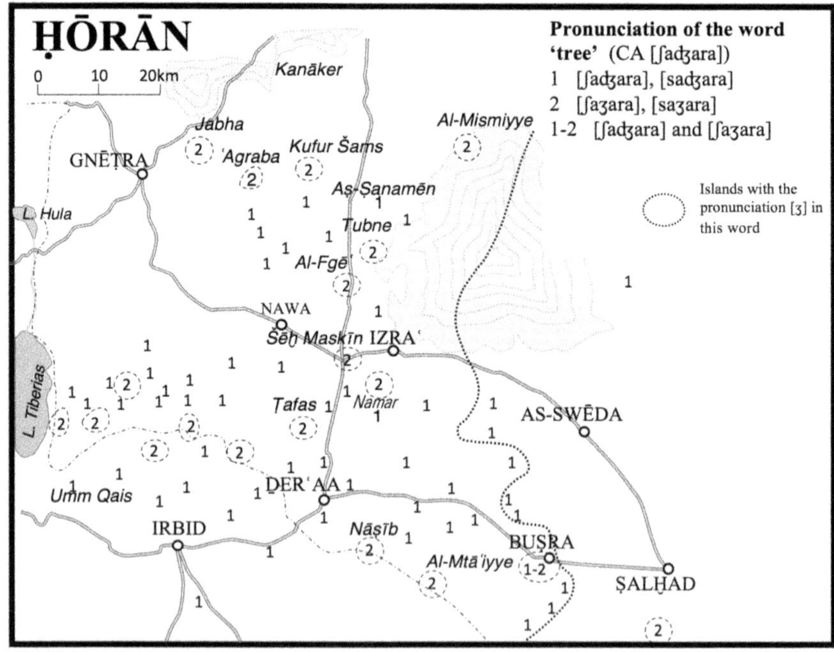

Map 8.8 Reflexes of /ʤ/ in Horan (based on Cantineau 1940, courtesy of Michael A, Jones)

with [ʒ]. Yet even this speaker was aware that other speakers in the region would pronounce the same words with [dʒ], which he considers rural. Further, Cantineau names a number of villages in the periphery of Horan, nearer to Damascus, where both pronunciations are used.

The maps presented so far are only two examples of relative linguistic uniformity across Horan. This is probably related to Horan being a continuous area, consisting mostly of a series of connected plains. This kind of topography is conducive to linguistic homogeneity, as it lacks physical barriers that may hamper communication. This is further supported by the fact that we often find in Cantineau's atlas that dialects spoken in elevated areas, mountains as well as higher plateaus, differ from the norms prevalent in the core of the Horan plains. One such example is Jabal al-Druze 'mountain of the Druze' (known officially as Jabal al-Arab 'mountain of the Arabs'), which contains several peaks, ranging in altitude from 1,138 to 1,803 metres. This region is the traditional home of the Druze community, and their unique social, religious and ethnic make-up is probably another contributing factor to some of the dialectal differences between speakers in this area and the rest of Horan (see Chapter 6). Cantineau's atlas includes many more examples, not only of phonological features but also of morphological and lexical ones.

Recall that in the aftermath of the First World War, Horan was divided between what later became two separate countries, namely Jordan and Syria. Turning to the linguistic effects of this political division, in some cases, members of a single tribe became citizens of two different countries, such as the Zuʿbi tribe of Derʿaa in Syria and Ramtha in Jordan. Apparent signs of divergence can be gleaned from Cantineau's atlas. Map 8.9 deals with the affrication of /k/ in the word /kitəf/ 'shoulder'. As in many other dialects in the Levant and elsewhere, this phoneme can be realised as an affricate [ʧ]. In this map we notice that the affricate variant in this word is almost confined to the Jordanian side of the border, while the prevailing pronunciation on the Syrian side is a velar stop [k], which is also the norm in Damascus. It is quite possible that what Cantineau's map captures here is a natural pattern of change in the direction of an urban dialect, that of Damascus. This pattern of change in the direction of dialects whose speakers are models of modernity and prosperity is widespread cross-linguistically. Subsequently, the isogloss seen on this map that separates the two forms in the southwest and straddles the political border does not necessarily mean that the Horani dialects are diverging because of this political separation. Rather, it may be interpreted to suggest that, along the border, some communities have adopted the change in the direction of the speech of Damascus, while others remained unaffected.

Research over the past four decades in various Horani localities on the Jordanian side has shown radically different patterns of linguistic development

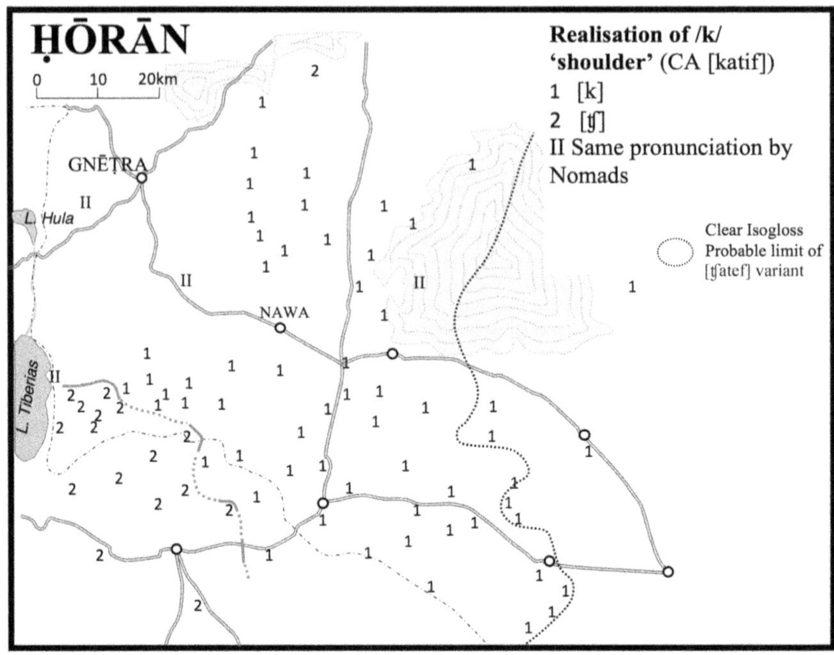

Map 8.9 Reflexes of /k/ in Horan (based on Cantineau 1940, courtesy of
Michael A. Jones)

compared to Cantineau's data (which were collected in the 1930s). For
instance, Map 8.9 shows invariant affrication of /k/ in the word /kitəf/ in and
around the Jordanian town of Ajloun, whereas data collected by Enam Al-Wer
in 1987 in Ajloun and its surroundings, confirm that affrication of /k/ was not
consistent (Al-Wer 1991). Additional data reported by Areej Al-Hawamdeh in
2016 in the town of Sūf, roughly in the same region, provide definitive evidence that this feature is undergoing a change in progress towards the non-
affricated variant [k]. In this case, we should note that the more recent changes
in Jordanian Horani dialects, *happen* to resemble the changes in Syrian Horan
documented in 1940. However, in interpreting this process in northern Jordan
we must note that in the intervening years, a new dialect has developed in the
Jordanian capital Amman, in which affrication does not occur at all. Therefore,
the change in these Jordanian communities should be understood as a result
of alignment with a new local standard – that of Amman. The totality of the
results of research in Jordanian Horan confirms very clearly that other features
as well are changing in the direction of the Ammani dialect. In other words,
younger Horani generations – especially from Irbid, the largest city in the
north, in the heart of Jordanian Horan – increasingly sound like Ammanis.

Unfortunately, we do not have comparable data stemming from contemporary research in Syrian Horani dialects. It is nonetheless noticeable, even by lay people in the region, that the younger generations of Syrian Horani speakers gradually adopt features of the Damascene dialect and that their speech increasingly sounds like that of speakers from Damascus itself. There is therefore evidence that a hundred years on from political separation, the dialects of Horan in Syria and Jordan are diverging and hence becoming more distinguishable from each other.

We thus see that human intervention in physical space can alter the linguistic profile of a region. In the case of Horan, the imposition of a political border seems to have had similar effects to that of natural, physical barriers, such as mountains and valleys. There is, in fact, a physical element in many political borders. This can be seen in cases where the border crossing has a physical presence in the form of buildings, military personnel, and administrative procedures at the border. These may pose psychological as well as practical impositions on the community, thus reducing the frequency of face-to-face interaction between people on opposite sides of the border. It is not implausible to assume that even without severe physical obstacles, the mere political division creates new environments, which, in successive generations, become real or imagined realities. These new realities inevitably affect linguistic configurations through the gradual abandonment of linguistic features distinctive of the original grouping and their replacement with features typical of the new communities to which they have been assigned.

In essence, the conditions that can lead to the creation of differences between dialects across a newly created political border, such as the one imposed in Horan, often lead to the emergence of social dialects, or *sociolects*, too. What we mean by this is the existence of differences within the same dialect that are due to speakers belonging to different socio-economic classes, ethnicities, and religious groups. In Chapters 4 and 5, we made the point that patterns of social interaction can create and perpetuate linguistic differentiation along socio-economic lines. People with similar socio-economic characteristics tend to communicate more frequently with one another than with members of other social strata. The same can be true of speakers belonging to different ethnic or religious groups. What this means is that frequency and patterns of social interaction contribute to the configuration of sociolinguistic variation.

8.5 Waterways as Carriers of Linguistic Features

In Section 8.2, we mentioned the case of the Alsace province as a German-speaking enclave within France and the role of the River Rhine as a channel of communication that helped preserve the linguistic profile of the province.

The effect of the Rhine as a means of transporting linguistic features and innovations can be further demonstrated with reference to the linguistic border between the two main types of German dialects: those that descend from Low German (*Plattdeutsch*) – spoken in northern Germany and the eastern part of the Netherlands – and those that descend from High German (*Hochdeutsch*), which are spoken for the most part in the central and southern regions of Germany as well as in Austria and Switzerland. The linguistic border between the two types of dialects is marked by a bundle of isoglosses that run across east and west Germany and the Netherlands. The isoglosses delimiting Low and High German varieties are more or less regular all along the route until they hit the Rhine. At this location, the isoglosses separate out into what is known as 'the Rhenish Fan', such that southern features can be found north of the isogloss and vice versa. The common explanation for this is that the Rhine, as a waterway, facilitated communication between speakers south and north of the isogloss, and through this line of communication southern features slowly moved northwards along the river.[4]

For Arabic, we have an excellent illustration of the effect of waterways as trade routes on the geographical configuration of linguistic features from the Nile Delta in Egypt. North of Cairo, the Nile divides into two main branches, the Rosetta to the west (*Rashid*) and the Damietta (*Dumyat*) to the east. The river branches have been used as trade routes linking the Nile Valley with the Mediterranean throughout ancient and modern times, but during the Middle Ages the town of Damietta on the Mediterranean became Egypt's main port of trade with the Levant. This important mediaeval trade route has resulted in the emergence of a bundle of linguistic features, covering phonology, morphology, and lexis, which are shared between the dialects spoken along the eastern side of the Delta in opposition to the dialects spoken further east and west. The dialect atlas of Egypt (Behnstedt and Woidich 1985) shows that many of these features originated from the major urban settlement of Cairo and from there they diffused to all of the settlements up to and including Damietta on the Mediterranean coast. Map 8.10 shows the distribution of the two most salient features that diffused from Cairo along this route: reflexes of /q/ and reflexes of /dʒ/.

The shaded area on the map shows a concentration of dialects that use the Cairo forms [ʔ] for /q/ and [g] for /dʒ/ on the eastern side and all along this trade route up to the port, whereas the dialects further east have different forms ([g] for /q/ and [dʒ] for /dʒ/). That the Damietta route was key to the diffusion of innovations from Cairo is supported by the fact that the locations along the

---

⁴ For further details about the Rhenish Fan, see Petyt (1980) and Chambers and Trudgill (1980, chapter 7).

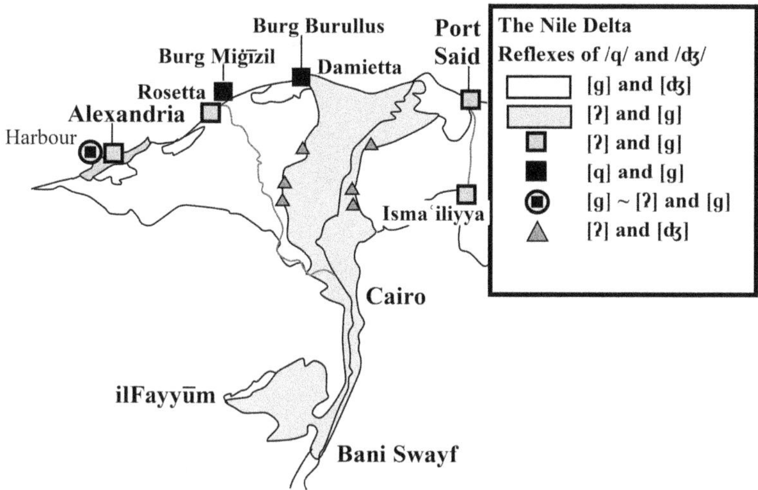

Map 8.10 Distribution of reflexes of /q/ and /dʒ/ in the Nile Delta (based on Behnstedt and Woidich 1985, maps 15 and 34, courtesy of Peter Behnstedt and Michael A. Jones)

western branch, the Rosetta, have not been affected by the Cairo forms even though many of them are considerably closer to the focal area (Cairo).

In addition to functioning as a facilitator of communication and thus as a route and mechanism for the diffusion of the Cairo innovations, the Damietta waterway seems to have functioned as a barrier to the encroachment of linguistic features arriving with a second wave of migration of Arabic-speaking Bedouin tribes into Egypt during the twelfth century from Sinai and Palestine in the east and during the thirteenth century from the Maghreb. Map 8.11 clarifies this point.

As illustrated by the white area on Map 8.11, the Cairo–Damietta trade route created a corridor along the eastern side of the Delta, which has fended off linguistic incursions from both sides. For instance, the second wave of migration of Bedouin tribes during the twelfth and thirteenth centuries consisted of dialects that had [g] for /q/ and [dʒ] for /dʒ/; these features were established and became characteristic of the majority of the dialects in adjacent areas but failed to diffuse to the dialects along the trade route (which have [ʔ] for /q/ and [g] for /dʒ/; see Map 8.10). Furthermore, the settlements along the trade route became increasingly similar in social structure and lifestyle through urbanisation, which seems to have consolidated the status of their dialects.

It is also interesting to note that linguistic borders can coincide with aspects of human geography and cultural practices. For example, in discussing another isogloss in the Nile Valley, Woidich (1996) points out that south

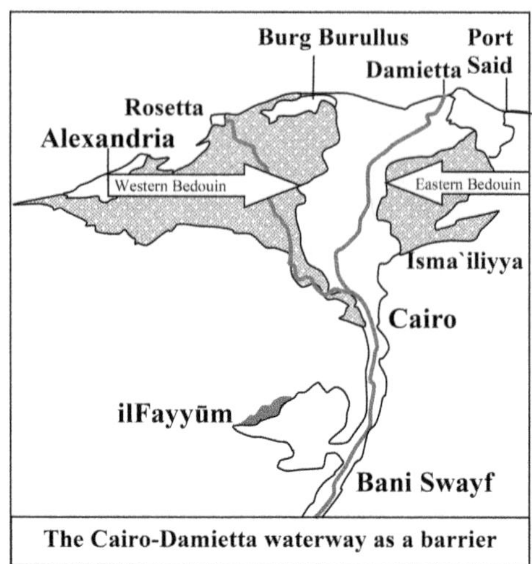

Map 8.11 The Cairo-Damietta route as a barrier (based on Behnstedt and Woidich 2005: 158, map 70, courtesy of Michael A. Jones)

of this isogloss, ovens are bell-shaped whereas on the northern side they are cube-shaped. Similarly, in the south, bread is loaf-shaped, and in the north, bread is unleavened; in the south the pitchfork is two-pronged whereas it is five-pronged in the north.

In the cases reviewed above we saw that increased contact leads to convergence: in Alsace convergence is seen through maintenance of the linguistic habits of the people (the German-speaking populations to the east) with whom a channel of communication (the Rhine) was available. In the Rhine Valley and the Nile Delta, the waterways were shown to be conduits for facilitating access to linguistic targets and thus the dialects ended up sharing a larger number of linguistic features (i.e. they converged). The other side of the coin is that geographical isolation and the absence of means of communication, and thus contact, result in the emergence of *linguistic enclaves* and *relic areas* in which archaic linguistic features survive as *relic features* (see Chapter 9) .

8.6   Focal and Relic Areas

Dialectologists make a distinction between *focal* and *relic* areas. Geographically, focal areas tend to be located centrally and are often urban centres characterised by cultural diversity and lively economic activity. Such areas are hubs of linguistic innovation. Capital cities such as Amman in Jordan and Beirut in Lebanon, as well as other financially and culturally significant cities, such as Casablanca in

Morocco and Jeddah in Saudi Arabia, function as focal areas. Relic areas, on the other hand, tend to be isolated, either geographically or socially, such as the area of southern Arabia discussed above.

In this section, we shall elaborate on both types of areas through detailed discussions of several prominent focal and relic areas.

8.6.1   *Focal Areas*

In Arab countries, the dialects of capital cities or, more generally, large metropolitan centres often assume the status of standard varieties. In Egypt, for instance, the dialect of Cairo, which is used throughout the country, is a standard variety, as summarised by Manfred Woidich:

Cairene, which is often equated with 'Egyptian Arabic', is only one of numerous Egyptian dialects, albeit the most important. It assumes to all intents and purposes the status of a standard language. It is also spoken by the middle and upper classes outside of Cairo. It plays a significant role in radio and television, such that the need for Standard Arabic becomes restricted to reading the news bulletins and commenting on specific topics in the domains of religion and politics. Nowhere in the Arab world is the dialect of the capital as prominent as it is in Egypt.

(Woidich 2006: 1)[5]

In Morocco, a number of important developments have altered the social significance of the country's main urban centres. In particular, the vast and rapid expansion of the city of Casablanca has had significant sociolinguistic ramifications. Research focussing on the capital Rabat and on Casablanca, the largest city in the country, has shed light on the emergence of the latter as a linguistic focal area, beginning in the mid-twentieth century. Unlike Rabat, Casablanca did not grow organically as the metropolis that it is today, but rather its expansion was intentionally planned by the French colonial power (in the first half of the twentieth century) and involved mass migration from the countryside as well as from other cities. Research by Atiqa Hachimi includes a detailed analysis of migrants who came to Casablanca from Fez, an old traditional city, which for centuries served as the capital of Morocco and had a unique dialect often associated with its old urban elite. Hachimi argues that these developments in Casablanca led to the 'disruption of the rural/urban dichotomy that once dominated Moroccan dialects and identities' (Hachimi 2007: 97).

Rabat, the current capital, was also home to a traditional urban dialect. Leila Messaoudi, in her research, analyses the transition from this old traditional urban dialect into a koineised variety, which resembles that of Casablanca. Messaoudi's findings present further evidence of the increasing consolidation of Casablanca as a focal area. The Moroccan case shows that sociolinguistic

---

[5] Translated from German by the authors.

processes respond to social and economic changes. It also demonstrates that the attributes 'rural' and 'urban', which are widely used in Arabic sociolinguistics, are merely labels, devoid of explanatory value. Such terms do not always connote the same social meaning, nor do they correspond uniformly to specific linguistic features. For example, the phoneme /q/ is variable in several Arabic dialects. Among its variants are [q], [g], and [ʔ], which are often stereotyped as 'rural', 'Bedouin', and 'urban', respectively. While such labels may be convenient for the purpose of classifying dialects and describing their genealogies, we must be careful how we use them in sociolinguistic analysis. The social evaluation of each of these realisations varies from community to community and may change over time. Thus we find that while [q] is dominant in Tunisia and associated with urbanity (e.g. in the capital Tunis), it is generally marginal and recessive in the Levant, bearing an association with minority sectarian groups. In Morocco, [ʔ] is stigmatised, despite its association with the traditional elite community of Fez, whereas it is the dominant and prestigious variant in Egypt and the Levant. The realisation [g] is gaining ground in new city dialects in Morocco despite its rural origin within Morocco. The same realisation, [g], is losing ground in other regions, for instance in Jordan's city dialects (e.g. Amman, Irbid, and Salt), among women particularly.

Research over the last decade in various locations in Saudi Arabia has uncovered patterns of koineisation that suggest that there are two distinctive norms that influence linguistic developments in their respective regions. In the western region, the dialect of Jeddah, to all intents and purposes, functions as a standard variety. In the central region, there is anecdotal evidence that Riyadh, the capital, is emerging as a focal area, and its dialect is becoming a standard variety.

8.6.2   *Relic Areas and Language Islands*

Relic areas are typically located on the periphery or in geographically remote and inaccessible (e.g. mountainous) regions. These areas preserve old or archaic linguistic forms because they are generally immune to influence from the outside by virtue of their geographical location. As mentioned in Section 8.2, in the mountains of the southwest corner of the Arabian Peninsula, archaic linguistic features of Arabic survive, some of which are even thought to have been preserved for millennia.

A specific type of area that we can call relic is represented by language varieties that for historical reasons became isolated. Such areas are commonly referred to by dialectologists as language islands (from the German *Sprachinseln*). There are numerous examples of language islands where Arabic is spoken in areas detached from majority Arabic-speaking communities. The list includes (but is not limited to) the varieties of Arabic spoken in parts of

Central Asia (e.g. Uzbekistan and Afghanistan), sub-Saharan Africa (e.g. Nigeria and Chad), and the Mediterranean islands of Malta, Cyprus, and Sicily. Language islands typically preserve older forms of the language in question owing to their isolation from developments in the mainstream varieties of the language. At the same time, they may diverge further from the mainstream varieties as a result of contact with other languages.

Maltese is a good example of a variety of Arabic that for centuries has remained isolated from the contiguous Arabic-speaking region. As such, it was not influenced by changes that affected mainland Arabic dialects, but rather developed independently. These independent developments were also possible in Maltese, given the absence of any role for Standard Arabic in the lives of the Maltese community. Having escaped the ramifications of the presence of a superimposed standard, Maltese itself was free to undergo natural standardisation and codification as an official language in its own right. Part of this freedom was also manifest in the incorporation of extensive borrowings, from Italian in particular, due to prolonged contact with the nearby island of Sicily, as well as through Catholicism, the religion of the vast majority of the Maltese population.

Maltese and North African varieties of Arabic are spoken in relatively close geographical proximity to one another and share several core features. These similarities have prompted many scholars to suggest that Maltese itself is typologically a variety of North African Arabic, while some research also acknowledges the presence of a number of eastern Arabic features in Maltese.

Over the centuries, Maltese has diverged from other varieties of Arabic. At the same time, we must remember that other dialects of Arabic have also continued to undergo changes. Some of these changes have been contact-induced (e.g. contact between Egyptian Arabic and Coptic, or between Levantine varieties of Arabic and Aramaic). Other changes were internal within each dialect (e.g. affrication of velar stops in the environment of front vowels in Najdi dialects). We can thus view this situation as one in which the non-isolated ('mainstream') dialects of Arabic are the ones that diverged, while varieties such as Maltese have, in fact, retained certain archaic forms.

Maltese is one of very few Arabic varieties in which a relic of the old Semitic verb /raʔa/ 'to see' is preserved. In most other dialects, both eastern and western, a form of the verb /ʃaːf/ is used in this meaning (see Ferguson 1959). In Maltese, the bare form (perfective 3rd person masculine singular) is /ra/ 'to see', and it inflects for all tenses, persons, numbers, and the two genders. Table 8.1 represents the paradigm for this verb.[6]

---

[6] The authors wish to thank Maris Camilleri for providing this table and additional information about Maltese.

Table 8.1 *Paradigm of /ra/ 'to see' in Maltese (provided by Maris Camilleri)*

Perfective	
1sg	rajt
2sg	rajt
3sgm	ra
3sgf	rat
1pl	rajna
2pl	rajtu
3pl	raw
Imperfective	
1sg	nara
2sg	tara
3sgm	jara
3sgf	tara
1pl	naraw
2pl	taraw
3pl	jaraw

In addition to maintaining the use of forms which have become obsolete in other Arabic dialects, Maltese has undergone several internal structural changes that increased the gap between Maltese and other varieties of Arabic. As an example, in Table 8.2 we consider the paradigm for the verb <qagħad> /ʔaːd/ 'to stay, endure, fit', in both Standard Maltese and in the local dialect of Mosta. What we see is that the pharyngeal segment /ʕ/ (written in Maltese with the grapheme <għ>) is deleted, a process that has applied across the board in Maltese, with the exception of a few dialects. In some persons in the imperfective, the deletion of /ʕ/ is accompanied by lengthening of the following vowel, e.g. noʔoːd (< noʔʕod). This compensatory lengthening of the vowel applies across the board in the standard variety, whereas a further development in the dialect of Mosta results in deletion of the vowel in the plural forms, e.g. noʔdu (< noʔʕodu).

In addition to the loss of the pharyngeal consonant /ʕ/ in standard Maltese, the uvular fricative /ɣ/ has also been lost. The standard writing system of Maltese shows traces of these two phonemes. They are both represented by the combination <għ>, probably indicating that prior to them being lost from the phonemic inventory, there was a period of time during which they were merged. By contrast, several sounds that do not occur regularly in Arabic varieties have been added to the Maltese inventory. Among these are /p/ and /v/, which entered Maltese through extensive borrowings from Italian, e.g. /ponn/ 'fist' (Italian *pugno*), /veːra/ 'true (f)' (Italian *vera*).

Table 8.2 *Paradigm of <qagħad> 'to stay, endure, fit' in Maltese (provided by Maris Camilleri)*

Morphosyntactic features	Standard Maltese	Mosti dialect	Maltese Orthography
Perfective			
1sg	/ʔadt/	/ʔadt/	qgħadt
2sg	/ʔadt/	/ʔadt/	qgħadt
3sgm	/ʔaːd/	/ʔaːd/	qagħad
3sgf	/ʔaːdet/	/ʔaːdet/	qagħdet
1pl	/ʔadna/	/ʔadna/	qgħadna
2pl	/ʔadtu/	/ʔadtu/	qgħadtu
3pl	/ʔaːdu/	/ʔaːdu/	qagħdu
Imperfective			
1sg	/noʔoːd/	/noʔoːd/	noqgħod
2sg	/toʔoːd/	/toʔoːd/	toqgħod
3sgm	/joʔoːd/	/joʔoːd/	joqgħod
3sgf	/toʔoːd/	/toʔoːd/	toqgħod
1pl	/noʔoːdu/	/noʔdu/	noqogħdu
2pl	/toʔoːdu/	/toʔdu/	toqogħdu
3pl	/joʔoːdu/	/joʔdu/	joqogħdu

Additional processes in Maltese include the merger of the emphatic consonants with their plain counterparts (e.g. $s^ˤ > s$, $t^ˤ > t$) and a rather complex process of partial neutralisation of the distinction between /x/, /ħ/, and /h/. For example, /saːr/ 'he became' (Arabic /sˤaːr/), /aːbt/ 'underarm' (Arabic /ʔibtˤ/), /haredʒ/ 'he went out' (Arabic /xaradʒ/), /wiːhed/ 'one (m)' (Arabic /waːħid/).[7]

Malta includes two main populated islands: Malta and Gozo. Some 90 per cent of the population live on the island of Malta, which is where Standard Maltese as well as several local dialects are spoken. The island of Gozo may be described as a relic area within Malta. Some of its dialects preserve the Arabic sounds [ɣ] and [h], which in Standard Maltese have been dropped or merged with other sounds (Mifsud 2008; Trimble 1971).

The other reason that relic areas diverge over time from dialects spoken in the core areas is that they often come in contact with a different set of languages. As mentioned above, Maltese has maintained prolonged contact with Italian leading to extensive borrowing of lexical items, which has led to permanent structural changes as well.

Cypriot Arabic is another example of an Arabic dialect that has developed in isolation from other dialects. Its presence in Cyprus dates back to the seventh

---

[7] These examples are from Borg (1997).

century and is currently spoken by approximately 1,300 speakers, mostly in the village of Kormakiti in northern Cyprus. All of the current speakers are at least bilingual in this variety of Arabic and Cypriot Greek (some also speak Turkish). The community most probably came originally from Lebanon. They follow the Christian Maronite order, and their language is therefore often referred to as Maronite Cypriot Arabic. Similar to Maltese, Standard Arabic never had an influence on the development of Cypriot Arabic. Unlike Maltese, however, it does not enjoy the status of a national language, is not standardised or written, and is considered to be an endangered language. Since the admission of Cyprus to the European Union, there have been measures taken to protect Maronite Cypriot Arabic as a minority language of Europe.

The influence of Cypriot Greek on this variety of Arabic is evident in phonology, morphology, and syntax, as well as lexicon. At the same time, it preserves relic features of Levantine Arabic. Some of these features are no longer attested in any other dialect in the Levant, and some have traces in speech communities in the region, which have also experienced some degree of isolation. As an example of the latter, we may consider the possessive marker /ʃait/ (or /ʃat/). This particle is reported to have been widespread in the Levant (e.g. in Damascus), but its use nowadays seems to be restricted. Data collected in the city of Salt in Jordan include a few instances of /ʃeːt/ in the speech of very old speakers, which indicates that the particle might have been more widely used in the dialects of the region but has become almost obsolete. By contrast, in a number of Palestinian cities, e.g. Jaffa and Ramle, the particle /ʃeːt/ is the default analytic genitive marker, while elsewhere in Palestine and the Levant in general, the genitive particles used are /tabaʕ/ and /taːʕ/. The interesting aspect of this distribution in the Levant is that /ʃeːt/ (and its derivatives) are in active use only in areas which have been isolated by the political turmoil in the region. The parts of historical Palestine where these forms are still commonly used have been cut off from the rest of the Arab world by the colonisation of Palestine by Israel in 1948. Both the Palestinian case and the Cypriot case illustrate how speech communities that, by different means, have become isolated from their historical linguistic habitat can preserve relic features.

The influence of Cypriot Greek on Maronite Cypriot Arabic is quite significant and extends to all linguistic levels. In phonology, the influence of Cypriot Greek results in the elimination of Arabic sounds that do not occur in Cypriot Greek, e.g. the emphatics. It also leads to convergence towards Cypriot Greek by carrying over phonotactic constraints from Cypriot Greek to Cypriot Arabic. A good example of such a process is the epenthetic /k/ in the Cypriot Arabic words /apkjað/ 'white' (< Arabic /ʔabjadˤ/) and /θkjep/ 'clothes' (< Arabic /θjaːb/) (see Borg 1997: 224).

Additionally, a number of original Arabic sounds have lost their phonemic status in Cypriot Arabic and now only exist as allophones. Consider these examples (from Borg 1997: 228): Levantine Arabic /tuːte/ 'mulberry tree' and /duːde/ 'worm' are both rendered in Cypriot Arabic as /tute/, illustrating that Arabic /t/ and /d/ have merged in Cypriot Arabic as /t/. Similarly, Levantine Arabic /daːr/ 'he turned around' and /tˤaːr/ 'he flew' are /tar/. In this example, we notice that the emphatic /tˤ/ has also merged with /t/. What in Levantine and most other varieties of Arabic was a three-way distinction, d–t–tˤ is a single phoneme in Cypriot Arabic. Note that the phoneme /t/ is voiced to [d] in certain environments, e.g. [indi] for /inti/ 'you (sg.f.)'. This means that the sound [d] does exist in Cypriot Arabic, albeit not as a separate phoneme, while [tˤ] has disappeared completely, as have the rest of the Arabic emphatics.

Among the several syntactic influences of Cypriot Greek on Cypriot Arabic we find the basic structure of the noun phrase. In mainstream Arabic, the phrase meaning 'the big house' has the structure DEF-NOUN DEF-ADJ:

(1)   l-   bajt   li-   kbiːr   (Levantine Arabic)
          DEF-   house   DEF-   big
          'the big house'

The Cypriot Arabic equivalent would be DEF ADJ NOUN:

(2)   li   kbir   páit
          DEF   big   house
          'the big house'

For comparison, the Cypriot Greek phrase would be *to meálo spítin*, which is identical in its structure to the Cypriot Arabic phrase in (2) (Newton 1964: 47–48).

The cases of Maltese and Cypriot Arabic are examples of varieties of Arabic that have existed in isolation for a long time. They demonstrate a general tendency often cited by linguists for such varieties to preserve older features of the dialect family from which they originate. We can think of parallel examples from the modern era that would be expected to produce a similar outcome, such as Arabic spoken by migrant groups in Europe and North and South America. While most of the available research has focussed on the widespread phenomenon of code-switching, a promising area for future research would be the examination of structural features in the Arabic spoken by such communities in comparison with their parent dialects. Indeed, Peter Trudgill, among many other scholars, has shown that isolated varieties tend to be 'more conservative linguistically than the parent variety' (1986: 130).

8.7   Arabic-Based Creoles

Arabic-based creoles are an object of study that involves Arabic in contact with other languages, but one which is usually investigated within the discipline of creole linguistics, rather than within mainstream sociolinguistics.

Creoles, in general, represent the most dramatic possible outcome of language contact, namely the emergence of totally new languages. The creoles which have been documented and analysed emerged as a direct result of various contact situations around the world, to serve the need for a common language of communication.[8] Many creoles are based on the languages of colonial nations, e.g. Tok Pisin (English-based, in Papua New Guinea), Cape Verdean Creole (Portuguese-based, in Cape Verde), and Haitian Creole (French-based, in Haiti). The structure of creole languages typically includes lexical elements from the language of the colonisers (lexifier languages) and grammatical features from the native languages of the colonised or enslaved peoples. Creoles are natural human languages, which emerged under rather unusual social and historical circumstances (see Trudgill 2000, chapter 9).

The best-known Arabic-based creoles emerged in Africa and include Juba Arabic in South Sudan, and Nubi in Uganda and Kenya. According to Owens (1997), these two creoles emerged within just over one generation of the expulsion of the Egyptian rule in the region, in the second half of the nineteenth century. Their formation occurred in 'a social milieu where native speakers of Arabic constituted no more than 10–25% of the total population' (Owens 1997: 136). These creoles exhibit several similarities, representing features inherited from the original Arabic varieties of Sudan.

Below are examples from Arabic-based creoles:

(3)   *ána kélim le íta* 'I speak to you'
       (Juba Arabic, from Manfredi and Bizri 2019)

(4)   *úwo fí le ána* 'he is at my house' (lit. 'he exists at me')
       (Juba Arabic, from Owens 2001)

(5)   *'ina gi 'katifu* 'we are writing'

(6)   *'itakum gi 'katifu* 'you (pl.) are writing'

(7)   *'umwon gi 'katifu* 'they are writing'
       (Examples 5–7 are from Nubi Creole Arabic, Owens 2001)

We notice that the lexical material is derived from Arabic, thus in Juba, *kélim* comes from the Arabic root k.l.m. 'to speak', and in Nubi, *'katifu* from Arabic k.t.b. 'to write'. However, the grammar is distinct from that of Arabic. We see that the verb form is invariant for all persons and numbers, and, typically for a creole language, a particle (here *gi*) is used to express verbal aspect (here PROG). Person and number are marked by independent pronouns, which, too, are derived from the Arabic pronouns, e.g. in Juba *ána* (from Arabic *'ana*) 'I', and in Nubi *'ina* (from Arabic *'iḥna*) 'we'.

---

[8] For detailed definitions and analysis of creole languages, see Holm (2000).

For detailed information about Arabic-based creoles, the reader is referred to Owens (1997), Tosco and Manfredi (2013), and Manfredi and Bizri (2019).

8.8   Further Reading

Behnstedt and Woidich (2013) – This chapter in *The Oxford Handbook of Arabic Linguistics* surveys the history and development of Arabic dialectology and the contribution of this sub-discipline to the understanding of Arabic linguistics more generally.

Britain (2009, 2012) – In these two articles, the author reviews and critiques the use of labels such as 'rural' and 'urban' in dialectology and sociolinguistics, with particular attention to Arabic in the 2009 article.

Camilleri (2019) – This chapter in *The Routledge Handbook of Arabic Sociolinguistics* presents an innovative approach to the contextualisation of Maltese within the western group of Arabic dialects, without losing sight of connections between Maltese and eastern varieties of Arabic as well. Camilleri's is the first account of the connection between Maltese and other varieties of Arabic on a morphosyntactic basis.

Chambers and Trudgill (1998) – This is the second edition of the authors' classic 1980 textbook *Dialectology*, which in fact can serve as a foundational text also for many of the issues that are of interest to variationist sociolinguists.

Manfredi and Tosco (2014) – This is a special issue of *Journal of Pidgin and Creole Languages* devoted to Arabic-based pidgins and creoles. It includes, among others, articles by Jonathan Owens on East African Nubi and by Catherine Miller on written Juba Arabic.

Trudgill (2000) – This is a classic introduction to sociolinguistics. Many of its chapters cover topics dealt with in the current book. Chapter 8 is dedicated to language and geography.

8.9   Exercises for Chapter 8

1. Having studied the importance of considering social factors in the analysis of both variation and change, what do you think are the benefits and the limitations of using dialectological materials (such as atlases and dialect descriptions) for sociolinguistic research?

2. Think of your own country or region. Identify areas that can be described (linguistically) as focal and relic areas. Investigate the circumstances (geographical, historical, social, political, etc.) that led them to acquire these statuses. What are the criteria you might use to make this decision?

3. To what extent do you think the terms 'rural', 'urban', and 'Bedouin', which are commonplace in the dialectological literature, can be useful in sociolinguistic research? How can they be used without losing sight of the social dynamics that occur in the community and drive language change?

9   Contact and Diffusion

9.1   Introduction

We need to remind ourselves that linguistic features spread from place to place through the agency of speakers. When we say that a feature A diffuses from area X to another area Y, what we mean is that people who live in area Y come to adopt the feature A which is typical of the speakers in area X. This means that spatial diffusion and geographical configuration of linguistic features are ultimately determined by contact and patterns of interaction between speakers. In turn, opportunities and frequency of contact are continually manipulated by human agency; for instance through construction of roads and railways, building of new towns, reclamation and habitation of formerly uninhabitable land, etc. Therefore, contact between speakers is the basic mechanism via which linguistic diffusion from place to place occurs. Furthermore, linguistic features can undergo changes along their journey and arrive at their destination in modified or different forms.

In this chapter we discuss additional types of contact-induced phenomena, the models used in linguistics to represent processes of diffusion, and the principles that govern them.

9.2   Regional Standards

The diffusion of linguistic forms and innovations from focal areas to neighbouring or more distant locations can create what is called a *regional standard*, i.e. a linguistic norm that characterises the speech of a whole region. This process typically happens in the following way. Linguistic forms characteristic of the dialect spoken in the focal area (normally the largest city in the region) or innovations that originated in the focal area are adopted by speakers in nearby towns. Provided enough speakers adopt the incoming forms and use them frequently, over time the new forms replace the local traditional forms; i.e. the local forms are levelled out. Levelling-out of localised features is one form of linguistic *koineisation*. For regional standards to emerge, koineisation does not necessarily have to result in total replacement of all local features, but if enough features diffuse from the focal area to replace the most localised and most traditional forms in the neighbouring dialects, the focal area and its surroundings end up sharing many linguistic features. To outsiders, different dialects in the same region may sound indistinguishable although local residents are normally able to distinguish between the local dialects even if the salient local features have been levelled out.

For instance, a major division in Arabic dialectology is that between the eastern (*Mashreqi*) dialects spoken from the Nile Valley eastwards and the western (*Maghrebi*) dialects in most of North Africa. Laypersons are typically aware of this division and able to identify dialects within this broad classification. Noticeably, however, while speakers are able to identify finer differences between dialects within their own region, they are often unable to identify such differences among dialects outside their region. For example, a layperson from Jordan will be able to tell that a speaker's dialect is of the Maghrebi group but not specify which dialect exactly (e.g. Moroccan versus Algerian). The same holds true the other way around: a Moroccan layperson is likely to identify a Levantine speaker but not to pinpoint their specific dialect within that group (e.g. Syrian versus Palestinian).

Regional standards can also develop across political borders, provided contact between speakers in the different countries is frequent enough and is not hampered. In other words, linguistic innovations do not only diffuse from place to place within the same country but can also transcend political boundaries. In some parts of the Middle East, diffusion across political borders has resulted in large-scale regional koineisation[1]. In the Levant region, a well-established dimension of dialectal differentiation is based on urban versus rural communities. It is common to find cities whose dialects are completely different from the dialects spoken in a village just a few miles away. For example, the Arabic dialect of the city of Jerusalem differs at every level from the traditional dialects of all of the villages which surround it (e.g. Silwan, Bet Safafa, Al-Malha), even though the city and the countryside dialects all descend from the same type of Arabic dialects (the sedentary type).

Most probably, the divide between urban and rural dialects emerged as a result of the social distance commonly created among communities who lead different lifestyles, which has acted as a barrier to linguistic convergence between the urban and rural dialects. Some 70 km to the north of Jerusalem is the city of Nablus whose traditional dialect has undergone a total sound shift in the pronunciation of /q/, from the old pronunciation [q] to the new form [ʔ] which is the pronunciation found in the dialect of Jerusalem (see

---

[1] Many Middle Eastern countries became separate political entities only in the twentieth century, and contact between the populations in different countries has been interrupted on many occasions by the political upheavals in various parts of the region (see Section 8.4.2).

Section 9.6.2). As a result of this shift ([q] > [ʔ]), the dialect of Nablus became identical in its consonantal inventory (i.e. its system of consonants) to the dialect of Jerusalem and all other city dialects in the Levant region as a whole. Similarly, the dialects of Bethlehem and Ramallah, two Palestinian cities that border Jerusalem, which are known to be rural in origin, have also been transitioning towards the urban norm typical of Jerusalem.[2] In recent decades, and probably accelerated by the Oslo Accords of 1993, all three cities – Jerusalem, Bethlehem, and Ramallah – have expanded, creating a contiguous urban sprawl. In fact, any rural communities that existed on the outskirts of these cities have been pretty much diluted.

In the city of Amman, which has no traditional dialect but where a new dialect has recently been formed, the consonantal features of this new dialect are now identical to those found in Jerusalem, Damascus, and Beirut. In the Gulf region, dialectologists and sociolinguists working on various aspects of dialectal changes in the region have found that some linguistic features are changing in the same direction in different countries, e.g. [ʤ] > [j] and gender neutralisation in the 2nd and 3rd person verbal and nominal endings, which has led to the conclusion that a Gulf-wide koine (i.e. a shared norm) is emerging.

9.3   Diffusion across the Language Barrier

Linguistic features can also transcend the language barrier by diffusing from one language to a different language spoken in a neighbouring country. A well-known case is the diffusion of uvular /r/, [ʁ], apparently from Parisian French, to dialects of German, Dutch, and the Scandinavian languages. The diffusion of uvular /r/ seems to have followed a pattern whereby it appears in cities first and from there it diffuses to other locations within each country.[3] We shall return to this point, namely, the importance of urban centres as focal areas of linguistic diffusion, in later sections.

The long history of Arabic being spoken outside its original geographical base has led over the centuries to various types of contact between Arabic and other languages. In numerous cases, Arabic became a mother tongue for populations that had been speakers of other languages. In such cases, we often find linguistic influence of the language spoken formerly on the new language, which we call *substrate* influence. Substrate influence is a type of transfer of linguistic features from one language to another. Examples of substrate

---

[2] See Seeger (2013) for a detailed description of the original rural dialect spoken in and around Ramallah.

[3] A detailed account of the history of uvular /r/ in French can be found in Haden (1955). Further details about the geographical diffusion of this feature in European languages can be found in Chambers and Trudgill (1998: 170–175).

languages that have had this kind of effect on Arabic are Aramaic, Amazigh, and Coptic, as they are the main languages that were spoken in the Levant, North Africa, and Egypt, respectively, prior to the spread of Arabic. We will shortly cite examples of substrate influences on some Arabic varieties.

In the sections to follow, we shall focus on the effect of other languages on Arabic varieties. The effect in the opposite direction, viz. of Arabic on other languages, spans many centuries and includes a diverse range of languages. The two primary vehicles of transmission in this direction are military conquests and the spread of Islam. The most obvious linguistic effect that Arabic has had on these languages is the incorporation of multiple Arabic lexical items into languages such as Persian, Turkish, Spanish, and several languages of South Asia. Some languages have also adopted modified versions of the Arabic script, e.g., Persian, Ottoman Turkish, Urdu, and Uyghur. As far as Arabic is concerned, these are macro-sociolinguistic issues that deserve treatment in their own right.

9.4   Borrowing and Substrate Effects

Some of the languages with which Arabic has been in contact belong, like Arabic itself, to the Semitic language family, while others belong to different families. Each of the next two subsections will be devoted to a different region where Arabic has been in contact with other languages. We first illustrate these substrate phenomena with examples from Arabic–Aramaic contact in the east Mediterranean, and later we turn to Amazigh and its role as a substrate language in North Africa.

9.4.1   *The Levant: Aramaic as a Substrate Language*

Within Semitic, Arabic has been in contact with Aramaic for at least two and a half millennia. In many cases, similarities between Arabic varieties and varieties of Aramaic are due to inherited features from their parent languages, e.g. certain similarities in the sound system. Other cases of shared features between the two languages are attributable to their long-term co-territorial existence in a relatively small area. This has led to widespread bilingualism, the primary mechanism through which features diffuse from one language to another. The outcome of the contact between Aramaic and Arabic has resulted in almost seamless borrowing of vocabulary items and structural features. For instance, in some parts of the Levant, where Aramaic used to be the dominant language but is now confined to small pockets, mainly in Syria and Lebanon, the local dialects contain numerous such Aramaic features. Retsö (2006) provides a long list of lexical items borrowed from Aramaic into the Arabic dialects of these areas. We shall only provide a small sample of these. As an example, we cite the Levantine Arabic word for 'heat' (referring specifically to hot weather), /ʃawb/ (or /ʃoːb/), from Aramaic /ʃawba/ 'summer heat'. The Levantine dialects also derive verbal forms such as /ʃawwab/ 'he got hot', /ʃawwabat/ 'she got hot' or 'the weather got hot', and the participle /mʃawwib/ 'he is feeling hot'. Arabic dialects outside this area generally use derivations of /ħaːrr/ or /ħamm/ 'hot'.

A second interesting example is the root /n.tˤ.r./, which in Aramaic means 'to guard'. All Levantine dialects use the derived agentive noun /naːtˤuːr/ to mean 'guard'. Additionally, several Levantine dialects, e.g. Lebanese, have borrowed this Aramaic root to derive the verb /natˤar/ 'to wait (for someone)'. Other varieties of Arabic have the derivation /ʔintaðˤar/ 'to wait', which is cognate with Aramaic /natˤar/. However, in Levantine Arabic it is only the Aramaic-derived form /natˤar/ that is used to mean 'to wait'. Similarly, the Levantine verb /ʃalaħ/ 'he undressed' has been borrowed from Aramaic /ʃlaħ/, 'take off clothes', and it is used in this meaning in all Levantine dialects. The original Aramaic verb also means 'lay aside'. Some Levantine Arabic dialects have also incorporated this meaning in the root /ʃ.l.ħ./, e.g. *ʃlaħ-o həniːk* 'chuck it there'. The Aramaic root /ʃ.l.ħ./ represents the following sound correspondences: Arabic /s/ ↔ Aramaic /ʃ/ and Arabic /x/ ↔ Aramaic /ħ/. We thus also find the Arabic root /s.l.x./ 'to pull off.' This root survives in Levantine dialects in the verb /salax/ to mean specifically 'to skin an animal' but not to mean 'take off clothes'. Both the use of the Aramaic corresponding sounds and the meaning derived from the Aramaic form are evidence that this root was borrowed into Arabic from Aramaic, rather than being a shared form inherited by both Arabic and Aramaic from a parent language.

The next two cases will illustrate what appears to be substrate influence from Aramaic on the *structure* of Arabic dialects of the Levant and Iraq. These dialects have a history of contact with Aramaic, which in this region – known as the Fertile Crescent – continued to be spoken as a majority language well into the fourteenth century.[4]

Our first structural example comes from morphology. Arabic uses pronominal suffixes to augment both nouns (for possession) and verbs (to refer to objects). These suffixes inflect for number, gender, and person. Some Arabic dialects distinguish between feminine and masculine genders in the plural, while others do not. Where gender distinction exists, the feminine usually ends with /n/, while the masculine ends with /m/. Most Arabic dialects that do not have a gender distinction in the plural use /m/ for all plural forms. The following are a few examples to illustrate these patterns.

---

[4] See Versteegh (2014: 127) and Arnold and Behnstedt (1993: 92). It must be emphasised that Arabic, too, was spoken in the Fertile Crescent before the arrival of Islam.

(1)   Syrian Horan
       a.   be:t-kum 'your (m.pl) house'
       b.   be:t-kin 'your (f.pl) house'
       c.   be:t-hum 'their (m) house'
       d.   be:t-hin 'their (f) house'

(2)   Amman
       a.   be:t-kum 'your (pl) house'
       b.   be:t-hum 'their house'

What we see in some dialects in the Levant that are known to have had an Aramaic substrate is the use of /n/ suffixes to mark the plural, regardless of gender.

(3)   Damascus
       a.   be:t-kon 'your (pl) house'
       b.   be:t-hon 'their house'

There is some controversy as to the origin of the /n/ forms in dialects such as that of Damascus.[5] Scholars who subscribe to the Aramaic influence on Levantine dialects base their thesis on the fact that the Syriac (the historic local dialect of Aramaic) suffixes end in /n/. Consider the examples in (4).

(4)   Syriac (Aramaic)[6]
       a.   di:n-ko:n 'your (m.pl) judgement'
       b.   di:n-ke:n 'your (f.pl) judgement'
       c.   di:n-ho:n 'their (m) judgement'
       d.   di:n-he:n 'their (f) judgement'

As we see, Syriac (4) has /n/ for all plural suffixes, similar to Damascus Arabic (3). We also notice that the Damascus common form is derived from the Syriac masculine form, as it has /o:/ rather than /e:/. This pattern of neutralising gender distinction in the plural forms towards the masculine form is common throughout the Levant. We see this happening in Jordanian cities such as Salt, Irbid, and Kerak, where the gender distinction maintained in the traditional dialects is neutralised from -*ku* (m.pl) and -*kin* (f.pl) to gender-neutral -*ku*.

Aramaic has two syntactic structures that seem to have diffused into the Arabic dialects of the Levant. Both structures are often referred to by linguists as 'clitic doubling'. They involve the use of a pronominal suffix followed by the preposition *l-* (or *la-*). One structure is used to express possession and the

---

[5] A counterargument to the Aramaic origin of the /n/ in these suffixes comes from the presence of such forms in some Yemeni dialects as well, as discussed by Owens (2006: 244).

[6] These Syriac examples come from Chrichton (1904: 87). Chrichton's is an English translation of Nöldeke (1898).

other to link a transitive verb with its direct object. The first can be exemplified
with the following Syriac noun phrase:[7]

(5)   Syriac
         šm   *–ēh*   *l–*   *gabr–ā*
         name-   3SG.M   to   man-DEF
         'the man's name'

The second structure can be used to form a full sentence:

(6)   Syriac
         bnā–   *y*   *l–*   *bayt–*   *ā*
         build.PRF.   3SG.M   3SG.M   to-house   DEF
         'He built the house.'

Several Levantine and Iraqi dialects have the same structures, which scholars
believe represent substrate influences from Aramaic. Consider the following
examples.[8]

(5')   Christian Baghdadi Arabic
         maɣt–   *u*   *l–*   *axū–*   *yi*
         wife-   3SG.M   to–   brother–   OBL.1SG
         'my brother's wife'

(6')   Damascene Arabic
         ḥabbēt–   *o*   *la–ʿamər*
         love.PRF.1.SG–   3SG.M   to-Amr
         'I loved Amr (personal name)'

These constructions occur in the Arabic dialects spoken in at least five other
regions as well. In addition to the Levant, they are found in parts of Algeria
and Morocco, Malta, Central Asia, and Oman (Dhofar). Souag (2017) analyses
these cases and points out that in all of them (perhaps with the exception of
Dhofar), there exists some other language with which Arabic had been in contact and which had similar constructions. The Algerian and Moroccan Arabic
constructions resemble those in some Amazigh varieties; Maltese appears to
have been influenced by Sicilian; dialects in Uzbekistan, Afghanistan, and Iran
have constructions that are similar to ones found in Tajik and Uzbek. As we
see, there is a variety of languages – and indeed, language families – that are
the source of these structures in the various Arabic dialects mentioned above.
Nonetheless, what they all have in common is intimate prolonged contact with
a language that also has these structures. Some of these contact languages are
currently spoken in neighbouring regions, and some are substrates.

---

[7] The Syriac examples are from Hopkins (1997) and Rubin (2005), as cited by Procházka (2020).
[8] The Arabic examples are taken from Abu-Haidar (1991), for Baghdad, and Berlinches (2016),
   for Damascus, both cited by Procházka (2020).

9.4.2   *North Africa: Substrate Effects of Amazigh*

The Amazigh languages (also known as Berber) constitute a branch of the Afroasiatic language group. They are spoken across North Africa, from Morocco and Western Sahara in the west to western Egypt in the east. Amazigh languages are indigenous to this region and continue to be spoken by some 25 million people, the vast majority of whom live in Algeria and Morocco. Arabic arrived in North Africa in multiple waves of migration beginning in the seventh century, gradually becoming the majority language. Not only has Arabic expanded westward into North Africa, but its arrival there has also led to large-scale language shift. The effect of Amazigh on the Arabic varieties that emerged in the region is analogous to the effect that Aramaic had on Arabic in the Fertile Crescent, in the sense that features of the former native language of the population were transferred onto the local varieties of the incoming language. But while Arabic has almost totally obliterated Aramaic, Amazigh continues to be spoken by a relatively sizeable population. Moreover, in the twenty-first century it has been accorded official status – alongside Arabic – in both Algeria and Morocco.

In addition to a relatively large number of lexical borrowings from Amazigh to North African varieties of Arabic (e.g. *agméz* 'thumb', *aġrūm* 'bread', and *fakrūna* 'turtle', see Versteegh 2014: 141; Benkato 2020: 9), many structural substrate effects have been recorded as well. In phonology, perhaps the most striking feature is the shortening of vowels. In Moroccan Arabic, historically long vowels are shortened, and historically short vowels are deleted or reduced to /ə/, particularly in open syllables. We thus have /ktab/ 'book' (cf. Cairene Arabic /kitaːb/), /fʒəl/ 'radishes' (cf. Cairene Arabic /figl/), and /kbərˤ/ 'larger' (cf. Cairene Arabic /akbar/).

Phonological effects of Amazigh varieties on a Moroccan Arabic dialect can be seen at the local level as well. Consider the following example from the Arabic spoken by the Ghomara tribes in northwest Morocco. Unlike most Moroccan Arabic dialects, the variety spoken by the Ghomara has interdental fricatives: [θ], [ð], and [ðˤ]. It is important to note that the presence of these sounds in the phonetic system of this variety is not attributable to possible retention of historical Arabic interdentals but to contact with local varieties of Amazigh. Consider the following examples from Ghomara Arabic.[9]

(7)   [maːθəθ] 'she died' (< /maːtat/)

(8)   [ðaːba] 'now' (< /daːba/)

(9)   [mihfaːðˤa] 'backpack' (< [mihfaːdˤa])

---

[9] Examples are from Naciri-Azzouz (2016) and Mourigh (2015). Additional examples and analysis are available therein.

The interdental fricatives in Ghomara Arabic function as allophones of their stop counterparts /t/, /d/, and /dˤ/. In the case of the phoneme /t/, it is spirantised in postvocalic and word-final positions, as in example (7). In other positions it remains a stop [t], as in [tsannəθ] 'she listens'. The phoneme /d/ is spirantised in the same environments as /t/, and also in word-initial position, as in example (8). The two phonemes /t/ and /d/ show the exact same phonological conditions for spirantisation as in Ghomari Amazigh. As for the emphatic phoneme /dˤ/, it is difficult to discern what the precise conditions are for spirantisation due do the rarity of this phoneme and its allophones in both Ghomara Arabic and Ghomara Amazigh.

We now turn to morphology, where a very interesting influence of Amazigh on varieties of Algerian and Moroccan Arabic is the derivation of abstract nouns denoting professions by using the Amazigh pattern for forming feminine nouns, namely *tā*–NOUN–*t*. Consider the following examples.[10]

(10)   *tā-nəžžāṛ-t* 'carpentry' (Moroccan Arabic), from Arabic *nažžār* 'carpenter' (Kossmann 2013)

(11)   *tā-ḥəddād-t* 'blacksmithing'

(12)   *tā-ṭəbbāx-t* 'the art of cooking'

(13)   *tā-xəḍḍār-t* 'the profession of being a greengrocer'

(14)   *tā-gəzzār-t* 'the profession of being a butcher'

This morphological pattern is productive, meaning that *tā* ... *t* can be applied to many other nouns to derive abstract nouns. Two good examples of this are the Moroccan Arabic word *tā-mʿəllmī-t* 'a pretentious attempt to be a master', from *mʿəllim* 'master',[11] and *tā-šʿbi-t* 'a desire to be "one of the people"' (Hachimi 2007: 117).

9.5   Areal Groupings

Situations where Arabic and other languages have coexisted in the same geographic area for centuries are prime locations for observing areal groupings of languages.[12] What this means is that different languages that have a long history of coexistence in the same geographical area develop shared linguistic features. The emergence of such features is usually attributed to extensive multilingualism and frequent code-switching in these languages. Such

[10] Examples (11) to (14) were kindly provided by our colleague Moncef Lahlou, a native speaker of Fessi Moroccan Arabic (personal communication).

[11] Thanks to Moncef Lahlou for this example as well.

[12] See Huehnergard and Rubin (2011: 266) for the use of this term.

situations exist at the Semitic–Indo-European–Altaic language borders in West and Central Asia, where the languages involved include Arabic and Neo-Aramaic (Semitic); Persian, Kurdish, Dari, and Pashto (Iranian, a sub-branch of Indo-European); Turkish, Uzbek, Azeri, and Turkmen (Turkic, a sub-branch of Altaic). Another important border that Arabic came to share with other languages families is in sub-Saharan Africa. Here the languages with which Arabic has been in close contact include members of the Chadic, Nilo-Saharan, and Niger-Congo language families, as discussed in detail by Jonathan Owens.[13]

Owens (2020) discusses contact-induced changes in the Arabic dialects spoken in the Lake Chad region (in Nigeria, Cameroon, and Chad). Some of these features appear to be results of prolonged contact across numerous (as many as a hundred or so) languages in the region, earning them the status of *areal features*. One of the features that Owens analyses within this category is the versatility of the demonstrative *da*. He identifies the following contexts in which *da* is used in Nigerian Arabic and its related dialects:
1. Marking the end of dependent (adverbial, conditional, relative) clauses
2. Text referential, cataphoric
3. Deictic
4. Marking pronouns

Importantly, Owens points out, these 'expanded functions' of the demonstratives are not available in other dialects of Arabic but do mirror the use of demonstratives in the non-Arabic languages of the Lake Chad region, e.g. Kanuri, Bagirmi, Wandala, and Fali. An additional, crucial fact mentioned by Owens is that only some of these languages have been in direct contact with Arabic, lending further support to the hypothesis that this feature is an areal one.

The next set of examples of areal features comes from Uzbekistan Arabic. Central Asian Arabs, including Uzbekistani Arabs, arrived in the region during the seventh and eighth centuries. The dialect shows close affinity with Mesopotamian varieties. This variety has been for centuries surrounded by the Turkic language Uzbek and the Iranian language Tajik. It contains many divergent features vis-à-vis other Arabic dialects, which is typical of dialects that have existed in isolation from Arabic-speaking regions.

Unlike most varieties of Arabic, where definite nominals are preceded by an article while indefinite nominals are unmarked, in Uzbekistan Arabic it is the other way around, viz. it is the indefinite that is marked by the article *fat*. This arrangement is shared with the Turkic and Iranian languages spoken in the same area. Consider the following examples (from Jastrow 2005: 135).

---

[13] The data cited in this section are extrapolated from Owens (2020), especially section 3 (pp. 179–189).

(15)   Uzbekistan Arabic
        fat   mara   kōnet
        ART   woman   was.F.SG
        'There was a woman.'

(16)   Uzbekistan Arabic
        mara   qōlet
        woman   asked.F.SG
        'The woman asked.'

(17)   Turkish
        bir   kadın   vardı
        ART   woman   was
        'There was a woman.'

(18)   Turkish
        kadın   dedi
        woman   said
        'The woman said.'

(19)   Persian
        yec   zan   bud
        ART   woman   was
        'There was a woman.'

(20)   Persian
        zan   gofft
        woman   said
        'The woman said.'

Another important feature that has crossed the language barrier in Uzbekistan is word order. Unlike the majority of Arabic dialects that have a Subject–Verb–Object (SVO) word order, in Uzbekistan Arabic sentences typically have an SOV or OSV order, as in the following example (from Versteegh 1984: 448).

(21)   xaṭīb   ṣayyōt   ǧāb-u
        mullah   fisherman   brought.3M.SG-ACC.3.SG
        'The fisherman brought the mullah.'

As in the case of marking indefiniteness, which Uzbekistan Arabic shares with its co-territorial languages Tajik and Uzbek, the word order of Uzbekistan Arabic is also a consequence of its long-term contact with these languages. In Tajik and Uzbek, the default sentence structure has the verb at the end of the sentence, and its complements (e.g. objects and adverbials) always precede it. According to Versteegh (1984: 452), constant exposure of Uzbekistan Arabic speakers to Tajik and Uzbek has contributed to the predominance of such structures in Uzbekistan Arabic as well.

Bruce Ingham reports very similar phenomena in the variety of Arabic spoken in Afghanistan. The speakers of this variety probably arrived in the area several hundred years after the Arabs of Uzbekistan, i.e. in the fourteenth century (Ingham 2006: 28). The languages with which this variety has been in contact also include Iranian and Turkic languages, specifically Pashto and Dari – the Iranian languages native to Afghanistan – and Uzbek, the Turkic language of the region. The outcomes of this contact situation are quite similar to those of the Uzbekistan case described above. In Afghanistan Arabic as well, definite nouns are unmarked morphologically, while indefinite nouns are marked. One form of indefinite marking is the use of the particle *fad*, and the other is nunation, i.e. the suffixation of -*in*. For example (Ingham 2006: 33):

(22)   fad maktab 'an office'

(23)   ḥintatin ḥamra 'a red wheat'

(24)   fad gappin maḥqūl 'reasonable words'.

In this dialect, too, word order is influenced by the neighbouring languages. Thus, we find in Afghanistan Arabic verb-final constructions as in the Iranian and Turkic languages (Ingham 2006: 34).

(25)   darwīšin šuft 'I saw a dervish'

(26)   šīrviyya li-xōja šāfu 'Shīrviyya saw Khāja'

(27)   hint tintah-mi 'will you give it to him?'

Note that in addition to the aforementioned word order, examples (26) and (27) show two additional areal features: the use of the particle *li-* to mark a direct object and the postposed interrogative -*mi*, which comes from Turkic, respectively.

A fascinating outcome of contact between different languages as a result of their existence in close geographical proximity, or what Chambers and Trudgill (1980) call the 'neighbourhood effect', is the development of a *linguistic area*, also known by its original German coinage *Sprachbund* (literally 'language league'). One of the most famous linguistic areas is the Balkans, which has had a long history of bilingualism and multilingualism. The languages of the Balkans, which belong to different branches of the Indo-European language family, have developed common features in phonology, morphology, syntax, and lexis.[14] These shared linguistic features, which emerge as a result of coexistence in the same geographical location, are called *areal features*.

For a linguistic area to emerge, it is necessary to have a long history of frequent contact between neighbouring communities and for bilingualism or multilingualism to be widespread among the speakers of these communities.

---

[14] These include Bulgarian and Macedonian, part of the Serbo-Croatian grouping (all Slavic), Romanian (Romance), Albanian and Modern Greek.

Scholars working with Arabic data from similarly multilingual regions have seldom raised the question of whether the notion of *linguistic areas* applies to these data. Nonetheless, the array of situations of contact involving varieties of Arabic is extremely rich. The examples cited in this section demonstrate clear instances of linguistic convergence at points of contact.

An important observation in the study of language contact is that the outcome can sometimes be described as structurally simpler than the input and sometimes as more complex. The literature on world languages shows many examples of both types, and linguists (mostly historical linguists) have debated which of these outcomes is more readily described as a direct result of contact. Peter Trudgill proposes a solution to this puzzle from the perspective of *sociolinguistic typology*, an approach that integrates 'sociolinguistic insights into the distribution of linguistic features over the world's languages; (Trudgill 2009: 177; also see Trudgill 2011). Trudgill relates these two opposing outcomes, viz. simplification and complexification, to the type of contact experienced by the communities in question. Put simply, Trudgill suggests that simplification will tend to occur in contact situations that involve primarily adult populations, while complexification, or additive complexity – as in cases of areal features – develops in cases of co-territorial, prolonged, and stable bilingualism that involve children as well. This is because young children are much more flexible than adults in their ability to acquire new linguistic features, as is widely accepted and repeatedly affirmed in studies of language acquisition.

9.6 Types and Models of Diffusion

There are three basic models of representation of linguistic diffusion from place to place. These models are dealt with below, with examples and illustrations from empirical research.

9.6.1 The Wave Model

This model of expansion of linguistic features across space is based on the principles of the 'Wave Theory' (*Wellentheorie*) first suggested by Johannes Schmidt in 1872. According to the Wave Model, a linguistic feature spreads in waves outward from a focal (or central) area in a series of concentric circles (i.e. circles sharing the same centre). The metaphor of the 'wave' likens the process of linguistic diffusion to the effect of throwing a stone into a body of water, which produces ever weakening circles (ripples) around the point where the stone fell. The principle is that a linguistic innovation that occurs in a given place will affect the areas nearer to the centre of innovation before it affects more distant areas; the further a locale is from the centre, the weaker the effect will be. Distance from the focal point is thus the key factor.

This model accounts for the overall pattern found after a change has spread over a relatively large area. In this pattern, typically the areas that have been affected are continuous, in the sense of being connected, whereas relic areas, or areas which have not yet been affected, are discontinuous. The effect of distance from the focal area can be seen in Map 9.1, which shows an areal representation of the spread of *h-deletion* in pronominal suffixes in Syrian varieties of Arabic.

This example comes from the linguistic atlas of Syrian dialects (*Sprachatlas von Syrien*, Behnstedt 1997) concerning the innovative feature of *h-deletion* in the pronominal suffixes -*ha*, -*hon*; thus /be:thon/ > /be:ton/ 'their house'. This feature was studied quantitatively in the dialect of Damascus by Hanadi Ismail (2008). She found that deletion of [h] in the dialect of the capital was predominant, occurring in over 95% of the total number of tokens for this variable. Comparisons with earlier records of the dialect indicated that the rate of usage in Damascus has not changed for one hundred years. Map 9.1, which is based on the Atlas data, shows the geographical distribution of this feature in Syria (and parts of Lebanon).

A cluster of dialects without [h] can be immediately noticed, covering all of the coastal area and extending further inland in a continuous pattern (shaded

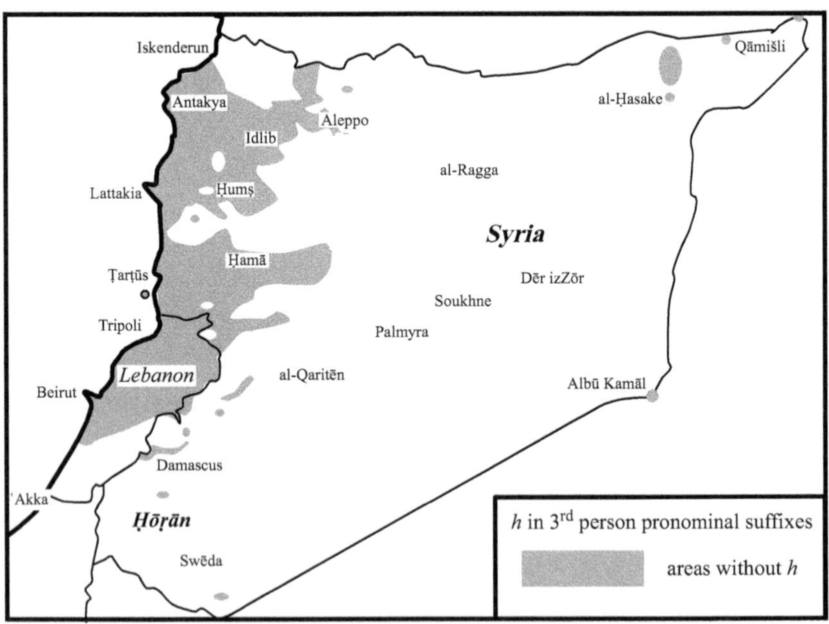

Map 9.1 Areal view of h-deletion in Syria (Based on Ismail 2007: 200, courtesy of Peter Behnstedt and Michael A. Jones)

on the map). This sort of pattern strongly indicates that the innovation started somewhere along the coast, not in the capital city, which is located inland in the south. The data from Damascus show that the coastal innovation had diffused to the capital a long time ago (possibly over one hundred years ago). We do not have information on how the innovation reached Damascus, but the pattern resembles a wave-like diffusion from the coast inwards. We shall assume that since the innovation has been firmly established in Damascus, the city became an inland focal area.[15] South of Damascus, the innovation appears in a couple of places only. Both of these places are towns located by the main road to Damascus. The fact that only two locations are plotted here as having the innovation is a bias in the localities selected for data collection. Traditional dialectological research tended to seek the most conservative and most isolated communities, in the hope of finding the original 'pure' dialectal forms. Moving to the east and south, there is no sign of the innovation for 500 km until it appears in the southeastern city of Albu Kamal on the Euphrates (100,000 inhabitants). Although the map shows three further areas without [h] in the far northeastern corner, the form without [h] in these towns is indigenous to the local dialects and does not originate from the coastal dialects. In these towns (Al-Hasakah, Qamishli, and Al-Malkiyah) an Anatolian type of Arabic dialect is spoken in which [h] is also dropped, i.e. it just happens to be identical to the form used in the coastal Levantine dialects.[16]

The Wave Model has been used quite extensively by historical linguists, but for sociolinguistics the model is of limited utility given that it relies on distance alone and does not incorporate the social factors and their role in accelerating or hindering diffusion. Nonetheless, the principle that geographical proximity is a key factor has been maintained in the formulation of more recent and socially more sensitive models.

9.6.2   The Gravity Model

As early as 1933, the famous linguist Leonard Bloomfield pointed out that the amount of interaction between two localities is not only dependent on geographical distance but also on the size or density of their populations. While distance shows an inverse relationship with interaction (the larger the distance, the less the interaction), population size and density have a direct relationship with amount of interaction, thus diminishing the effect of distance.

Sociolinguists noticed that, contrary to what the Wave Model predicts, linguistic innovations sometimes hop from one large urban centre to another,

---

[15] Damascus is not necessarily the *only* inland focal area. The central and northern cities (e.g. Homs, Hama, Aleppo) may also be focal areas for their respective regions.

[16] Peter Behnstedt provided the clarification in relation to the three towns in the north-east (personal communication). On Anatolian Arabic dialects, see Jastrow (1981) and Wittrich (2001).

and from there to other urban centres, bypassing smaller communities or rural areas, even those located nearer the centre of innovation. In other words, innovations make their way down a hierarchy: from large city to large town to smaller town and so on. This is why this model is also called the Urban Hierarchy Model. Chambers (1993: 150) uses the metaphor of 'skipping a stone across a pond' to describe what happens in this process. The rationale behind the model is that in modern societies interaction between larger cities is more frequent than between cities and rural areas. A larger population naturally increases opportunities for contact. Cities are also better connected by transport networks (roads, railways, etc.). They normally have better infrastructure and offer better opportunities for employment and commuting. They are thus altogether economically and culturally dominant localities.

A hierarchical pattern of diffusion can be seen in both historical and contemporary innovations in various Arabic dialects. A case in point is the Palestinian dialect of Nablus (see Section 9.2). Characteristic of this old city dialect was the pronunciation of /q/ as [q]. This realisation is still used by some groups and in specific contexts. In 1987, Abdel-Jawad reported that the change from [q] to [ʔ] in Nablus was very advanced in the younger generation, especially among women. Data from a small-scale ethnography we conducted in 2020 among two Nabulsi families suggest that, within a generation, the traditional form [q] moved from being used variably to becoming obsolete. Figure 9.1 illustrates this rather rapid transition. Importantly, the parents' generation had acquired [q] from their parents but replaced it with [ʔ] under social pressures. These pressures were felt when speaking outside the home, e.g. in school.

One of the speakers we interviewed recalls being ridiculed in primary school for using [q]. She adds that this incident made her conscious of the stigma attached to this pronunciation. On the other hand, when speaking with family members, she was able to revert to her native variant [q]. Members of the younger generation in this sample did not acquire [q] at all; their native dialect only has [ʔ]. But, by and large, the Nabulsi speech community now use the [ʔ] variant, similar to all other Palestinian city dialects. The villages surrounding the city have retained the traditional [k] realisation typical of central and north-central rural Palestinian dialects. The change in Nablus, therefore, has not originated in neighbouring communities but most likely spread to it from other cities (e.g. Jerusalem, 70 km south of Nablus), bypassing the villages along the way.

The validity of the Urban Hierarchy Model – and thus the importance of ecological factors – is evidenced very clearly in recent changes in several Saudi Arabian dialects. In western Saudi Arabia, features diffuse from the cosmopolitan city of Jeddah outwards, affecting the dialect of Medina. For instance, Medina is changing its realisation of /dʒ/ from [dʒ] to [ʒ], as well as undergoing change in syllable structure, in the direction of the Jeddah dialect. We find the same pattern of linguistic features diffusing from one large urban

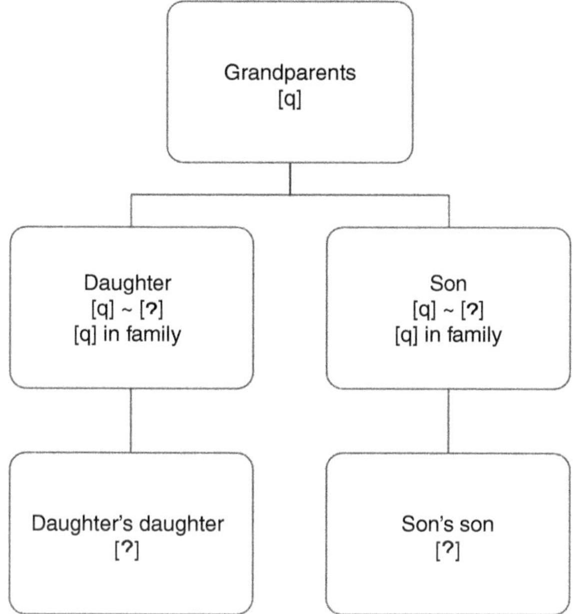

Figure 9.1 Transition from [q] to [ʔ] across generations in a Nabulsi family

centre to another, bypassing smaller communities in between, all over Saudi Arabia. Riyadh, the capital and largest city in Saudi Arabia, is the source of linguistic innovations in cities in northern, central, and eastern regions, such as Ha'il, Dammam, and Al-Ahsa.[17]

9.6.3 *Contra-Hierarchical Diffusion*

Elsewhere in the world, researchers found a few cases where innovations diffused against the urban hierarchy. For instance, in a study by Peter Trudgill (1986: 47–50), 'smoothing', i.e. monophthongisation of triphthongs (diphthong + /ə/), was found to be spreading *to* London from small towns in East Anglia, as in the following examples.

(28)   /aʊ/ + /ə/ > /ɑː/, tower /taʊə/ > /tɑː/

(29)   /ai/ + /ə/ > /ɑː/, fire /faiə/ > /fɑː/

(30)   /æ/ + /ə/ > /æː/, player /plæiə/ > /plæː/

Smoothing also affects diphthongs in

(31)   *pure* /pʉə/ > /pɜ:/

(32)   *going* /guːən/ > /gɔːn/.

Another example of such a pattern was found in the *Survey of Oklahoma Dialects* (G. Bailey et al. 1993) with regard to the quasi-modal construction *fixin' to*. In Southern American English 'fixin' to' is used to mean 'intending to' or 'preparing to', e.g. *he's fixin' to go* (he's preparing to go). This feature in Oklahoma was found to be diffusing outwards from rural areas to urban centres, i.e. in a contra-hierarchical fashion.

This finding is explained with reference to two waves of migration. Following World War I, and even more so following World War II, urbanisation led to extensive population movement from the Oklahoma countryside – where the form *fixin' to* is concentrated – into the state's larger cities. The second wave of migration began in the 1970s and consisted of migrants from the north of the United States moving into Oklahoma and other Southern states. As a result of the arrival of large numbers of migrants from outer regions, the use of traditional rural forms became symbols of native status, assertion of local identity and Southern heritage.

A similar situation that has resulted in originally rural features becoming characteristic of a city dialect because of extensive migration from the countryside has been documented in Casablanca. During French colonisation (in the first half of the twentieth century), Casablanca grew from a small town into Morocco's largest city, gradually leading to distinctly rural features, such as [g] as a reflex of /q/, becoming the norm.

The models of linguistic diffusion outlined above show that there is a complex interaction between geographical and social factors in the spatial configuration of linguistic features.

9.7   Transitional Zones and Interdialectal Forms

The isoglosses we saw on some of the maps presented in Chapter 8 are imaginary lines, used as a convenient way of delimiting the borders of linguistic features. In reality, borders between different dialects are not abrupt, discrete, or invariable. On the contrary, we normally find a higher than usual degree of variability in the forms used at border points between different dialects, as well as new forms not found elsewhere. The reason for this is that inhabitants of such areas normally have contact with both sides of the border and are therefore much more likely to be exposed to and come into contact with the full range of variation used on both sides. Borders are corridors that form transitional zones between different dialects. They share linguistic characteristics with two or more areas in their vicinity and can have distinctive linguistic characteristics.

Mixed and phonetically intermediate forms have been found in transitional zones in many parts of the world. For example, in England, one of the most important isoglosses is the one that separates southern and northern dialects with respect to the vowel in words such as *strut*, *cup*, and *stud*. Southern dialects have a central vowel /ʌ/ in these words, /strʌt/, /kʌp/, /stʌd/, thus making a distinction between *stood* /stʊd/ and *stud* /stʌd/. Northern dialects do not make this distinction, and they lack this central vowel altogether. In northern dialects, both *stood* and *stud* are pronounced as /stʊd/, *strut* /strʊt/, and *cup* /kʊp/.

In the transitional area that runs from the Wash in the east to mid Wales, many types of intermediate forms can be found. For instance, consider the data listed in Table 9.1 (Trudgill 1986: 59–61). The term 'fudged' is used by Trudgill to refer to a 'phonetically intermediate form'.

As can be seen, in the mixed varieties there is a distribution of variants from both sides: *cup* and *love* used with the southern variant and *but* with the northern variant, and both variants can occur in the same lexical item, *up*, *butter*. In the fudged form, the general distribution resembles the southern pattern, but the vowel used for southern /ʌ/ is phonetically intermediate between southern /ʌ/ and northern /ʊ/ (lower than northern and higher than southern). This pattern in the mixed and fudged varieties is only found in transitional areas.

Two of the regions cited in Chapter 8 represent such transitional zones. The Rhenish Fan area is a typical example of a transitional zone, containing dialects that use a mixture of features from both norms, Low German and High German. In other words, many of the dialects in this region share features with the northern and southern German varieties. Notice that although the features themselves are found in other dialects (northern and southern), the *combination* of features in this region represents a *new pattern* not found in the southern proper or the northern proper dialects.

The Nile Delta is the other transitional zone mentioned in Chapter 8. Through this region runs the most important linguistic border between the two major groups of Arabic dialects: the eastern or *Mashreqi* type, from the Delta eastwards; and the western or *Maghrebi* type, from the Delta westwards. The isoglosses that divide the two groups run through the Delta as represented by the bundles of the isoglosses in Map 9.2.

Table 9.1 *Intermediate forms in England (based on Trudgill 1986: 59–61, Tables 2.2 and 2.4)*

	put	*bull*	*push*	*but*	*up*	*cup*	*butter*	*love*
Northern	ʊ	ʊ	ʊ	ʊ	ʊ	ʊ	ʊ	ʊ
Mixed	ʊ	ʊ	ʊ	ʊ	ʊ/ʌ	ʌ	ʊ/ʌ	ʌ
Fudged	ʊ	ʊ	ʊ	ʊ	ɤ	ɤ	ɤ	ɤ
Southern	ʊ	ʊ	ʊ	ʌ	ʌ	ʌ	ʌ	ʌ

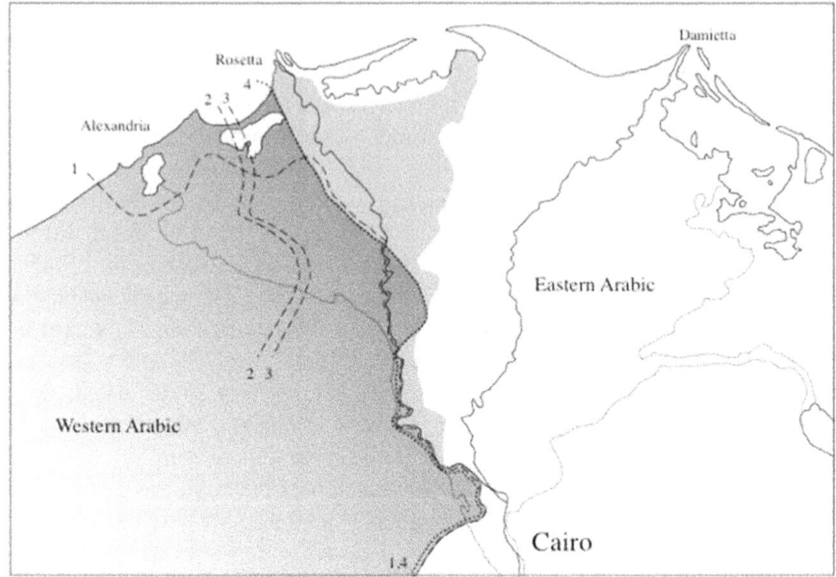

Map 9.2 The Nile Delta as a transitional zone: (based on Behnstedt and Woidich 2005: 103, map 34)

The most important linguistic feature that distinguishes between the eastern and western types is the 1st person singular and plural imperfect verb forms. In the western type these forms are *niktib* 'I write', *niktibu* or *nikitbu* 'we write'. In the eastern type the forms are *aktib* 'I write', *niktib* 'we write'. There are no exceptions to this pattern in the heartland of either group, as can be seen on the map (the white and dark-shaded areas). In the transitional zone (grey shade), a mixture of both patterns can be found, thus *aktib-niktibu*. In addition to the mixing of verbal forms, the transitional zone, especially the central and southern parts, contains a mixture of other features, delineated by lines 1–4, which represent isoglosses of four further features. The type of mixture shown in this map is similar to the one we saw above in the Rhine transitional zone in that the pattern is characterised by new combinations of features.

A different type of development can be seen in Map 9.3 (also from the Nile Delta), which shows the distribution of diphthongal and monophthongal variants of the diphthongs /ai/ and /au/. Unlike the 1st person verbal forms cited above, both types (diphthongs and monophthongs) can be found in the eastern type as well as in the western type.

As can be seen, in the Delta transitional zone all realisations of the diphthongs can be found, but notice in particular the central region. Here, we find a

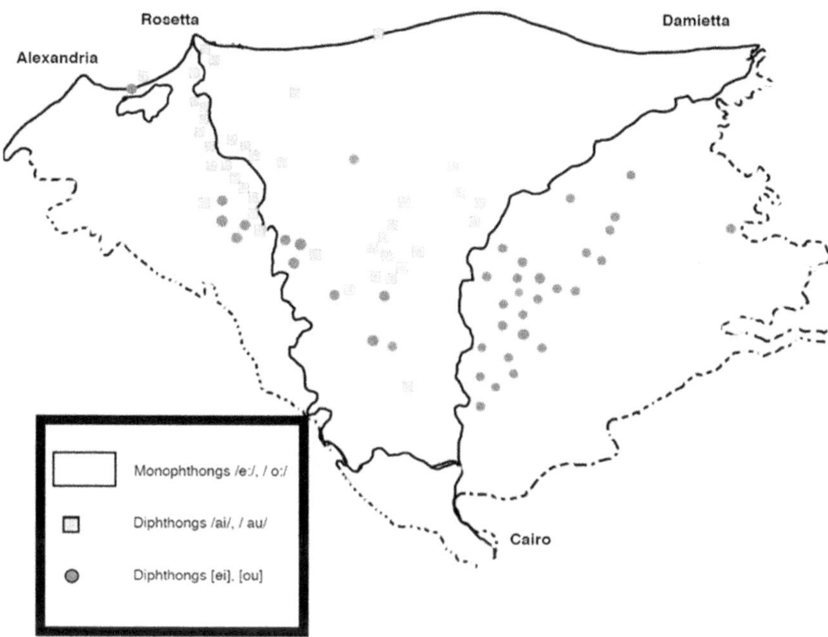

Map 9.3 The diphthongs in the Nile Delta (based on Behnstedt and Woidich 2005: 98, map 27, courtesy of Peter Behnstedt and Michael A. Jones)

concentration of dialects in the western part with /ai/ and /au/ in all positions; but in the eastern part, especially immediately east of the Damietta, we find a group of dialects which have the monophthongs /eː/, /oː/, as well as the diphthongs (used specifically in pausal position). So, this group of dialects uses more variants of these features (not one, but two variants for each diphthong). Furthermore, the quality of the diphthongs in this group is considerably narrower, thus /ai/ > /ei/, /au/ > /ou/. The narrower realisations are phonetically midway between a broad diphthong, with open first element /ai/, /au/, and a monophthong /eː/, /oː/. This means that the narrow diphthongs found in this transitional zone are intermediate forms: [ai] > [ei] > [eː]; [au] > [ou] > [oː]. A similar range of intermediate variants was found in a contact situation in Mecca. Najla Alghamdi (2014; also see Chapter 5) found that among the Ghamdi migrant group, whose heritage dialect has diphthongs [aɪ] and [aʊ], a range of intermediate variants is used (e.g. [ɛɪ] and [ɔu]), in addition to the target monophthongal realisations [ɛː] and [ɔː]. In transitional zones (as in the Nile Delta), the fudged and mixed forms become stabilised as features characteristic of the local dialects. In contact situations such as Mecca, the mixed and fudged forms most likely represent stages in the transition to the target variants and have significant social correlates.

The types of linguistic developments found in transitional zones, as areas which are normally characterised by higher-than-average contact between speakers of different dialects, are commonly found in contact situations that lead to the formation of new dialects. In many parts of the world, new dialects are formed from scratch, e.g. in new towns where the population is for the most part made up of migrants and thus speakers of dialects from different dialectal stock. A case in point is the capital city of Jordan, Amman. As an Arabic-speaking community, Amman's history only began during the first two decades of the twentieth century. With such a recent history and only four generations of native inhabitants, Amman naturally does not have a traditional dialect, but a new dialect has recently emerged. The ingredients that went into the formation of the new dialect are a range of Jordanian and Palestinian dialects, which are mutually intelligible dialects of the Levantine type but can be distinguished from each other by many features.[18]

The linguistic developments that led to the stabilisation of the forms used for the feminine ending (ah) in the formation of this dialect demonstrate rather aptly the process of mixing and fudging that we saw in transitional zones. The input dialects, Palestinian and Jordanian dialects, differ in the phonology and phonetics of (ah). The Jordanian dialects use /a/ in all environments except after coronal sounds, in which case the ending is raised to a half-open vowel [ɛ] (i.e. /a/ is the default choice), as in the following examples.

(33)   /ħilwa/ 'pretty', /biʃʕa/ 'ugly'; *but* /madanijjɛ/ 'modern', /riːʃɛ/ 'feather',
         /sanɛ/ 'year'

On the other hand, in urban Palestinian dialects, the feminine ending is realised as /e/ (which can be [e] or [ɪ]), except after velarised, emphatic, and pharyngeal sounds, where /a/ is used (i.e. /e/ is the default choice). The examples below illustrate this pattern.

(34)   /ħilwe/ 'pretty', /sˤaʕbe/ 'difficult'; *but* /mantˤiʔa/ 'region', /ʒaːmʕa/
         'university'.

In Amman, the contact between speakers of the two types of dialects has resulted in the emergence of a fudged form, which combines Palestinian phonology and Jordanian phonetics, i.e. /a/ is raised everywhere except after velarised, pharyngeal, and emphatic sounds, and the raised variant is phonetically half open [ɛ]. Regional koineisation in this case also exerts an influence on the course of developments in Amman, seeing as the phonological pattern in urban Palestinian is the one prevalent in all city dialects in the Levant.

---

[18] 'Palestinian' in this context refers to urban Palestinian dialects only, and 'Jordanian' refers to central and northern dialects. For further details about the formation of the Amman dialect see Al-Wer (2007).

9.8 Summary and Concluding Remarks

In this chapter we have looked at some of the factors that influence the diffusion of linguistic features across space, as well as the linguistic repercussions of this diffusion. The basic observation that the geography of a place (its physical space) influences its linguistic configuration is a valid observation, but we need to keep in mind that space as a dimension of linguistic variation includes the *social* as well as the physical aspects of human societies (Britain 2002). For instance, in the data from Oklahoma and Casablanca, (see Sections 9.6.3 and 8.6.1) we saw the influence of non-physical spatial factors, namely 'urbanisation', which in some cases has led to the disappearance of traditional local linguistic features, and 'assertion of local identity', which has led to the revival and diffusion of traditional forms from rural areas to urban centres (see Section 9.6.3).

We have also discussed the various models of representation of spatial diffusion used in sociolinguistics. As we have seen, these models can be supported by empirical data, but no single model accounts adequately for all of the linguistic facts on the ground. For instance, the Wave Model (see Section 9.6.1), which predicts that areas nearer to the focal point will be affected before areas located further away from the focal point, does not account for linguistic features which hop from city to city before reaching smaller towns and villages that may be nearer to the focal point (see Section 8.6.1). In some cases, predictions made on the basis of a certain model are contradicted by the empirical data, as in the case of linguistic diffusion contra-hierarchically (see Section 9.6.3). Findings that contradict a certain model of diffusion do not mean that the model is altogether invalid but that there may be other, yet undiscovered factors that influence diffusion.

In the final section (see Section 9.7), we focussed on transitional zones and demonstrated the continuity of linguistic features as they travel across space. We have seen that the transition from form A to form B does not happen abruptly. Typically, what we find in transition zones is that both forms A *and* B may be present, as well as a range of intermediate forms, intermediate patterns, and in some cases, totally new forms and patterns not found elsewhere.

9.9 Further Reading

> Al-Jallad (2019) – This, among several other publications by the same author, presents a state-of-the-art account of current knowledge about the origin of Arabic. According to the evidence he presents, it is discerned that the Syrian Steppe (in today's terms, north-east Jordan and southern Syria) is the original home of Arabic. A more detailed account of the grammar of the Arabic variety found in the Safaitic inscriptions in this area is Al-Jallad (2015).

Al-Wer (2020) – This is a concise summary of the principal mechanisms of the formation of the new dialect in Amman. In addition, a large-scale research project on this dialect was completed in 2020, and a monograph is in preparation.

Behnstedt and Woidich (2018) – This chapter in the volume *Arabic Historical Dialectology* is a thoughtful historical account comprising a synthesis of the authors' decades-long research on the formation of Egyptian Arabic.

Chambers and Trudgill (1998) – This is the second edition of the authors' 1980 classic textbook *Dialectology*, which in fact can serve as a foundational text also for many of the issues that are of interest to variationist sociolinguists.

Grigore (2019) – This is a succinct yet detailed overview of peripheral varieties of Arabic, many of which are located in Central Asia and have been in long-term contact with the other languages of the region.

Holes (2000, 2005, 2016) – These three volumes present the culmination of Clive Holes's extensive research on dialect, culture, and society in eastern Arabia. The first volume is an extensive glossary; the second includes ethnographic texts; and the third deals with linguistic variation in phonology, morphology, syntax, and style.

Huehnergard and Rubin (2011) – This is a comprehensive, up-to-date review of models of classification of the Semitic Languages, incorporating traditional historical linguistic genealogical classifications with a fresh look at language contact as an important component to be considered in the grouping of these languages.

Owens (2006) – In this groundbreaking book, Owens presents an account of the history of Arabic, basing his analysis on a large corpus of data drawn from varieties of Arabic of all time periods and across a wide geographical distribution.

Thomason and Kaufman (1988), Thomason (2001) – These are two of the foundational texts on language contact. The former is a detailed synthesis of many studies in the field from a historical linguistic perspective. The latter is an introductory textbook.

Trudgill (2004) – This is an analysis of the formation of the New Zealand variety of English, in which Trudgill lays out the mechanisms, principles, and theoretical foundations of the study of new-dialect formation and koineisation.

Trudgill (2011) – This book proposes a novel theoretical approach combining sociolinguistics and typology. It includes examples from a wide variety of languages, including detailed examples from Arabic (also discussed in Trudgill 2009, which is devoted to Arabic).

9.10   Exercises for Chapter 9

1. Political borders and linguistic borders rarely coincide. However, as we have seen, the creation of new political borders may have linguistic consequences. Think of examples from a region you are familiar with where there is instability or dispute regarding the political boundaries. What, if any, have the linguistic repercussions of political developments around these borders been?

2. It is a common but not inevitable outcome that migrant communities accommodate linguistically to their host communities. For instance, the Gulf region in particular has been home to generations of migrants from all over the Arab world. Design a research project in which you will investigate the patterns of linguistic modification that different migrant groups exhibit. What makes some groups more susceptible than others to linguistic assimilation to their host communities? Can this be predicted? How can different generations within the same community be affected differently? What role do education and socialisation patterns play in such processes?

3. Sociolinguists are well positioned to provide expert advice on forensic linguistic questions, such as police investigations, healthcare, and immigration. How can our understanding of language and dialect contact put society's perceptions in perspective, such that they inform authorities on matters pertaining to social justice?

References

Abu Ain, Noora. 2016. *A sociolinguistic study in Saḥam, Northern Jordan.* PhD thesis, University of Essex.

Abu-Haidar, Farida. 1991. *Christian Arabic of Baghdad.* Wiesbaden: Harrassowitz.

Akkuş, Faruk and Elabbas Benmamoun. 2016. Clause structure in contact contexts: The case of Sason Arabic. In Youssef Haddad and Eric Potsdam (eds.). *Perspectives on Arabic Linguistics,* Volume 28. Amsterdam: John Benjamins. 153–172.

Al Sheyadi, Sara. 2022. *Sociolinguistic variation in the Yāl Saʿad dialect in northern Oman.* PhD thesis, University of Essex.

Al-Azraqi, Munira. 2007. The Use of *kaškašah/kaskasah* and alternative means among educated urban Saudi speakers. In Catherine Miller, Enam Al-Wer, Dominique Caubet, and Janet C. E. Watson (eds.). *Arabic in the city: Issues in dialect contact and language variation.* London: Routledge. 230–245.

Al-Bohnayyah, Moayyad. 2019. *Dialect variation and change in eastern Arabia: Al-Ahsa dialect.* PhD thesis, University of Essex.

Al-Essa, Aziza. 2008. *Najdi speakers in Hijaz: A sociolinguistic investigation of dialect contact in Jeddah.* PhD Thesis, University of Essex.

Al-Essa, Aziza. 2009. When Najd meets Hijaz: Dialect contact in Jeddah. In Enam Al-Wer and Rudolf de Jong (eds.). *Arabic dialectology: In honour of Clive Holes on the occasion of his sixtieth birthday.* Leiden: Brill. 203–222.

Al-Essa, Aziza. 2019. Phonological and morphological variation. In Enam Al-Wer and Uri Horesh (eds.). *The Routledge handbook of Arabic sociolinguistics.* London: Routledge. 151–168.

Al-Hawamdeh, Areej. 2016. *A sociolinguistic investigation of two hōrāni features in Sūf, Jordan.* PhD thesis, University of Essex.

Al-Jallad, Ahmad. 2015. *An outline of the grammar of the Safaitic inscriptions.* Leiden: Brill.

Al-Jallad, Ahmad. 2019. The classification of Arabic and sociolinguistic variation in the pre-Islamic period. In Enam Al-Wer and Uri Horesh (eds.). *The Routledge handbook of Arabic sociolinguistics.* London: Routledge. 15–29.

Al-Jehani, Nasir. 1985. *Sociostylistic stratification of Arabic in Makkah.* PhD dissertation, The University of Michigan.

Al-Khatib, Mahmoud. 1988. *Sociolinguistic change in an expanding urban context: A case study of Irbid city.* PhD thesis, University of Durham.

Al-Qahtani, Khairia. 2015. *A sociolinguistic study of the Tihami Qahtani dialect in Asir, southern Arabia.* PhD thesis, University of Essex.

Al-Qouz, Muna. 2009. *Dialect contact, acquisition and change among Manama youth, Bahrain*. PhD thesis, University of Essex.

Al-Rohili, Mohammad. 2019. Depalatalisation of /gʲ/ and /kʲ/ in the Ḥarbi dialect in Medina: Patterns of variation and change. PhD thesis, University of Essex.

Al-Shareef, Jamal. 2002. *Language change and variation in Palestine: A case study of Jabalia refugee camp*. PhD thesis, University of Leeds.

Al-Shawi, Wisam. 2020. *A sociolinguistic study of a southern Iraqi dialect: fortition of the variants [j] and [ʧ]*. PhD thesis, University of Essex.

Al-Shehri, Abdullah. 1993. Urbanization and linguistic variation and change: A sociolinguistic study of the impact of urbanization on the linguistic behaviour of urbanized rural immigrants in Hijaz, Saudi Arabia. PhD. thesis, University of Essex.

Al-Tamimi, Feda'. 2001. *Phonetic and phonological variation in the speech of rural migrants in a Jordanian city*. PhD thesis, University of Leeds.

Al-Wer, Enam. 1991. *Phonological variation in the speech of women from three urban areas in Jordan*. PhD thesis, University of Essex.

Al-Wer, Enam. 1997. Arabic between reality and ideology. *International Journal of Applied Linguistics* 7 (2): 251–265.

Al-Wer, Enam. 1999. Why do different variables behave differently? Data from Arabic. In Yasir Suleiman (ed.). *Language and society in the Middle East and North Africa*. Richmond, Surrey: Curzon. 38–57.

Al-Wer, Enam. 2003. New dialect formation: The focusing of *-kum* in Amman. In David Britain and Jenny Cheshire (eds.). *Social dialectology: In honour of Peter Trudgill*. Amsterdam: John Benjamins. 59–57.

Al-Wer, Enam. 2007. The formation of the dialect of Amman. In Catherine Miller, Enam Al-Wer, Dominique Caubet, and Janet C. E. Watson (eds.). *Arabic in the city: Issues in dialect contact and language variation*. London: Routledge. 55–76.

Al-Wer, Enam. 2013. Sociolinguistics. In Jonathan Owens (ed.). *The Oxford handbook of Arabic linguistics*. Oxford: Oxford University Press. 241–263.

Al-Wer, Enam. 2014. Language and gender in the Middle East and North Africa. In Susan Ehrlich and Miriam Meyerhoff (eds.). *Handbook of language, gender and sexuality*, 2nd edition. Somerset, NJ: John Wiley & Sons. 396–411.

Al-Wer, Enam. 2020. New dialect formation: the Amman dialect. In Christopher Lucas and Stefano Manfredi (eds.). *Arabic and contact-induced change*. Berlin: Language Science Press. 551–566. DOI: 10.5281/zenodo.3744549.

Al-Wer, Enam and Bruno Herin. 2011. The lifecycle of *qaf* in Jordan. *Langage et Société* 138 (4): 59–76.

Al-Wer, Enam and Rudolf de Jong. 2018. Dialects of Arabic. In Charles Boberg, John Nerbonne, and Dominic Watt (eds.). *Handbook of dialectology*. Oxford: Wiley. 523–534.

Al-Wer, Enam and Uri Horesh. 2019. Arabic sociolinguistics: Principles and epistemology. In Enam Al-Wer and Uri Horesh (eds.). *The Routledge handbook of Arabic sociolinguistics*. London: Routledge. 1–11.

Al-Wer, Enam, Uri Horesh, Bruno Herin, and Maria Fanis. 2015. How Arabic regional features become sectarian features. Jordan as a case study. *Zeitschrift für Arabische Linguistik* 62: 68–87.

Al-Wer, Enam, Uri Horesh, Deema AlAmmar, Hind Alaodini, Aziza Al-Essa, Areej Al-Hawamdeh, Khairia Al-Qahtani, Abeer A. B. Hussain. 2022. Probing linguistic change in Arabic vernaculars: A sociohistorical perspective. *Language in Society* 51: 29–50. DOI: 10.1017/S0047404520000706.

AlAmmar, Deema. 2017. *Linguistic variation and change in the dialect of Ha'il Saudi Arabia: Feminine suffixes*. PhD thesis, University of Essex.

Alaodini, Hind. 2019. *A sociolinguistic study of the Dawāsir dialect in Dammam, Eastern Arabia: Affrication of /j/ and unrounding of /a:/*. PhD thesis, University of Essex.

Alghamdi, Najla. 2014. *A sociolinguistic study of dialect contact in Arabia: Ghamdi immigrants in Mecca*. PhD thesis, University of Essex.

Arnold, Werner and Peter Behnstedt. 1993. *Arabisch-Aramaische Sprachbeziehungen Im Qalamun (Syrien): Eine Dialektgeographische Untersuchung*. Wiesbaden: Harrassowitz.

Ash, Sharon. 2013. Social class. In J. K. Chambers and Natalie Schilling (eds.). *The handbook of language variation and change*, 2nd edition. Oxford: Wiley. 350–367.

Badawi, El-Said. 1985. Educated spoken Arabic: A problem in teaching Arabic as a foreign language. In Kurt R. Jankowsky (ed.). *Scientific and humanistic dimensions of language: Festschrift for Robert Lado on the occasion of his 70th birthday on May 31, 1985*. Amsterdam: John Benjamins. 15–22.

Bagamba, Bukpa Araali. 2007. *A Study of language shift in rural Africa: The Hema of the northeast of the Democratic Republic of Congo*. PhD thesis, University of Essex.

Bailey, Charles-James N. 1973. *Variation and linguistic theory*. Arlington, VA: Center for Applied Linguistics.

Bailey, Guy, Thomas Wikle, Jan Tillery, and Lori Sand. 1993. Some patterns of linguistic diffusion. *Language Variation and Change* 5: 359–390.

Baranowski, Maciej and Danielle Turton. 2020. TD-deletion in British English: New evidence for the long-lost morphological effect. *Language Variation and Change* 32: 1–23.

Barontini, Alexandrine and Karima Ziamari. 2009. Comment des (jeunes) femmes Marocaines parlent 'masculine': tentative de definition sociolinguistique. In Ángeles Vicente (ed.). *Women's world – women's word: Female life as reflected in the Arabic dialects*. Zaragoza: Instituto de Estudios Islámicos y del Oriente Proximo. 153–172.

Behnstedt, Peter. 1985. *Die nordjemenitischen Dialekte*, Teil 1, *Atlas*. Wiesbaden: Reichert.

Behnstedt, Peter. 1997. *Sprachatlas von Syrien*. Wiesbaden: Harrassowitz.

Behnstedt, Peter. 1998. Zum Arabischen von Djerba (Tunesien) I. *Zeitschrift für Arabische Linguistik* 35: 52–83.

Behnstedt, Peter. 2016. *Dialect Atlas of North Yemen and adjacent areas*, Leiden: Brill.

Behnstedt, Peter and Manfred Woidich. 1985–1999. *Die ägyptisch-arabischen Dialekte*. Wiesbaden: Ludwig Riechert.

Behnstedt, Peter and Manfred Woidich. 2005. *Arabische Dialektgeographie: eine Einführung*. Leiden: Brill.

Behnstedt, Peter and Manfred Woidich. 2010–2021. *Wortatlas der arabischen Dialekte*. Leiden: Brill.

Behnstedt, Peter and Manfred Woidich. 2013. Arabic dialectology. In Jonathan Owens (ed.). *The Oxford handbook of Arabic linguistics*. Oxford: Oxford University Press. 300–325.

Behnstedt, Peter and Manfred Woidich. 2018. The formation of the Egyptian Arabic dialect area. In Clive Holes (ed.). *Arabic historical dialectology: Linguistic and sociolinguistic approaches*. Oxford: Oxford University Press. 64–95.

Benkato, Adam. 2020. Maghrebi Arabic. In Christopher Lucas and Stefano Manfredi (eds.). *Arabic and contact-induced change*. Berlin: Language Science Press. 197–212. DOI: 10.5281/zenodo.3744517.

Bentahila, Abdelali and Eirlys E. Davies. 1983. The syntax of Arab–French codeswitching. *Lingua* 59: 301–330.

Bentahila, Abdelali, Eirlys E. Davies, and Jonathan Owens. 2013. Codeswitching and related issues involving Arabic. In Jonathan Owens (ed.). *The Oxford handbook of Arabic linguistics*. Oxford: Oxford University Press. 326–347.

Bergsträsser, G. 1915. *Sprachatlas von Syrien und Palästina*. Leipzig: Hinrichs.

Berlinches, Carmen. 2016. *El dialecto árabe de Damasco (Siria): Estudio gramaticaly textos*. Zaragoza: Prensas de la Universidad de Zaragoza.

Blake, Renée and Meredith Josey. 2003. The /ay/ diphthong in a Martha's Vineyard community: What can we say 40 years after Labov? *Language in Society* 32: 451–485.

Blanc, Haim. 1953. Studies in north Palestinian Arabic: Linguistic inquiries among the Druzes of Western Galilee and Mt. Carmel. Jerusalem: Israel Oriental Society.

Blanc, H. 1964. *Communal dialects in Baghdad*. Cambridge, MA: Harvard University Press.

Bloomfield, Leonard. 1933. *Language*. New York: Holt.

Borg, Alexander. 1997. Cypriot Arabic phonology. In Alan S. Kaye (ed.). *Phonologies of Asia and Africa (including the Caucasus)*, Volume 1. Winona Lake, IN: Eisenbrauns. 219–244.

Boumans, Louis. 1998. *The syntax of codeswitching: Analysing Moroccan Arabic/ Dutch conversations*. Tilburg: Tilburg University Press.

Boumans, Louis and Dominique Caubet. 2000. Modelling intrasentential codeswitching: A comparative study of Algerian/French in Algeria and Moroccan/Dutch in the Netherlands. In Jonathan Owens (ed.). *Arabic as a minority language*. Berlin: De Gruyter. 117–180.

Bourdieu, Pierre. 1977. *An outline of a theory of practice* (translated by Richard Nice). Cambridge: Cambridge University Press.

Britain, David. 2002. Diffusion, levelling, simplification and reallocation in past tense BE in the English Fens. *Journal of Sociolinguistics* 6: 16–43.

Britain, David. 2009. 'Big bright lights' versus 'green and pleasant land'?: The unhelpful dichotomy of 'urban' versus 'rural' in dialectology. In Enam Al-Wer and Rudolf de Jong. *Arabic dialectology: In honour of Clive Holes on the occasion of his sixtieth birthday*. Leiden: Brill. 223–248.

Britain, David. 2012. Countering the urbanist agenda in variationist sociolinguistics: Dialect contact, demographic change and the rural-urban dichotomy. In Sandra Hansen, Christian Schwarz, Philipp Stoeckle, and Tobias Streck (eds.). *Dialectological and folk dialectological concepts of space*. Berlin: De Gruyter. 12–20.

Brunot, Louis. 1930. Topographie dialectale de Rabat. *Hespéris* 10: 7–13.

Camilleri, Maris. 2019. Morphosyntactic variation: Focus on Maltese and other western varieties. In Enam Al-Wer and Uri Horesh. (eds.). *The Routledge handbook of Arabic sociolinguistics*. London: Routledge. 214–226.

Campbell, Lyle. 2004. *Historical linguistics: An introduction*, Edinburgh University Press: Edinburgh.

Cantineau, Jean. 1938. Le parler Drŭz de la montagne *Ḥōrânains*. *Annales de l'Institut d'Étude Orientales* 4: 157–183.

Cantineau, Jean. 1940. *Les parlers arabes du Ḥōrân: Atlas*. Paris: C. Klincksieck.

Cantineau, Jean. 1946. *Les parlers arabe du Ḥōrân: Notions générales, grammaire*. Paris: C. Klincksieck.

Chambers, J. K. 1993. Sociolinguistic dialectology. In Dennis R. Preston (ed.). *American dialect research*. Amsterdam: John Benjamins. 134–164.

Chambers, J. K. 2000. Region and language variation. *English World-Wide* 21: 169–199.

Chambers, J. K. 2003. *Sociolinguistic theory: Linguistic variation and its social significance*, 2nd edition. Oxford: Blackwell.

Chambers, J. K. 2009. *Sociolinguistic theory: Linguistic variation and its social significance*, revised edition. Chichester, UK: Blackwell.

Chambers, J. K. and Natalie Schilling. 2013. *The handbook of language variation and change*, 2nd edition. Oxford: Wiley-Blackwell.

Chambers, J. K. and Peter Trudgill. 1980. *Dialectology*. Cambridge: Cambridge University Press.

Chambers, J. K. and Peter Trudgill. 1998. *Dialectology*, 2nd edition. Cambridge: Cambridge University Press.

Chen, Matthew. Y. and William S-Y. Wang. 1975. Sound change: Actuation and implementation. *Language* 51: 255–281.

Cheng, Chin-Chuan and William S-Y. Wang. 1977. Tone change in Chao-Zhou Chinese: A study in lexical diffusion. In William S-Y. Wang (ed.). *The lexicon in phonological change*. Berlin: De Gruyter. 86–100.

Cheshire, Jenny. 2005. Syntactic variation and beyond: Gender and social class variation in the use of discourse-new markers. *Journal of Sociolinguistics* 9: 479–508.

Chrichton, James. 1904. *Compendious Syriac grammar*. [Reprinted 2001]. Winona Lake, IN: Eisenbrauns. [English translation of Nöldeke 1898].

Cotter, William. M. 2013. *Dialect contact and change in Gaza City*. MA. dissertation, University of Essex.

Cotter, William. M. 2016. (q) as a sociolinguistic variable in the Arabic of Gaza City. In Youssef. A. Haddad and Eric Potsdam (eds.). *Perspectives on Arabic linguistics*, Volume 28, *Papers from the Annual Symposium on Arabic Linguistics, Gainesville, Florida, 2014*. Amsterdam: John Benjamins. 229–246. DOI: 10.1075/sal.4.10cot.

Cotter, William M. and Uri Horesh. 2015. Social integration and dialect divergence in coastal Palestine. *Journal of Sociolinguistics* 19: 460–483.

Cukor-Avila, Patricia and Guy Bailey. 2013. Real time and apparent time. In J. K. Chambers and Natalie Schilling (eds.). *The handbook of language variation and change*, 2nd edition. Oxford: Wiley. 239–262.

D'Anna, Luca. 2017. Agreement with plural controllers in Fezzānī Arabic. *Folia Orientalia* 54: 101–122.

De Jong, Rudolf. 2000. *A grammar of the Bedouin dialects of the northern Sinai littoral, bridging the linguistic gap between the Eastern and Western Arab world*. Leiden: Brill.

De Jong, Rudolf. 2011. *A grammar of the Bedouin dialects of central and southern Sinai*. Leiden: Brill.

De Jong, Rudolf. 2013. Northern Sinai: Identifying the transitional area between Bedouin and sedentary Arabic dialects using methods of multi-dimensional scaling. In Alena Barysevich, Alexandra D'Arcy, and David Heap (eds.). *Bamberger Beiträge zur Englischen Sprachwissenschaft / Bamberg Studies in English Linguistics*, Volume 57, *Proceedings of Methods 14: Papers from the Fourteenth International Conference on Methods in Dialectology, 2011*. Frankfurt: Peter Lang. 215–227.

Eckert, Penelope. 1980. Separate and unequal. *Linguistics* 18: 1053–1064.

Eckert, Penelope. 1989. *Jocks and burnouts: Social categories and identity in the high school*. New York: Teachers College Press.

Eckert, Penelope. 1997a. Age as a sociolinguistic variable. In Florian Coulmas (ed.). *The handbook of sociolinguistics*. Oxford: Blackwell. 151–167.

Eckert, Penelope. 1997b. Why ethnography? In Ulla-Britt Kotsinas, Anna-Brita Stenstrom, and Anna-Malin Karlsson (eds.). *Ungdomssprak i Norden*. Stockholm: Stockholm University. 52–62.

Eckert, Penelope. 2000. *Linguistic variation as social practice*. Oxford: Blackwell.

Eckert, Penelope. 2006. Communities of practice. In Jacob L. Mey (ed.). *Concise encyclopedia of pragmatics*, 2nd edition. Oxford: Elsevier. 109–112.

Eckert, Penelope. 2012. Three waves of variation study: The emergence of meaning in the study of sociolinguistic variation. *Annual Review of Anthropology* 41: 87–100.

Eckert, Penelope and Sally McConnell-Ginet. 1992. Think practically and look locally: Language and gender as community-based practice. *Annual Review of Anthropology* 21: 461–490.

Edwards, John. 1985. *Language, society, and identity*. Oxford: Basil Blackwell.

Edwards, John. 2009. *Language and identity: An introduction*. Cambridge: Cambridge University Press.

Edwards, John. 2010. *Minority languages and group identity: Cases and categories*. Amsterdam: John Benjamins.

Ehrlich, Susan and Miriam Meyerhoff (eds.). 2014. *Handbook of language, gender and sexuality*, 2nd edition. Chichester, UK: John Wiley & Sons.

El Salman, Mahmoud. 2003. The use of the [q] variant in the Arabic dialect of Tirat Haifa. *Anthropological Linguistics* 45: 413–425.

El-Hassan, Shahir. A. 1977. Educated spoken Arabic in Egypt and the Levant: A critical review of diglossia and related concepts. *Archivum Linguisticum Leeds* 8(2): 112–132.

Ferguson, Charles. A. 1959. Diglossia. *Word* 15: 325–340.

Fowler, Joy. 1986. The social stratification of (r) in New York City department stores, 24 years after Labov. Manuscript, New York University.

Gafter, Roey J. and Uri Horesh. 2020. Two languages, one variable? Pharyngeal realizations among Arabic–Hebrew bilinguals. *Journal of Sociolinguistics* 24: 369–387.

Gauchat, Louis. 1905. L'unité phonetique dans le patois d'une commune. *Aus romanischen Sprachen und Literaturen: Festschrift Heinrich Morf*. Halle: Max Niemeyer. 175–232.

Germanos, Marie-Aimée. 2007. Greetings in Beirut: Social distribution and attitudes towards different formulae. In Catherine Miller, Enam Al-Wer, Dominique Caubet, and Janet C. E. Watson (eds.). *Arabic in the city: Issues in dialect contact and language variation*. London: Routledge. 147–165.

Germanos, Marie-Aimée and Catherine Miller. 2015. Is religious affiliation a key factor of language variation in Arabic-speaking countries? *Language & Communication* 42: 86–98.

Geva-Kleinberger, Aharon and Peter Behnstedt. 2019. *Atlas of the Arabic dialects of Galilee (Israel)*. Leiden: Brill.

Gorman, Kyle and Daniel Ezra Johnson. 2013. Quantitative Analysis. In Robert Bayley, Richard Cameron, and Ceil Lucas (eds.). *The Oxford handbook of sociolinguistics*. Oxford: Oxford University Press. 214–240.

Grigore, George. 2019. Peripheral varieties. In Enam Al-Wer and Uri Horesh (eds.). *The Routledge handbook of Arabic sociolinguistics*. London: Routledge. 117–133.

Hachimi, Atiqa. 2005. *Dialect leveling, maintenance and urban identity in Morocco: Fessi immigrants in Casablanca*. PhD Dissertation, University of Hawai'i.

Hachimi, Atiqa. 2007. Becoming Casablancan: Fessis in Casablanca as a case study. In Catherine Miller, Enam Al-Wer, Dominique Caubet, and Janet C. E. Watson (eds.). *Arabic in the city: Issues in dialect contact and language variation*. London: Routledge. 97–122.

Hachimi, Atiqa. 2011. Réinterprétation sociale d'un vieux parler citadin maghrébin à Casablanca. *Langage et Société* 138: 21–42.

Hachimi, Atiqa. 2012. The urban and the urbane: Identities, language ideologies, and Arabic dialects in Morocco. *Language in Society* 41: 321–341.

Haden, Ernest F. 1955. The uvular *r* in French. *Language* 31: 504–510.

Haeri, Niloofar. 1987. Male/female differences in speech: An alternative interpretation. In Keith M. Dennig, Sharon Inkelas, Faye McNair-Knox, and John R. Rickford (eds.) *Variation in language: NWAV-XV*. Stanford, CA: Department of Linguistics, Stanford University. 173–182.

Haeri, Niloofar. 1994. A linguistic innovation of women in Cairo. *Language Variation and Change* 6: 87–112.

Haeri, Niloofar. 1996. *The sociolinguistic market of Cairo: Gender, class, and education*. London: Kegan Paul International.

Haeri, Niloofar. 1997. The reproduction of symbolic capital: Language, state and class in Egypt. *Current Anthropology* 38: 795–805.

Haeri, Niloofar. 2000. Form and ideology: Arabic sociolinguistics and beyond. *Annual Review of Anthropology* 29: 61–87.

Haeri, Niloofar and William M. Cotter. 2019. Form and ideology revisited. In Enam Al-Wer and Uri Horesh (eds.). *The Routledge handbook of Arabic sociolinguistics*. London: Routledge. 243–258.

Hassan, Batoul. 2009. *Ideology, identity, and linguistic capital: A sociolinguistic investigation of language shift among the Ajam of Kuwait*. PhD thesis, University of Essex.

Hassanein, Ahmad Taher. 2009. Youth speech. In Kees Versteegh, Mushira Eid, Alaa Elgibali, Manfred Woidich, and Andrzej Zaborski (eds.). *Encyclopedia of Arabic language and linguistics*, Volume 4. Leiden: Brill, 764–767.

Heath, Jeffrey. 2002. *Jewish and Muslim dialects of Moroccan Arabic*. London: Routledge Curzon.

Herin, Bruno. 2010. *Le parler arabe de Salt (Jordanie): Phonologie, morphologie et éléments de syntaxe*. PhD thesis, Université Libre du Bruxelles.

Herin, Bruno. 2019. Traditional dialects. In Enam Al-Wer and Uri Horesh (eds.). *The Routledge handbook of Arabic sociolinguistics*. London: Routledge. London: Routledge. 93–105.

Herin, Bruno and Enam Al-Wer. 2013. From phonological variation to grammatical change: Depalatalisation of /č/ in Salti. In Clive Holes and Rudolf de Jong (eds.). *Ingham of Arabia: A collection of articles presented as a tribute to the career of Bruce Ingham*. Leiden: Brill. 55–73.

Hock, Hans Henrich. 1986. *Principles of historical linguistics*, Berlin: De Gruyter.

Hoffman, Katherine E. 2007. *We share walls: Language, land, and gender in Berber Morocco*. Oxford: Wiley-Blackwell.

Højrup, Thomas. 1983. The concept of life-mode: A form-specifying mode of analysis applied to contemporary western Europe. *Ethnologia Scandinavica* 13: 15–50.

Højrup, Thomas. 2003. *State, culture and life-modes: The foundations of life-mode analysis*. London: Routledge.

Holes, Clive. 1987. *Language variation and change in a modernising Arab state: The case of Bahrain*. London: Kegan Paul International.

Holes, Clive. 1995. Community, dialect and urbanisation in the Arab-speaking Middle East. *Bulletin of the School of Oriental and African Studies* 58: 270–287.

Holes, Clive. 2000. *Dialect, culture, and society in Eastern Arabia*, Volume 1, *Glossary*. Leiden: Brill.

Holes, Clive. 2004. *Modern Arabic: Structures, functions, and* varieties, revised edition. Washington, DC: Georgetown University Press.

Holes, Clive. 2005. *Dialect, culture, and society in Eastern Arabia*, Volume 2, *Ethnographic texts*. Leiden: Brill.

Holes, Clive. 2011. Language and identity in the Arabian Gulf. *Journal of Arabian Studies* 1: 129–145.

Holes, Clive. 2016. *Dialect, culture, and society in Eastern Arabia*, Volume 3, *Phonology, morphology, syntax, style*. Leiden: Brill.

Holes, Clive. 2018. Introduction to Clive Holes (ed.). *Arabic historical dialectology: Linguistic and sociolinguistic approaches*. Oxford: Oxford University Press. 1–28.

Holes, Clive. 2019. Confessional varieties. In Enam Al-Wer and Uri Horesh (eds.). *The Routledge handbook of Arabic sociolinguistics*. London: Routledge. 63–80.

Holm, John. 2000. *An introduction to pidgins and creoles*. Cambridge: Cambridge University Press.

Hopkins, Simon. 1997. On the construction *šmēh l-gabrā* 'the name of the man' in Aramaic. *Journal of Semitic Studies* 42: 23–32.

Horesh, Uri. 2014. *Phonological outcomes of language contact in the Palestinian Arabic dialect of Jaffa*. PhD thesis, University of Essex.

Horesh, Uri. 2015. Structural change in urban Palestinian Arabic induced by contact with Modern Hebrew. In Aaron M. Butts (ed.). *Studies in Semitic language contact*. Leiden: Brill. 198–233.

Horesh, Uri. 2021. Sociolinguistic variation and variation in sociolinguistics. In Karin Ryding and David Wilmsen (eds.). *The Cambridge handbook of Arabic linguistics*. Cambridge: Cambridge University Press. 181–198.

Horesh, Uri and William M. Cotter. 2015. Sociolinguistics of Palestinian Arabic. In Rudolf de Jong and Lutz Edzard (eds.). *Encyclopedia of Arabic language and linguistics online*. Leiden: Brill. DOI: 10.1163/1570-6699_eall_SIM_001007.

Horesh, Uri and William M. Cotter. 2016. Current research on linguistic variation in the Arabic-speaking world. *Language and Linguistics Compass* 10/8: 370–381.

Huehnergard, John and Aaron D. Rubin. 2011. Phyla and waves: Models of classification of the Semitic languages. In Stefan Weninger (ed.). *The Semitic languages: An international handbook*. Berlin: De Gruyter Mouton. 259–278.

Hussain, Abeer. 2017. *The sociolinguistic correlates of dialect contact and koineisation in Medini Arabic: Lenition and resyllabification*. PhD thesis, University of Essex.

Ibrahim, Muhammad Hassan. 1986. Standard and prestige language: A problem in Arabic sociolinguistics. *Anthropological Linguistics* 28: 115–126.

Ingham, Bruce. 1994. *Najdi Arabic: Central Arabian*. Amsterdam: John Benjamins.

Ingham, Bruce. 2006. Afghanistan Arabic. In Kees Versteegh, Mushira Eid, Alaa Elgibali, Manfred Woidich, and Andrzej Zaborski (eds.). *Encyclopedia of Arabic language and linguistics*, Volume 1. Leiden: Brill. 28–35.

Ismail, Hanadi. 2007. Patterns of linguistic variation and change in Damascus. In Catherine Miller, Enam Al-Wer, Dominique Caubet, and Janet C. E. Watson (eds.). *Arabic in the city: Issues in dialect contact and language variation*. London: Routledge. 188–212.

Ismail, Hanadi. 2008. *Suburbia and the inner-city: Patterns of linguistic variation and change in Damascus*. PhD thesis, University of Essex.

Jabeur, Mohamed. 1987. *A sociolinguistic study in Tunisia: Rades*. PhD thesis, University of Reading.

Jassem, Zaidan Ali. 1993. *Impact of the Arab-Israeli wars on language & social change in the Arab World: The case of Syrian Arabic*. Kuala Lampur: Pustaka Antara.

Jastrow, Otto. 1981. *Die mesopotamisch-arabischen qəltu Dialekte*, Band 2, *Volkskundliche Texte in elf Dialekten*. Wiesbaden: Steiner J.

Jastrow, Otto. 2005. Uzbekistan Arabic: A language created by Semitic-Iranian-Turkic linguistic convergence. In Éva Ágnes Csató, Bo Isaksson, Carina Jahani (eds.). *Linguistic convergence and areal diffusion: Case studies from Iranian, Semitic and Turkic*. London: RoutledgeCurzon. 133–140.

Johnson, Daniel Ezra. 2009. Getting off the GoldVarb standard: Introducing Rbrul for mixed effects variable rule analysis. *Language and Linguistics Compass* 3: 359–383.

Johnstone, T. M. 1963. The affrication of 'kaf' and 'gaf' in the Arabic dialects of the Arabian Peninsula. *Journal of Semitic studies* 8: 210–226.

Kossmann, Maarten. 2013. *The Arabic influence on northern Berber*. Leiden: Brill.

Krumbacher, Karl. 1902. *Das Problem der neugriechischen Schriftsprache*. Munich: K. B. Akademie in kommission des G. Franz'schen verlags.

Labov, William. 1963. The social motivation of a sound change. *Word* 19: 273–309.

Labov, William. 1966. *The social stratification of English in New York City*. Washington D. C. Center for Applied Linguistics.

Labov, William. 1972. *Sociolinguistic patterns*, Philadelphia: University of Pennsylvania Press.

Labov, William. 1981. Field methods of the project on linguistic change and variation. In John Baugh and Joel Sherzer (eds.) *Language in use: Readings in sociolinguistics*. Englewood Cliffs, NJ: Prentice Hall. 28–66.

Labov, William. 1982. Objectivity and commitment in linguistic science: The case of the Black English trial in Ann Arbor. *Language in Society* 11: 165–201.

Labov, William. 1994. *Principles of linguistic change*, Volume 1, *Internal factors*. Oxford: Blackwell.

Labov, William. 2001. *Principles of linguistic change*, Volume 2, *Social factors*. Malden, MA: Blackwell.

Labov, William and Dennis R. Preston. 2013. Foreword. *Journal of Linguistic Geography* 1: 93–95.

Lahlou, Moncef. 1991. *A morpho-syntactic study of code switching between Moroccan Arabic and French*. PhD dissertation, University of Texas at Austin.

Lass, Roger. 1997. *Historical linguistics and language change*. Cambridge: Cambridge University Press.

Macaulay, Ronald. 1977. *Language, social class, and education: A Glasgow study*. Edinburgh: Edinburgh University Press.

Mallinson, Christine. 2009. Sociolinguistics and sociology: Current directions, future partnerships. *Language and Linguistics Compass* 3/4: 1034–1051.

Mallinson, Christine, Becky Childs, and Gerard Van Herk. 2018. *Data collection in sociolinguistics methods and applications*, 2nd edition. London: Routledge.

Mallinson, Christine and Robin Dodsworth. 2009. Revisiting the need for new approaches to social class in variationist sociolinguistics. *Sociolinguistic Studies* 3: 253–278.

Manfredi, Stefano and Fida Bizri. 2019. Arabic-based pidgins and creoles. In Enam Al-Wer and Uri Horesh (eds.). *The Routledge handbook of Arabic sociolinguistics*. London: Routledge. 134–147.

Manfredi, Stefano and Mauro Tosco. 2014. *Arabic-based pidgins and creoles*, Special issue of *Journal of Pidgin and Creole Languages* 29 (2).

Marçais, William. 1930. *Le Dialecte arabe parlé à Tlemcen; grammaire, textes et glossaire*. Paris: E. Leroux.

Messaoudi, Leila. 2019. Urban sociolinguistics. In Enam Al-Wer and Uri Horesh (eds.). *The Routledge handbook of Arabic sociolinguistics*. London: Routledge. 203–213.

Meyerhoff, Miriam. 2018. *Introducing sociolinguistics*, 3rd edition. London: Routledge.

Mifsud, Manwel. 2008. Maltese. In Kees Versteegh, Mushira Eid, Alaa Elgibali, Manfred Woidich, and Andrzej Zaborski (eds.). *Encyclopedia of Arabic language and linguistics*, Volume 3. Leiden: Brill. 146–159.

Miller, Catherine. 2007. Arabic urban vernaculars: Development and change. In Catherine Miller, Enam Al-Wer, Dominique Caubet, and Janet C. E. Watson (eds.). *Arabic in the city: Issues in dialect contact and language variation*. London: Routledge. 1–31.

Miller, Catherine. 2014. Juba Arabic as a written language. *Journal of Pidgin and Creole Languages* 29: 352–384.

Miller, Catherine, Enam Al-Wer, Dominique Caubet, and Janet C. E. Watson (eds.). 2007. *Arabic in the city: Issues in dialect contact and language variation*. London: Routledge.

Milroy, James, Lesley Milroy, and Susan Hartley. 1994. Local and supra-local change in British English – the case of glottalisation. *English World-Wide* 15: 1–33.

Milroy, Lesley. 1987. *Language and social networks*, 2nd edition. Oxford: Blackwell.

Milroy, Lesley and Matthew Gordon. 2003. *Sociolinguistics: Method and interpretation*. Oxford: Blackwell.

Milroy, Lesley and James Milroy. 1992. Social network and social class: Towards an integrated sociolinguistic model. *Language in Society* 21: 1–26.

Mitchell, T. F. 1978. Educated spoken Arabic in Egypt and the Levant, with special reference to participle and tense. *Journal of Linguistics* 14: 227–258.

Mourigh, Khalid. 2015. *A grammar of Ghomara Berber*. PhD thesis, Leiden University.

Naciri-Azzouz, Amina. 2016. Les variétés arabes de Ghomara? *s-sāḥəl* vs. *əǧ-ǧbəl*: (la côte vs. la montagne). In George Grigore and Gabriel Biţună (eds.). *Arabic varieties – Far and wide: Proceedings of the 11th international conference of AIDA – Bucharest, 2015*. Bucharest: Universităţii din Bucureşti. 405–412.

Newton, Brian. 1964. An Arabic-Greek Dialect. *Papers in memory of George C. Pappageot*. Supplement to *Word* 20: 43–52.

Nichols, Johanna. 1996. The geography of language origins. *Annual meeting of the Berkeley Linguistics Society* 22: 267–278.

Nöldeke, Theodor. 1898. *Kurzgefasste syrische Grammatik*. Leipzig: Tauchnitz.

Owens, Jonathan. 1997. Arabic-based pidgins and creoles. In S. G. Thomason (ed.). *Contact languages: A wider perspective*. Amsterdam: John Benjamins. 125–172.

Owens, Jonathan. 2001. Arabic sociolinguistics. *Arabica* 48: 419–469.

Owens, Jonathan. 2006. *A linguistic history of Arabic*. Oxford: Oxford University Press.

Owens, Jonathan. 2011. Arabic sociolinguistics. In Stefan Weninger, Geoffrey Khan, Michael. P. Streck, and Janet C. E. Watson (eds.). *The Semitic languages: An international handbook*. Berlin: De Gruyter. 970–981.

Owens, Jonathan. 2013. A house of sound structure, of marvelous form and proportion: An introduction. In Jonathan Owens (ed.). *The Oxford handbook of Arabic linguistics*. Oxford: Oxford University Press. 1–22.

Owens, Jonathan. 2014. The morphologization of an Arabic creole. *Journal of Pidgin and Creole Languages* 29: 232–298.

Owens, Jonathan. 2020. Nigerian Arabic. In Chris Lucas and Stefano Manfredi (eds.). *Arabic and contact-induced change*. Berlin: Language Science Press. 175–196.

Paunonen, Heikki. 1996. Suomen kielen ohjailun myytit ja stereotypiat. *Virittäjä* 100: 544–544.

Petyt, Keith Malcolm. 1980. *The study of dialect: An introduction to dialectology*. Boulder: Westview Press.

Prichard, Hilary. 2016. *The role of higher education in linguistic change*. PhD dissertation, University of Pennsylvania.

Prichard, Hilary and Meredith Tamminga. 2012. The impact of higher education on Philadelphia vowels. *University of Pennsylvania Working Papers in Linguistics* 18: 87–95.

Procházka, Stephan. 2020. Arabic in Iraq, Syria, and Southern Turkey. In Christopher Lucas and Stefano Manfredi (eds.). *Arabic and contact-induced change*. Berlin: Language Science Press. 83–114.

Prochazka, Theodor. 1988. *Saudi Arabian dialects*. London: Kegan Paul International.

Psichari, Jean. 1928. Un pays qui ne veut pas de sa langue. *Mercure de France* 207: 63–121.

Retsö, Jan. 2006. Aramaic/Syriac loanwords. In Kees Versteegh, Mushira Eid, Alaa Elgibali, Manfred Woidich, and Andrzej Zaborski (eds.). *Encyclopedia of Arabic language and linguistics*, Volume 1. Leiden: Brill. 178–182.

Rickford, John. R. and Thomas A. Wasow. 1995. Syntactic variation and change in progress: Loss of the verbal coda in topic-restricting as far as constructions. *Language* 71: 102–131.

Rouabah, Siham. 2020. *Language shift or maintenance in Tamazight: A sociolinguistic study of Chaouia in Batna, Algeria*. PhD thesis. University of Essex.

Rubin, Aaron. D. 2005. *Studies in Semitic grammaticalization*. Winona Lake, IN: Eisenbrauns.

Sadiqi, Fatima. 2003. *Women, gender and language in Morocco*. Leiden: Brill.

Sadiqi, Fatima. 2007. Language and gender. In Kees Versteegh, Mushira Eid, Alaa Elgibali, Manfred Woidich, and Andrzej Zaborski (eds.). *Encyclopedia of Arabic language and linguistics*. Leiden: Brill. 642–650.

Sankoff, Gillian. 2019. Language change across the lifespan: Three trajectory types. *Language* 95: 197–229.

Sayahi, Lotfi. 2011. Code-switching and language change in Tunisia. *International Journal of the Sociology of Language* 211: 113–133.

Sayahi, Lotfi. 2014. *Diglossia and language contact: Language variation and change in North Africa*. Cambridge: Cambridge University Press.

Schilling, Natalie. 2013. *Sociolinguistic fieldwork*. Cambridge: Cambridge University Press.

Schmidt, Johannes. 1872. *Die Verwandtschaftsverhältnisse der indogermanischen Sprachen*. Weimar: H. Böhlau.

Seeger, Ulrich. 2013. *Der arabische Dialekt der Dörfer um Ramallah*, Teil 3, *Grammatik*. Wiesbaden: Harrassowitz.

Shami, Seteney. 1982. *Ethnicity and leadership: the Circassians in Jordan*. PhD thesis, Berkeley, University of California.

Sibawayh, Abu Bishr. 1988. *Al-Kitāb* [the book]. Hārūn, A. M. (ed.). Cairo: Maktabat al-Ḫānǧi.

Souag, Lameen. 2017. Clitic doubling and language contact in Arabic. *Zeitschrift für Arabische Linguistik* 66: 45–70.

Stuart-Smith, Jane. 1999. Glottals past and present: A study of t-glottalling in Glaswegian. *Leeds Studies in English*, n.s. 30: 181–204.

Tagliamonte, Sali A. 2006. *Analysing sociolinguistic variation*. Cambridge: Cambridge University Press.

Tagliamonte, Sali A. 2012. *Variationist sociolinguistics: Change, observation, interpretation*. Oxford: Wiley-Blackwell.

Taqi, Hanan. 2010. *Two ethnicities, three generations: Phonological variation and change in Kuwait*. PhD thesis, University of Newcastle.

Thomason, Sarah Grey. 2001. *Language contact: An introduction*. Edinburgh: Edinburgh University Press.

Thomason, Sarah Grey and Terrence Kaufman. 1988. *Language contact, creolization, and genetic linguistics*. Berkeley: University of California Press.

Tosco, Mauro and Stefano Manfredi. 2013. Pidgins and creoles. In Jonathan Owens (ed.). *The Oxford handbook of Arabic linguistics*. Oxford: Oxford University Press. 495–519.

Trimble, Louis. P. 1971. Phonemic change and the growth of homophones in Maltese. *Journal of Maltese Studies* 7: 92–98.

Trudgill, Peter. 1974. *The social differentiation of English in Norwich*, Cambridge: Cambridge University Press.

Trudgill, Peter. 1986. *Dialects in contact*. Oxford: Blackwell.

Trudgill, Peter. 2000. *Sociolinguistics: An introduction to language and society*. London: Penguin.

Trudgill, Peter. 2004. *New-dialect formation: The inevitability of colonial Englishes*. Edinburgh: Edinburgh University Press.

Trudgill, Peter. 2009. Contact, isolation, and complexity in Arabic. In Enam Al-Wer and Rudolf E. de Jong (eds.). *Arabic dialectology: In honour of Clive Holes on the occasion of his sixtieth birthday*. Leiden: Brill. 174–185.

Trudgill, Peter. 2011. *Sociolinguistic typology: Social determinants of linguistic complexity*. Oxford: Oxford University Press.

Versteegh, Kees. 1984. *Pidginization and creolization: The case of Arabic*. Amsterdam: John Benjamins.

Versteegh, Kees. 2014. *Arabic language*, 2nd edition. Edinburgh: Edinburgh University Press.

Versteegh, Kees, Mushira Eid, Alaa Elgibali, Manfred Woidich, and Andrzej Zaborski (eds.). 2006–2009. *Encyclopedia of Arabic language and linguistics*. 5 volumes. Leiden: Brill.

Vitt, Lois A. 2011. Class. In George Ritzer and J. Michael Ryan (eds.). *The concise encyclopedia of sociology*. Chichester: Wiley-Blackwell. 65–66.

Walters, Keith. 1991. Women, men, and linguistic variation in the Arab world. In Bernard Comrie and Mushira Eid (eds.). *Perspectives on Arabic linguistics*, Volume 3, *Papers from the third Annual Symposium on Arabic Linguistics*. Amsterdam: John Benjamins. 199–229.

Wang, William. S.-Y. 1969. Competing changes as a cause of residue. *Language* 45: 9–25.

Wittrich, Michaela. 2001. *Der arabische Dialekt von Äzn*. Wiesbaden: Harrassowitz.

Woidich, Manfred. 1996. Rural dialect of Egyptian Arabic: An overview. *Egypte/Monde Arabe* 27: 325–354.

Woidich, Manfred. 2006. *Das kairenisch-Arabische: eine Grammatik*. Wiesbaden: Harrassowitz.

Woidich, Manfred and Liesbeth Zack. 2009. The g/ǧ -question in Egyptian Arabic revisited. In Enam Al-Wer and Rudolf E. de Jong (eds.). *Arabic dialectology: In honour of Clive Holes on the occasion of his sixtieth birthday*. Leiden: Brill. 41–62.

Zaborski, Andrzej. 2007. Jīm. In Kees Versteegh, Mushira Eid, Alaa Elgibali, Manfred Woidich, and Andrzej Zaborski (eds.). *Encyclopedia of Arabic language and linguistics*, Volume 3. Leiden: Brill. 494–496.

Ziamari, Karima. 2003. *Le code switching intra-phrastique dans les conversations des étudiants marocains de l'ENSAM: approche linguitique du duel entre l'arabe marocain et le français*. PhD thesis. INALCO-Fès.

Ziamari, Karima. 2007. Development and linguistic change in Moroccan Arabic-French codeswitching. In Catherine Miller, Enam Al-Wer, Dominique Caubet, and Janet C. E. Watson (eds.). *Arabic in the city: Issues in dialect contact and language variation*. London: Routledge. 275–290.

Subject Index

acoustic analysis, 38
affrication, 25, 55, 56, 112, 134, 146, 147, 148, 172, 173, 174, 181
Afroasiatic, 84, 133, 196
age, 6, 26, 29, 30, 31, 32, 33, 35, 36, 39, 40, 41, 47, 55, 57, 58, 59, 60, 62, 63, 64, 65, 66, 67, 69, 70, 73, 75, 97, 98, 102, 106, 115, 117, 118, 123, 124, 126, 136, 141, 142, 143, 144, 154, 155
   division, 31, 32
   middle, 66, 68, 69, 102, 124
   old, 15, 18, 47, 58, 62, 67, 69, 73, 102, 108, 123, 141, 143, 144, 161
   young, 18, 20, 30, 31, 32, 33, 43, 44, 49, 58, 59, 66, 67, 69, 71, 73, 75, 80, 82, 116, 120, 123, 124, 128, 137, 142, 144, 149, 201
age group, 29, 30, 31, 32, 33, 35, 36, 40, 55, 57, 58, 59, 62, 66, 68, 69, 70, 73, 76, 102, 123, 124, 141, 143, 144, 154
Ajam, 122, 123, 124, 125, 126
Akkadian, 133
Albanian, 200
Altaic, 198
Amazigh, 44, 84, 108, 129, 158, 192, 195, 196, 197
Amharic, 133
apparent time, 5, 30, 140, 141, 143, 154
approximation, 56, 101
ʿArab, 109, 113, 114, 115, 116
Aramaic, 132, 133, 134, 158, 181, 192, 193, 194, 195, 196, 198
archaic, 157, 178, 180, 181
areal features, 163, 165, 197, 198, 200, 201, 202
article, xvi, 4, 23, 24, 104, 129, 151, 157, 158, 165, 187, 198
assimilation, 32, 98, 213
atlas, 1, 19, 109, 129, 138, 139, 158, 159, 160, 161, 163, 167, 173, 176, 187, 202
auditory analysis, 38
awareness, 14, 48, 59, 65, 121, 131, 138, 146, 148, 167, 173, 190

Bagirmi, 198
Baharna, 113, 114, 115, 116
Bani Ḥasan, 134
barrier, 93, 107, 156, 157, 158, 170, 171, 173, 175, 177, 190, 191, 199
Basque, 134
Bedouin, 22, 56, 112, 113, 114, 122, 149, 157, 161, 163, 166, 177, 180, 188
Berber. See Amazigh
bilingualism, 4, 23, 31, 33, 85, 87, 88, 126, 127, 128, 184, 192, 200, 201
border, 157, 159, 171, 173, 175, 176, 177, 190, 191, 198, 206, 207, 213
borrowing, 3, 4, 25, 29, 45, 99, 145, 146, 147, 181, 182, 183, 192, 193, 196
boundary, 29, 35, 110, 111, 114, 129, 156, 158, 159, 161, 190, 213
Bulgarian, 200
bundle, 20, 114, 176

Cape Verdean Creole, 186
capital, 20, 32, 52, 66, 88, 89, 90, 114, 127, 137, 140, 158, 161, 174, 178, 179, 180, 202, 203, 205, 210
cartography, 7, 160
casual speech. See vernacular
categorical, 9, 24, 25, 26, 28, 54, 59, 64, 67, 73, 99
Chadic, 198
chain shift, 27, 42, 54, 148
change, 1, 2, 4, 5, 6, 7, 9, 11, 17, 20, 22, 23, 25, 29, 30, 38, 43, 45, 48, 49, 51, 54, 55, 56, 57, 60, 61, 63, 65, 66, 67, 68, 69, 70, 72, 73, 75, 76, 78, 79, 83, 85, 92, 96, 98, 101, 102, 103, 109, 113, 117, 118, 119, 121, 124, 125, 126, 128, 131, 132, 134, 135, 136, 137, 138, 139, 140, 141, 143, 144, 146, 147, 148, 149, 150, 151, 152, 153, 154, 155, 156, 167, 172, 173, 174, 180, 187, 188, 202, 204
   trajectory, 3, 4, 51, 148, 150
change from above, 146, 147, 148, 149

change from below, 146, 148, 149
change in progress, 5, 22, 55, 68, 75, 79, 118,
    121, 137, 144, 152, 154, 155, 174
Chechens, 126, 127, 128
Christian, 81, 106, 109, 110, 111, 112, 113,
    119, 120, 121, 122, 130, 184, 195
church, 81, 103, 106
Circassian, 125, 126, 127, 128
city, 3, 7, 9, 10, 14, 15, 19, 28, 30, 32, 33, 36,
    49, 50, 52, 53, 54, 55, 58, 59, 60, 61, 63,
    68, 69, 70, 75, 78, 79, 80, 81, 82, 88, 90,
    93, 96, 97, 98, 99, 100, 102, 104, 108,
    111, 113, 114, 117, 118, 121, 122, 123,
    127, 142, 145, 146, 148, 149, 150, 158,
    161, 163, 174, 178, 179, 180, 184, 189,
    190, 191, 194, 203, 204, 205, 206, 210,
    211
class, 49, 55, 77, 85, 86, 92, 93, 94, 96, 102,
    104, 146
Classical Arabic, 51, 74, 76, 78, 90
clause, 22, 24, 198
clitic doubling, 112, 194
coast, 108, 133, 157, 176, 202
code-switching, 4, 5, 185, 197
coding, 4, 5, 35, 36, 37, 42, 185, 197
college, 80, 81, 88
colonialism, 184, 186, 206
community, 1, 3, 4, 5, 6, 7, 9, 10, 11, 12, 13, 16,
    18, 19, 20, 26, 27, 28, 31, 32, 33, 34, 35,
    36, 40, 42, 43, 44, 46, 47, 48, 49, 50, 51,
    52, 53, 54, 55, 56, 58, 59, 60, 61, 63, 65,
    67, 68, 69, 70, 71, 73, 74, 75, 76, 77, 78,
    79, 80, 81, 82, 83, 84, 85, 88, 89, 93, 94,
    96, 97, 98, 99, 100, 101, 102, 104, 105,
    106, 107, 108, 109, 110, 111, 113, 114,
    116, 117, 118, 119, 120, 122, 123, 124,
    126, 127, 128, 129, 130, 135, 137, 139,
    140, 141, 144, 146, 150, 151, 156, 158,
    161, 163, 166, 170, 173, 174, 175, 180,
    181, 184, 185, 188, 190, 200, 201, 203,
    204, 205, 210, 213
community of practice, 94, 102, 104
comparative method, 133, 134, 151
complexification, 61, 148, 201
consciousness, 11, 59, 94, 120, 143, 146, 148,
    204
conservative, 18, 63, 113, 141, 158, 185, 203
consonant, 27, 28, 33, 38, 40, 41, 42, 113, 118,
    133, 144, 147, 148, 159, 182, 183, 191
constraint
    external, 26
    internal, 26, 151
    linguistic, 26, 29
contact, 4, 16, 20, 23, 33, 43, 54, 56, 63, 65, 70,
    71, 76, 78, 79, 80, 92, 96, 97, 98, 101, 105,
    120, 122, 136, 142, 157, 158, 167, 178,
    181, 183, 185, 189, 190, 191, 192, 193,
    195, 196, 198, 199, 200, 201, 204, 206,
    209, 210, 212
    dialect, 7, 27, 54, 55, 109, 122, 157, 167, 213
    language, 7, 186, 201, 212
continuum, 17, 62, 159
contra-hierarchical diffusion, 205, 206, 211
convergence, 51, 56, 94, 114, 116, 118, 124,
    157, 178, 184, 190, 201
Coptic, 122, 181, 192
corpus, 17, 45, 151, 212
correlation, 33, 64, 78, 86, 87, 93, 94, 96, 97,
    99, 105, 106, 107, 141, 144, 209
creole, 134, 185, 186, 187
crossover, 57, 59, 73, 144, 145
cross-tabulation, 39, 57, 60, 75, 155
culture, 16, 18, 19, 31, 50, 52, 58, 63, 83, 84,
    93, 101, 102, 111, 127, 129, 158, 177,
    178, 212
Cypriot Greek, 184, 185

Dari, 198, 200
definiteness, xvi, 22, 23, 24, 29, 157, 158, 198,
    200
deictic, 198
deletion, 33, 36, 87, 182, 196, 202
demonstrative, 198
descriptive, 10, 39, 40, 107, 113
descriptive statistics, 39, 40
diachronic, 132, 141
dialect
    local, 4, 58, 61, 80, 122, 124, 149, 157, 182,
        183, 190, 192, 194, 203, 209
dialect geography, 7, 159, 160
dialectal, 2, 59, 75, 115, 122, 125, 142, 143,
    156, 159, 160, 173, 190, 191, 203, 210
dialectology, 1, 2, 7, 8, 12, 19, 107, 119, 139,
    159, 160, 161, 167, 178, 180, 187, 188,
    190, 191, 203, 212
diffusion, 7, 56, 57, 69, 77, 134, 135, 136, 146,
    156, 157, 176, 177, 189, 190, 191, 192,
    194, 201, 203, 204, 205, 206, 211
diglossia, 2, 4
diphthong, 46, 53, 58, 78, 99, 100, 101, 205,
    206, 208
divergence, 51, 54, 61, 89, 108, 122, 173, 175, 181
diversity, 65, 67, 79, 84, 98, 99, 106, 107, 122,
    133, 178, 192
Dōsari tribe, 98
Druze, 3, 109, 110, 111, 170, 172, 173
Dutch, 5, 191

education, 6, 12, 18, 24, 33, 50, 52, 55, 65, 67,
    69, 71, 72, 77, 78, 79, 80, 81, 82, 83, 84,
    85, 86, 87, 88, 89, 90, 92, 96, 97, 103, 108,
    116, 124, 126, 128, 137, 204, 213
    higher, 12, 61, 63, 67, 71, 78, 79, 80, 81, 82,
        83, 89

level, 77, 78, 79, 85, 89
type, 77, 85, 86, 87, 88, 89
Eimi, 123, 124, 125
elicitation, 13, 14, 15, 16, 17, 18, 46
emic, 32
emphatic, 28, 46, 131, 132, 172, 183, 184, 185, 197, 210
employment, 19, 58, 63, 65, 68, 79, 81, 88, 93, 97, 101, 102, 116, 139, 204
enclave, 122, 123, 128, 158, 163, 172, 175, 178
'Eneze tribe, 163
English, xv, 2, 13, 17, 29, 32, 45, 49, 52, 74, 82, 83, 84, 106, 123, 129, 131, 133, 163, 186, 194, 206, 212
escarpment, 156
ethics, 13, 42, 43, 44
ethnicity, 6, 19, 29, 35, 75, 92, 94, 106, 107, 109, 110, 114, 120, 121, 122, 124, 125, 126, 128, 129, 130, 137, 173, 175
ethnography, 15, 16, 19, 20, 42, 44, 69, 129, 212
etic, 32

factor weight, 41, 87
Fali, 198
feminine, xvi, 18, 21, 22, 28, 32, 40, 41, 46, 49, 50, 63, 65, 67, 74, 118, 119, 142, 147, 148, 154, 193, 197, 210
feminine ending, 18, 21, 22, 28, 33, 40, 41, 46, 63, 65, 67, 118, 119, 147, 154, 210
Finnish, 140
focal area, 177, 178, 179, 180, 188, 189, 191, 201, 202, 203, 211
formality, 11, 12, 15, 16, 17, 46
fortition, 69, 71
French, 5, 32, 83, 84, 111, 158, 171, 179, 186, 191, 206
fudged forms, 207, 209, 210

Gaelic, 128, 129
Gascon, 4
gender, 6, 17, 18, 21, 22, 26, 29, 35, 40, 41, 48, 49, 50, 51, 52, 53, 54, 55, 57, 59, 60, 62, 63, 64, 65, 66, 67, 70, 71, 72, 73, 74, 75, 76, 77, 98, 99, 102, 106, 117, 118, 119, 129, 136, 137, 142, 144, 147, 148, 154, 155, 161, 181, 191, 193, 194
grammatical, 78
genealogy, 107, 108, 109, 114, 133, 180, 212
generation. See age
genitive, xvi, 184
geography, 8, 52, 55, 111, 151, 156, 157, 158, 159, 160, 161, 163, 170, 176, 177, 178, 180, 181, 187, 188, 189, 191, 197, 200, 202, 203, 206, 211, 212
German, 83, 158, 161, 163, 175, 178, 179, 180, 191, 200, 207
High German, 176, 207
Hochdeutsch, 176
Low German, 176, 207
Plattdeutsch, 176
Ghamdi tribe, 58, 59, 99, 100, 209
Ghomara tribes, 196, 197
globalisation, 81, 83, 88
Gravity Model, 203
Greek, 132, 133, 184

Haitian Creole, 186
Ḥarb tribe, 75
heartland, 111, 123, 128, 208
Hebrew, 23, 32, 33, 87, 88, 107, 133, 134
heritage, 40, 50, 51, 54, 58, 59, 65, 75, 98, 100, 101, 116, 123, 124, 125, 126, 127, 128, 142, 143, 149, 206, 209
heterogeneity, 52, 78, 98, 99, 109, 117, 121, 127
Hijaz, 58, 150
historical linguistics, 5, 7, 132, 133, 134, 150, 151, 184, 201, 203, 212
homogeneity, 99, 120

Ibadi, 108, 109
identity, 43, 84, 85, 106, 115, 116, 117, 118, 119, 121, 124, 127, 129, 171, 206, 211
ideology, 50, 69, 81, 93, 120, 124, 128
immigration, 5, 50, 93, 107, 147, 213
income, 77, 92
index, xvi, 62, 77, 80, 85, 88, 96, 97, 98, 99, 100, 101, 102, 106, 134
indigenous, 32, 33, 84, 99, 100, 119, 128, 196, 203
Indo-European, 133, 198, 200
inferential statistics, 40
inner-city, 67, 69, 102, 144
innovation, 6, 7, 34, 40, 55, 57, 60, 64, 67, 68, 69, 72, 77, 86, 90, 92, 96, 102, 121, 132, 135, 143, 144, 146, 150, 153, 154, 156, 157, 176, 177, 178, 187, 189, 190, 201, 202, 203, 204, 205
inscription, 132, 211
insular, 111
interaction, 2, 10, 11, 15, 16, 17, 18, 27, 34, 35, 38, 48, 55, 57, 59, 65, 75, 76, 79, 85, 88, 92, 109, 114, 126, 135, 141, 151, 157, 160, 175, 189, 203, 204, 206
interdental, 10, 46, 51, 78, 108, 109, 110, 112, 132, 149, 150, 196, 197
interdialectal forms, 3, 206
interloper, 99, 100
intermediate, 58, 80, 99, 100, 101, 137, 167, 207, 209, 211
intermediate forms, 101, 167, 207, 209, 211
interview, 13, 14, 15, 16, 17, 18, 43, 46
Iranian languages, 123, 124, 198, 200
island, 108, 109, 128, 129, 180, 181, 183

isogloss, 159, 161, 163, 173, 176, 177, 206, 207, 208
isolation, 58, 70, 105, 107, 113, 157, 158, 178, 179, 180, 181, 183, 184, 185, 198, 203
Italian, 134, 181, 182, 183

Jewish, 88, 107, 108, 110, 111, 112, 113
Juba Arabic, 186, 187
Judaeo-Arabic, 107

Kanuri, 198
koine, 191
koineisation, 7, 20, 79, 120, 121, 179, 180, 189, 190, 210, 212
Kurdish, 158, 198

landscape, 156
language family, 133, 134, 192, 195, 198, 200
language isolates, 134
language shift, 7, 122, 124, 125, 127, 128, 129, 196
lateral, 131, 157
Latin, xv, 29, 133, 134
lenition, 33, 36, 56, 67, 87, 88, 144
levelling, 52, 60, 67, 101, 121, 189
lexicon, 1, 3, 4, 29, 30, 45, 108, 109, 111, 112, 120, 136, 152, 159, 160, 163, 173, 176, 183, 184, 186, 192, 196, 200, 207
lexifier, 186
life-mode, 68, 77, 93, 94, 101, 102, 104, 144
lifespan, 141
lifestyle, 29, 69, 92, 161, 177, 190
lingua franca, 3
linguistic area, 200
literacy, 80
localised, 2, 52, 53, 54, 55, 62, 63, 65, 67, 72, 74, 104, 189
log-odd, 87
longitudinal, 140, 141

Macedonian, 200
Maghrebi, 190, 207
maintenance, 96, 98, 100, 110, 121, 124, 128, 129, 148, 158, 178
majority, 81, 102, 110, 111, 114, 117, 120, 122, 125, 126, 128, 133, 137, 147, 150, 157, 177, 180, 181, 193, 196, 199
Maliki, 108
Maltese, 149, 181, 182, 183, 184, 185, 187, 195
man, 14, 18, 22, 31, 48, 49, 50, 51, 53, 54, 55, 56, 58, 59, 60, 62, 63, 64, 65, 66, 67, 68, 69, 70, 71, 72, 73, 74, 75, 85, 86, 94, 110, 120, 149, 195
map, 110, 159, 160, 161, 163, 165, 166, 167, 171, 172, 173, 174, 176, 177, 202, 203, 206, 207, 208

marginalisation, 84, 107, 120
Maronite, 110, 184
Maronite Cypriot Arabic, 183, 184, 185
marsh, 156
masculine, xvi, 21, 22, 49, 50, 74, 138, 147, 148, 167, 181, 193, 194
Mashreqi, 190, 207
meaning
    referential, 21
    social, 3, 20, 104
merger, 51, 78, 108, 132, 149, 182, 183, 185
methodology, 1, 6, 15, 20, 44, 45, 85, 89, 93
Middle English, 5
migration, 19, 53, 54, 58, 59, 60, 78, 89, 93, 96, 99, 104, 108, 113, 115, 120, 122, 127, 140, 142, 146, 150, 165, 166, 167, 177, 179, 185, 196, 206, 209, 210, 213
minority, 33, 64, 65, 106, 114, 119, 120, 122, 125, 127, 129, 180, 184
Mišlab tribe, 69
mobility, 67, 73, 76, 149, 167
Modern English, 5
Modern Greek, 200
Modern South Arabian, 133
monolingualism, 4, 126, 128
monophthong, 46, 53, 58, 59, 78, 99, 100, 101, 205, 208, 209
morpheme, xvi, 21, 25, 29, 32, 35, 118
morphology, 4, 8, 17, 21, 25, 29, 51, 78, 108, 111, 112, 114, 129, 159, 160, 167, 173, 176, 184, 193, 197, 200, 212
morphophonemics, 17, 21, 25, 35
morphosyntactic, 53, 96, 97, 183, 187
mosque, 99, 100
mountain, 109, 111, 129, 156, 157, 158, 173, 175, 180
multilingualism, 106, 197, 200
multivariate analysis, 26, 36, 38, 40, 113
Muslim, 81, 99, 106, 108, 109, 110, 111, 112, 113, 114, 119, 121, 122, 125, 130, 192, 193

Nabatean, 132
Najd, 25, 26, 27, 101, 115, 134, 146, 147, 148, 150, 181
nationalism, 123, 124
native speaker, 3, 11, 12, 21, 28, 45, 131, 147, 186, 197
neighbourhood, 10, 15, 19, 67, 69, 77, 85, 96, 97, 98, 99, 102, 108, 114, 116, 117, 123, 127, 157, 200
neighbourhood effect, 200
new-dialect formation, 20, 149, 186, 210, 212
Niger-Congo, 198
Nilo-Saharan, 198
nomad, 69, 166

non-standard, 44, 49, 52
norm, 2, 3, 18, 28, 48, 50, 52, 56, 63, 66, 71,
	96, 114, 116, 119, 120, 122, 141, 150,
	158, 161, 163, 172, 173, 180, 189, 191,
	206, 207
normative, 4, 17, 51, 131
Northern Cities Shift, 54
Nubi, 186, 187

observer's paradox, 13, 14, 15
occupation, 32, 35, 68, 77, 85, 92, 97, 111, 124
Oslo Accords, 191
Ottoman, 111, 126, 192

palatalisation, 26, 27, 55, 63, 75, 85, 86, 94,
	134
panel study, 139, 140
participant observation, 16
particle, 159, 184, 186, 200
Pashto, 198, 200
periphery, 72, 114, 172, 173, 180, 212
Persian, 122, 124, 133, 158, 192, 198, 199
Phoenician, 133
phoneme, xv, 2, 21, 24, 27, 34, 35, 51, 78, 87,
	90, 109, 124, 131, 132, 134, 148, 149,
	157, 161, 163, 171, 172, 173, 180, 182,
	184, 197
phonetics, xv, 35, 38, 100, 108, 109, 131, 144,
	147, 196, 210
phonology, 4, 7, 8, 17, 21, 25, 27, 28, 29, 33,
	35, 51, 53, 61, 75, 78, 87, 88, 96, 98, 99,
	108, 109, 111, 112, 114, 124, 129, 130,
	132, 148, 151, 159, 160, 171, 173, 176,
	184, 196, 197, 200, 210, 212
plateau, 109, 156, 157
plural, xvi, 17, 18, 21, 22, 66, 67, 78, 97, 142,
	148, 182, 193, 194, 208
politics, 6, 19, 50, 51, 74, 76, 77, 82, 84, 109,
	110, 114, 115, 116, 117, 119, 120, 127,
	130, 171, 173, 175, 179, 184, 188, 190,
	213
possessive, 112, 184
preposition, xvi, 159, 194
prescriptive, 10
prestige, 2, 48, 49, 51, 52, 56, 81, 88, 93, 114,
	145, 146, 172, 180
Principles of Commitment, 44, 47
privatisation, 83, 88
probability, 26, 33, 34, 38, 40, 41
pronominal suffix, 22, 142, 143, 167, 193, 194,
	202
pronoun, 22, 112, 115, 142, 143, 148, 159, 167,
	186, 193, 194, 198, 202
Proto-Indo-European, 133
proto-language, 133

proxy variable, 78, 79, 88
p-value, 41

qeltu, 112, 113
qualitative analysis, 26, 33, 138
quantitative analysis, 6, 24, 33, 34, 42, 44, 48,
	50, 55, 85, 97, 98, 101, 138, 154, 202

range of variation, 24, 25, 26, 46, 47, 72, 116,
	206
Rbrul, 36, 40, 44
reading, 7, 10, 15, 17, 73, 74, 179
real time, 114, 138, 139, 140, 141, 151, 152
reconstruction, 134
refugee, 32, 50, 53, 82, 120, 127, 149
regionality, xvi, 93, 94, 98, 99, 100, 101, 104
relic, 178, 179, 180, 181, 183, 184, 188, 202
religion, 6, 19, 29, 35, 40, 41, 64, 65, 80, 92,
	106, 107, 108, 109, 110, 111, 113, 114, 115,
	116, 117, 118, 119, 120, 121, 122, 129, 130,
	139, 161, 173, 175, 179, 180, 181
replacement, 101, 126, 147, 175, 189
Rhenish Fan, 176, 207
river, 122, 156, 157, 158, 175, 176
Romance, 4, 200
Romanian, 200
root, 133, 134, 159, 186, 193
round (vowels), 20, 63, 64, 117, 118, 119
rural, 3, 20, 26, 27, 31, 51, 53, 61, 96, 97, 108,
	128, 148, 149, 152, 161, 163, 173, 179,
	180, 187, 188, 190, 191, 204, 206, 211
Russian, 126, 133

Safaitic, 132, 211
Samā'na tribe, 167
Šammar tribe, 21, 66, 101
sampling, 6, 29, 31, 77
Sanskrit, 133
Scandinavian languages, 191
S-curve, 136
sedentary, 69, 112, 113, 114, 161, 163, 190
segregation, 108, 114, 116, 117
Semitic, 7, 35, 87, 133, 134, 181, 192, 198, 212
Sephardim, 107
Serbo-Croatian, 200
Sex. *See* gender
Shia, 41
sibilant, 108, 132, 149
Sicilian, 195
simplification, 201
Slavic, 200
social class, xvi, 6, 14, 26, 29, 49, 55, 67, 69,
	73, 77, 81, 85, 86, 88, 92, 93, 94, 96, 98,
	102, 104, 107, 146, 148, 175, 179
social integration, 96, 97, 101, 107, 127

social meaning, 6, 20, 31, 50, 61, 65, 69, 75, 81, 88, 93, 103, 116, 119, 137, 151, 180
social media, 17
social network, 6, 29, 59, 63, 77, 78, 79, 93, 94, 96, 98, 101, 103, 104
  loose, 98
  tight, 80, 96, 98
social value, 12, 49
socialisation, 59, 79, 89, 99, 213
socio-economic, 6, 26, 65, 67, 77, 83, 92, 93, 94, 96, 102, 104, 146, 175
sociohistorical, 165
sociolect, 175
sociolinguistic theory, 1, 4, 44, 73, 151
sound change, 134, 137, 146, 148
space, 7, 54, 76, 127, 156, 167, 175, 189, 201, 206, 211
Spanish, 84, 107, 134, 192
spectrogram, 38
speech community, 17, 20, 26, 28, 33, 34, 46, 50, 54, 55, 56, 81, 82, 87, 141, 146, 156, 204
Sprachbund, 200
Sprachinseln, 180
stable variation, 144
standard, 2, 3, 4, 7, 16, 25, 26, 35, 45, 48, 49, 51, 52, 53, 59, 62, 70, 74, 75, 108, 111, 116, 132, 134, 138, 147, 150, 159, 174, 179, 180, 181, 182, 183, 184, 189
Standard Arabic, 2, 3, 4, 25, 45, 138, 179, 181, 184
standardisation, 2, 3, 181, 184
statistical modelling, 9, 37, 38, 39, 42
statistical significance, 6, 9, 12, 15, 16, 32, 40, 41, 55, 56, 60, 64, 66, 77, 80, 81, 86, 87, 97, 98, 99, 100, 102, 113, 117, 118, 132, 137, 143, 144, 154, 156, 178, 179, 184, 209
statistics, 9, 19, 24, 26, 33, 34, 36, 37, 38, 39, 40, 42, 44, 45, 48, 52, 56, 63, 64, 66, 86, 102, 117, 122, 144
stem, 25, 29, 63, 147, 148, 159
stereotype, 6, 18, 44, 49, 67, 74, 150
stigmatisation, 27, 44, 49, 51, 61, 64, 65, 70, 72, 109, 116, 117, 119, 146, 150, 180, 204
stratification, 6, 31, 77, 82, 83, 89, 90, 92, 93, 101, 102, 104, 105, 119, 121, 175
style, 3, 17, 26, 28, 29, 33, 47, 55, 75, 76, 94, 129, 136, 141, 212
  casual, 10, 13, 14, 45, 146
  formal, 1, 3, 12, 14, 43, 51, 52, 53, 55, 74, 76, 77, 89, 126, 138
  informal, 11, 20
  narrative, 13, 34, 94

substrate, 191, 192, 193, 194, 195, 196
suburb, 20, 67, 68, 69, 96, 102, 103, 127, 144
Sumerian, 134
Sunna, 41, 64, 65, 114, 117, 118, 119, 122, 124, 125
supralocal, 2, 52, 53, 54, 55, 56, 60, 63, 65, 74, 77, 79, 98, 118, 154
survey, 7, 8, 67, 129, 151, 159, 172, 187, 206
syllable structure, 121
syntax, 4, 17, 21, 22, 23, 24, 51, 75, 111, 129, 147, 160, 184, 185, 194, 200, 212
Syriac. See Aramaic

Tajik, 195, 198, 199
Tifinagh, 85
Tok Pisin, 186
token, xvi, 17, 18, 24, 25, 33, 34, 36, 37, 38, 39, 40, 51, 57, 65, 87, 144, 147, 148, 202
topography, 157, 158, 173
traditional, 1, 2, 3, 7, 8, 23, 26, 28, 32, 40, 49, 53, 54, 56, 58, 59, 60, 61, 64, 66, 67, 68, 69, 70, 80, 82, 90, 96, 98, 99, 100, 104, 109, 110, 113, 117, 120, 121, 142, 143, 144, 148, 149, 154, 158, 159, 160, 171, 173, 179, 189, 190, 191, 194, 203, 204, 206, 210, 211, 212
transcription, xv, 35, 36
transitional zone, 159, 206, 207, 208, 210, 211
transmission, 30, 63, 69, 77, 128, 136, 192
transportation, 58, 61, 167
trend study, 59, 62, 116, 119, 137, 139, 140
tribe, 21, 23, 58, 66, 69, 71, 93, 105, 113, 115, 157, 163, 165, 166, 167, 170, 173, 177, 196
Turkic languages, 198, 200
Turkish, 158, 184, 192, 198, 199
Turkmen, 198
typology, 111, 122, 157, 181, 201, 212

Ugaritic, 133
university, 18, 45, 46, 60, 67, 71, 72, 78, 79, 80, 81, 82, 83, 84, 88, 89, 90, 210
urban, 3, 7, 20, 27, 32, 51, 54, 56, 60, 70, 97, 98, 108, 113, 121, 126, 137, 139, 142, 150, 161, 163, 173, 176, 178, 179, 187, 188, 190, 191, 203, 204, 205, 206, 210, 211
Urban Hierarchy Model, 204
urbanisation, 50, 93, 96, 97, 105, 127, 149, 177, 206, 211
Urdu, 192
Uyghur, 192
Uzbek, 195, 198, 199, 200

valley, 129, 156, 157, 158, 175, 176, 177, 178,
     190
variable
   linguistic, 5, 16, 21, 24, 26, 29, 34, 35, 36,
       38, 39, 40, 46, 61, 86, 97, 119, 124, 144,
       151, 167
   social, 6, 26, 29, 35, 46, 55, 57, 63, 64, 65,
       73, 75, 77, 80, 81, 85, 88, 97, 98, 109, 113,
       117, 118, 124, 139, 149, 150, 151, 154,
       161, 187, 203, 206
   speaker, 6, 29
variable rule, 26, 28
variant, 2, 3, 6, 10, 20, 21, 24, 26, 33, 34, 35,
       36, 38, 39, 40, 41, 45, 49, 50, 51, 53, 54,
       55, 56, 58, 59, 60, 61, 62, 64, 65, 66, 67,
       68, 69, 70, 72, 73, 75, 78, 79, 86, 87, 90,
       98, 99, 101, 102, 104, 108, 109, 116, 117,
       118, 119, 132, 137, 142, 143, 144, 147,
       149, 150, 152, 161, 163, 172, 173, 174,
       180, 204, 207, 208, 209, 210
variation, 4, 5, 18, 22, 26, 28, 131, 137, 143,
       144, 154, 164, 206
   language, 1, 4, 5, 6, 20, 38, 40, 42, 44, 45,
       54, 73, 78, 82, 83, 85, 96, 98, 110, 113,
       117, 130, 160
   regional, 1, 7, 52, 94, 107, 108, 110, 113,
       115, 116, 150, 163, 189, 190, 210

variationist paradigm, 2, 8, 9, 26, 27, 28, 45,
       48, 55, 77, 104, 113, 151, 160, 187, 212
variety, 2, 4, 8, 21, 23, 44, 51, 52, 84, 107, 108,
       109, 111, 112, 113, 130, 131, 132, 133,
       146, 148, 151, 176, 179, 180, 181, 182,
       185, 186, 187, 192, 193, 195, 196, 197,
       198, 201, 202, 207, 212
verb, 18, 21, 22, 29, 97, 112, 121, 152, 159, 181,
       182, 186, 191, 193, 195, 199, 200, 208
vernacular, 2, 3, 4, 9, 11, 12, 14, 16, 45, 46, 49,
       51, 55, 106, 133, 141, 142, 146
vowel, 25, 26, 27, 28, 32, 38, 40, 46, 54, 61, 62,
       63, 64, 112, 121, 134, 146, 147, 148, 159,
       167, 181, 182, 196, 207, 210
vowel raising, 32, 112

Wandala, 198
waterway, 175, 176, 177, 178
Wave Model, 201, 203, 211
Wave Theory, 201
woman, 15, 18, 22, 33, 48, 49, 50, 51, 52, 53,
       54, 55, 56, 58, 59, 60, 61, 62, 63, 64, 65,
       66, 67, 68, 69, 70, 71, 72, 73, 74, 75, 76,
       79, 81, 85, 86, 94, 143, 149, 180, 199, 204
word order, 199, 200

Zuʿbi tribe, 173

Place Index

Afghanistan, 181, 195, 199, 200
Algeria, 44, 84, 129, 149, 190, 195, 196, 197
Anatolia, 132, 203
Arabian Gulf, 72, 114, 116, 117, 130, 191,
    213
Arabian Peninsula, 26, 27, 114, 115, 133, 139,
    146, 149, 180, 204
Australia, 32
Austria, 176

Bahrain, 2, 18, 23, 72, 113, 114, 115, 116, 117,
    119, 132, 139, 140
  Manama, 49, 114, 116, 140
Balkans, 200

Cameroon, 198
Canada, 54, 98, 99
  Montreal, 140, 141
  Ontario, 98
  Quebec, 32, 98
Cape Verde, 186
Caucasus, 125, 126, 128
Central Asia, 23, 195, 198, 212
Chad, 181, 198
Cyprus, 181, 183
  Kormakiti, 184

Democratic Republic of Congo, 31, 198

Egypt, 1, 30, 52, 84, 122, 132, 139, 156, 160,
    164, 176, 177, 179, 180, 181, 186, 192,
    196, 212
  Al-Ṭūr, 167
  Cairo, 30, 52, 55, 77, 85, 88, 93, 94, 132,
    149, 176, 177, 179, 191, 196
  Damietta, 176, 177, 209
  Gaṭyah Oasis, 167
  Luxor, 122
  Nile Delta, 132, 176, 177, 178, 207, 208
  Rosetta, 176, 177
  Sinai Peninsula, 139, 156, 160, 164, 165,
    166, 167, 177

Siwa, 84
Tīh Plateau, 156
Ethiopia, 133
Euphrates, 203
Europe, 1, 5, 51, 80, 84, 101, 102, 132, 133,
    159, 184, 185, 191, 198, 200

Fertile Crescent, 171, 193, 196
Finland
  Helsinki, 140
France
  Alsace, 158, 175, 178
  Paris, 191
  Vosges, 158

Germany, 158, 159, 176

Haiti, 186
Horan, 1, 27, 60, 109, 110, 134, 139, 160, 167,
    170, 171, 172, 173, 175, 194

Iran, 114, 117, 122, 123, 124, 158, 195, 198,
    200
Iraq, 69, 70, 72, 107, 111, 113, 120, 123, 124,
    133, 149, 158, 193, 195
  Baghdad, 49, 69, 70, 101, 107, 111, 112, 113,
    114, 119, 195
  Mosul, 113
  Nasiriyya, 70
  Qalʿat Siker, 69, 72, 101
Ireland, 128, 129
Israel. *See* Palestine
Italy
  Sicily, 181

Jordan, 3, 12, 19, 21, 24, 25, 28, 31, 32, 49, 50,
    51, 53, 54, 60, 63, 74, 78, 79, 81, 82,
    83, 89, 90, 109, 110, 111, 113, 119, 120,
    121, 125, 126, 127, 128, 132, 134, 137,
    142, 143, 149, 150, 151, 159, 160, 163,
    170, 172, 173, 175, 178, 180, 184, 190,
    194, 210, 211

Ajloun, 90, 174
Amman, xv, 2, 10, 24, 27, 28, 30, 32, 53, 54,
       60, 63, 75, 81, 82, 90, 126, 127, 137,
       142, 143, 149, 152, 174, 178, 180, 191,
       194, 210, 212
Azraq, 109, 110
Balqā', 160
Ḥarra, 132
Irbid, 60, 61, 63, 149, 174, 180, 194
Jerash, 126
Kerak, 90, 163, 194
Kufrenğe, 163
Ramtha, 173
Saḥam, 60, 63
Salt, 28, 79, 90, 149, 180, 184, 194
South Azraq, 126, 128
Suf, 25, 63, 174
Sukhna, 126, 128
Umm al-Quttain, 110
Zarqa, 126, 127

Kenya, 186
Kuwait, 30, 72, 122, 123, 124, 125, 126
    Kuwait City, 122, 123

Lake Chad, 198
Latin America, 134
Lebanon, 28, 50, 52, 109, 110, 111, 130, 159,
       160, 178, 184, 192, 193, 202
    Beirut, 2, 10, 24, 50, 52, 53, 130, 142, 149,
       161, 172, 178, 191
    Chouf Mountains, 109, 111
Levant, 2, 19, 27, 28, 29, 32, 50, 53, 93, 109,
       110, 111, 126, 133, 139, 142, 143, 150,
       161, 163, 173, 176, 180, 181, 184,
       185, 190, 191, 192, 193, 194, 195,
       203, 210
Libya, 22, 84, 149
    Fazzan, 22

Maghreb, 4, 177
Malta, 181, 183, 195
    Gozo, 183
    Mosta, 182, 183
Mediterranean Sea, 133, 163, 176, 181, 192
Mesopotamia. *See* Iraq
Middle East, 31, 77, 88, 93, 129, 158, 190
Morocco, 1, 5, 20, 44, 49, 74, 75, 83, 84, 85,
       107, 108, 129, 139, 158, 179, 190, 195,
       196, 197, 206
    Atlas Mountains, 129, 158
    Casablanca, 80, 104, 178, 179, 206, 211
    Fez, xv, 49, 79, 104, 108, 179, 180, 197
    Ifrane, 83
    Meknes, 75, 108
    Rabat, 20, 139, 149, 179

Sous Valley, 129, 158
Zaer, 20

Netherlands, 176
Nigeria, 181, 198
Nile, 122, 176, 177, 178, 190, 207, 208, 209
North Africa, 4, 5, 44, 84, 88, 93, 107, 108,
       129, 133, 139, 158, 181, 190, 192, 196
North America, 32, 78

Oman, 23, 195
    Dhofar, 195

Palestine, 1, 3, 8, 19, 22, 23, 26, 27, 28, 32, 33,
       36, 50, 51, 54, 85, 87, 88, 109, 110, 111,
       120, 121, 137, 138, 139, 142, 143, 148,
       149, 150, 152, 159, 160, 163, 172, 177,
       184, 190, 191, 204, 210
    Al-Malha, 190
    Beit Jala, 148
    Bet Safafa, 190
    Bethlehem, 148, 191
    Gaza, 32, 36, 39, 40, 53, 54, 139, 149, 163
    Haifa, 3, 50
    Jaffa, 32, 33, 36, 39, 40, 53, 54, 85, 87, 88,
       163, 184
    Jenin, 163
    Jericho, 163
    Jerusalem, 2, 50, 53, 148, 161, 163, 190,
       191, 204
    Kufur Yasif, 109, 110
    Nablus, 163, 190, 204
    Ramallah, 148, 191
    Ramle, 163, 184
    Silwan, 190
    Taybeh, 23
    West Bank, 32
Papua New Guinea, 186

Red Sea, 157
River Rhine, 158, 175, 178, 208
Russia, 126, 133

Saudi Arabia, 158
    Abha, 158
    Al-Ahsa, 40, 41, 63, 117, 118, 205
    Al-Baha, 58, 59, 78, 99, 100
    al-Farša, 157
    Al-Jawwa, 158
    al-Sarāh mountains, 157
    ʿAsīr, 157, 158, 170
    Dammam, 71, 94, 98, 205
    Ha'il, 205
    Hijaz, 58, 150
    Jeddah, 18, 27, 49, 52, 56, 60, 101, 118, 146,
       147, 148, 149, 150, 179, 180, 204

Saudi Arabia (*cont.*)
  Mecca, xv, 58, 59, 78, 94, 99, 100, 101, 149,
    150, 209
  Medina, 56, 57, 59, 73, 75, 149, 150, 204,
    205
  Najd, 25, 26, 27, 101, 115, 134, 146, 147,
    148, 150, 181
  Qasim, 25, 134
  Riyadh, 9, 52, 66, 118, 154, 180, 205
  Shagra, 134
  Tihāmat Qaḥṭān, 157
Saudi Arabic
  Mecca, 99, 100
Scotland, 15, 129
South Asia, 106, 192
South Sudan, 186
  Juba, 186, 187
Spain, 107, 134
  Andalusia, 108
Sudan, 186
Switzerland, 176
  Charmay, 139
Syria, 1, 28, 50, 109, 110, 111, 120, 133, 134,
    139, 158, 159, 160, 163, 170, 172, 173,
    174, 175, 190, 192, 194, 202, 211
  Albu Kamal, 203
  Aleppo, 24, 203
  Al-Hasakah, 203
  Al-Malkiyah, 203
  Damascus, 2, 25, 27, 50, 53, 67, 79, 94, 101,
    142, 143, 144, 145, 149, 160, 161, 170,
    172, 173, 175, 184, 191, 194, 195, 202,
    203
    Dummar, 67, 68, 69, 102, 144
    Shaghoor, 67, 68, 69, 102, 144
  Golan Heights, 53
  Hama, 203
  Homs, 163, 203
  Jabal al-Druze, 109, 111, 170, 173
  Jaydur, 170

Palmyra, 163
Qalamūn, 158
Qamishli, 203
Sweda, 109

Tunisia, 5, 52, 53, 61, 79, 84, 96, 107, 180
  Djerba, 107, 108, 109
  Korba, 61, 62, 63, 79
  Rades, 53, 96, 97
  Tunis, 52, 53, 62, 79, 96, 108, 149, 180
Turkey, 132, 158
  Sason, 132
  Siirt, 132

Uganda, 186
United Arab Emirates, 30
United Kingdom, 2, 31, 49, 52, 78, 82, 83, 106,
    167, 171, 187, 211
  Belfast, 14, 16, 96
  East Anglia, 205
  Fens, 167
  Glasgow, 15, 49
  London, 9, 205
  Norwich, 13, 14, 17, 77
  The Wash, 207
  Wales, 207
United States, 2, 31, 32, 45, 52, 54, 80, 82, 83,
    88, 106, 206
  California, 9
  Detroit, 20, 44, 103
  New York, 9, 13, 15, 17, 45, 139
  North Carolina, 15
  Oklahoma, 206, 211
Uzbekistan, 181, 195, 198, 199, 200

Western Sahara, 196

Yemen, 1, 59, 139, 157, 160, 163, 194

Zagros Mountains, 158

Name Index

Abdel-Jawad, Hassan, 204
Abu Ain, Noora, 60, 61, 63
Abu-Haidar, Farida, 195
Al Sheyadi, Sara, 23, 24
Al-Azraqi, Munira, 55
Al-Bohnayyah, Moayyad, 40, 41, 63, 64, 117, 118, 119
Al-Essa, Aziza, 8, 18, 27, 60, 101, 146, 147, 148, 150
Al-Hawamdeh, Areej, 63, 110, 174
Al-Jallad, Ahmad, 132, 211
Al-Jehani, Nasir, 149
Al-Khatib, Mahmoud, 60, 149
Al-Qahtani, Khairia, 60
Al-Qouz, Muna, 114, 116, 139, 140
Al-Rohili, Mohammad, 75
Al-Shehri, Abdullah, 60, 150
Al-Wer, Enam, 8, 12, 27, 32, 50, 52, 53, 54, 74, 75, 78, 79, 88, 110, 119, 120, 121, 126, 128, 139, 149, 151, 152, 174, 210, 212
AlAmmar, Deema, 21, 65, 67, 80, 101, 154, 205
Alaodini, Hind, 71, 94, 98, 205
Alghamdi, Najla, 58, 59, 78, 94, 99, 100, 101, 150, 209
Alshawi, Wisam, 69, 70, 101
Arnold, Werner, 160, 193

Badawi, El-Said, 3
Bagambam Bukpa Araali, 31
Bailey, Guy, 206
Barontini, Alexandrine, 75
Behnstedt, Peter, 1, 107, 108, 139, 159, 160, 163, 176, 187, 193, 202, 203, 207, 208, 212
Benkato, Adam, 196
Benmamoun, Elabbas, 132
Bentahila, Abdelali, 5
Bergsträsser, Gotthelf, 1, 139, 159, 160, 161, 163
Bilbeisi, Moh'd, xiv
Bizri, Fida, 186, 187
Blanc, Haim, 107, 109, 111, 112, 113
Bloomfield, Leonard, 134, 203

Borg, Alexander, 183, 184
Boumans, Louis, 5
Bourdieu, Pierre, 122
Britain, David, 31, 52, 106, 167, 187, 211
Brunot, Louis, 139

Camilleri, Maris, 181, 182, 183, 187
Campbell, Lyle, 134, 151
Cantineau, Jean, 1, 109, 110, 139, 160, 171, 172, 173, 174
Caubet, Dominique, 5
Cedergren, Henrietta, 140
Chambers, J.K., 44, 48, 73, 98, 99, 141, 151, 157, 176, 187, 191, 200, 204, 212
Chrichton, James A., 194
Cotter, William M., 8, 32, 33, 36, 39, 53, 54, 139, 149

Davies, Eirlys, 5
De Jong, Rudolf, 8, 139, 156, 160, 164, 165, 167
Dodsworth, Robin, 104

Eckert, Penelope, 4, 6, 20, 32, 44, 73, 93, 102, 104
Edwards, John, 111, 127, 128, 129
El Salman, Mahmoud, 3
El-Hassan, Shahir, 3

Ferguson, Charles A., 4, 181

Gafter, Roey J., 88
Gauchat, Louis, 139
Germanos, Marie-Aimée, 129, 130
Gordon, Matthew, 44, 45, 89
Grigore, George, 212

Hachimi, Atiqa, 75, 79, 94, 102, 179, 197
Haeri, Niloofar, 7, 8, 52, 55, 77, 85, 86, 87, 88, 93, 94
Hassan II, King, 84
Hassan, Batoul, 51, 122, 123, 124, 125

Heath, Jeffrey, 107, 108
Herin, Bruno, 8, 27, 50, 75, 110, 119, 151
Hermann, Eduard, 139
Hock, Hans Henrich, 151
Hoffman, Katherine, 129, 158
Højrup, Thomas, 101
Holes, Clive, 2, 3, 7, 8, 18, 113, 114, 115, 116,
    129, 139, 140, 212
Holm, John, 186
Hopkins, Simon, 195
Horesh, Uri, 8, 32, 33, 36, 85, 87, 88, 110, 119,
    149, 152
Huehnergard, John, 197, 212
Hussain, Abeer, 56, 57, 73, 205

Ibrahim, Muhammad Hassan, 51, 52, 74
Ingham, Bruce, 27, 199, 200
Ismail, Hanadi, 25, 67, 68, 69, 94, 101, 102,
    143, 144, 202

Jabeur, Mohamed, 53, 94, 96, 97, 101
Jastrow, Otto, 198, 203
Johnson, Daniel Ezra, 36, 44, 87
Johnstone, T. M., 146
Jones, Michael Allen, 208

Kaufman, Terrence, 212

Labov, William, 2, 5, 9, 11, 13, 14, 15, 17, 32,
    44, 45, 48, 54, 74, 94, 135, 139, 146, 151,
    160, 167
Lahlou, Moncef, 4, 5, 83, 197
Lass, Roger, 151

Mallinson, Christine, 45, 104
Manfredi, Stefano, 186, 187
Marçais, William, 4
McConnell-Ginet, Sally, 102
Messaoudi, Leila, 20, 139, 179
Meyerhoff, Miriam, 73, 88, 103, 151
Mifsud, Manwel, 183
Miller, Catherine, 7, 74, 129, 187
Milroy, James, 52, 74, 101
Milroy, Lesley, 14, 16, 96, 101

Mitchell, T. F., 3
Mourigh, Khaled, 196

Naciri-Azzouz, Amina, 196
Newton, Brian, 185
Nöldeke, Theodor, 195

Owens, Jonathan, 7, 151, 186, 187, 194, 198, 212

Paunonen, Heikki, 140
Preston, Dennis R., 160
Procházka, Stephan, 195
Prochazka, Theodore, 139

Retsö, Jan, 192
Rouabah, Siham, 84, 129
Rubin, Aaron, 195, 197, 212

Sadiqi, Fatima, 74, 76
Sankoff, Gillian, 140
Sayahi, Lotfi, 4, 5
Schilling, Natalie, 44, 45
Schmidt, Johannes, 201
Sibawayh, 131, 132
Souag, Lameen, 195
Spitta, Wilhelm, 1
Stuart-Smith, Jane, 15

Tagliamonte, Sali, 45
Taqi, Hanan, 125
Thomason, Sarah Grey, 212
Tosco, Mauro, 187
Trudgill, Peter, 2, 13, 14, 17, 32, 77, 92, 157,
    176, 185, 186, 187, 191, 200, 201, 205, 212

Versteegh, Kees, 193, 196, 199

Walters, Keith, 61, 62, 63, 78
Wittrich, Michaela, 203
Woidich, Manfred, 1, 122, 132, 139, 159, 160,
    176, 177, 179, 187, 207, 208, 212
Wolfram, Walt, 15

Ziamari, Karima, 5, 75

www.ingramcontent.com/pod-product-compliance
Lightning Source LLC
La Vergne TN
LVHW021030190125
801667LV00009B/1007